Documenting the Beijing Olympics

This book focuses on the processes of documenting the Beijing Olympics — ranging from the visual (television and film) to radio and the written word — and the meanings generated by such representations. What were the 'key' stories and how were they chosen? What was dramatised? Who were the heroes? Which 'clashes' were highlighted and how? What sorts of stories did the notion of 'human interest' generate? Did politics take a backseat or was the topic highlighted repeatedly? Thus, the focus was not on the success or failure of this event, but on the ways in which the Olympic Games, as international and historic events, are memorialised by observers.

The key question that this book addresses is: How far would the Olympic coverage fall into the patterns of representation that have come to dominate Olympic reporting and what would China, as a discursive subject, bring to these patterns?

This book was previously published as a special issue of *Sport in Society*.

D. P. Martinez is Reader in Anthropology with special reference to Japan at the Department of Anthropology, SOAS.

Documenting the Beijing Olympics

Edited by
D. P. Martinez

Routledge
Taylor & Francis Group

LONDON AND NEW YORK

First published 2011
by Routledge
2 Park Square, Milton Park, Abingdon, Oxon, OX14 4RN

Simultaneously published in the USA and Canada
by Routledge
711 Third Avenue, New York, NY, 10017

Routledge is an imprint of the Taylor & Francis Group, an informa business

This book is a reproduction of *Sport in Society*, vol. 13, issue 5. The Publisher requests to those authors who may be citing this book to state, also, the bibliographical details of the special issue on which the book was based.

Typeset in Times New Roman by Taylor & Francis Books
Printed and bound in Great Britain by TJI Digital, Padstow, Cornwall

British Library Cataloguing in Publication Data
A catalogue record for this book is available from the British Library

ISBN13: 978-0-415-57548-5

Disclaimer
The publisher would like to make readers aware that the chapters in this book are referred to as articles as they had been in the special issue. The publisher accepts responsibility for any inconsistencies that may have arisen in the course of preparing this volume for print.

Contents

CONTENTS

SPORT IN THE GLOBAL SOCIETY – CONTEMPORARY PERSPECTIVES

Series Editor: Boria Majumdar

DOCUMENTING THE BEIJING OLYMPICS

Sport in the Global Society – Contemporary Perspectives
Series Editor: Boria Majumdar

The social, cultural (including media) and political study of sport is an expanding area of scholarship and related research. While this area has been well served by the Sport in the Global Society Series, the surge in quality scholarship over the last few years has necessitated the creation of *Sport in the Global Society: Contemporary Perspectives*. The series will publish the work of leading scholars in fields as diverse as sociology, cultural studies, media studies, gender studies, cultural geography and history, political science and political economy. If the social and cultural study of sport is to receive the scholarly attention and readership it warrants, a cross-disciplinary series dedicated to taking sport beyond the narrow confines of physical education and sport science academic domains is necessary. Sport in the Global Society: Contemporary Perspectives will answer this need.

Titles in the Series

SPORT IN THE GLOBAL SOCIETY - CONTEMPORARY PERSPECTIVES

Acknowledgement

I must acknowledge the important contribution made by my SOAS colleague Dr Kevin Latham, who helped organise the conference upon which this volume is based by bringing in Chinese experts. In addition, he shared the expertise gained through his ESRC project on media use during the Beijing Olympics. As well as writing a chapter for this volume, Dr Latham also helped with the editing of Chinese titles and names in the articles.

Introduction[1]

D.P. Martinez

School of Oriental and African Studies, University of London, Thornhaugh Street, Russell Square, London WC1H 0XG, UK

This introduction to the volume contextualises the theme of the conference and examines how all the papers included in this special issue address the theme of 'Documenting the Beijing Olympics'. The issue of what it means to document, especially in the twenty-first century in which the media must include new technologies, is considered in some detail. Types of documentation, the problem of intentional and unintentional meanings, are considered and the question 'what does it mean to represent an event?' is asked.

Hosting the Olympic Games is always a matter of pride for whichever country wins the right to do so on any particular occasion. However, the 2008 Games in Beijing were, as everyone was aware, an event of more than usual geopolitical and cultural significance because of China's emergence from isolation, burgeoning economic power and growing political influence. Even before the Games took place in Beijing, China, publications on them began to appear;[2] and, naturally, many studies have been published afterwards.[3] This special issue, however, does not attempt simply to document, but to ask what is involved in 'documenting', to consider how others were approaching the project of reporting on and representing the ceremonies and the games themselves. How far would the Olympic coverage fall into the patterns of representation that have come to dominate Olympic reporting and what would China, as a discursive subject, bring to these patterns?

These were two key questions put to the contributors to a panel at a conference on 'Documenting the Beijing Olympics' held at the School for Oriental and African Studies (SOAS), University of London, a few weeks after the Games finished. The essays in this collection give their own responses to these questions. A few introductory points need to be made here. First, the Chinese government saw the Games (as have other host nations) as a chance to demonstrate how far the country had travelled and changed in the last half of the twentieth century. So the building of facilities for the Games, the organization of the Games and all its ceremonies were an opportunity to represent the social change that has taken place in China in the last part of the twentieth century and at the beginning of the twenty-first century. Thus it was not just the Olympics that were being documented, but social change as represented vis-à-vis the Games through a global network of mass media. What does this mean? How is social change documented?

One could posit that there are two main categories that need distinguishing when it comes to the mass media, social change and its documentation: the intended and the unintended. To take the second category first, some stories are documented, told or fictionalized and somehow inadvertently capture a moment of change. The many novels about life in China during the last half of the twentieth century do this. It was to such incidental documentation that I referred when once I wrote[4] about the negotiation we see in popular culture: it is not that the mass media negotiates a change or even makes change (although this can sometimes happen), but that it represents the social concerns in some way so that, on the page, television or screen, audiences can see played out the various positions and possibilities they are faced with in daily life: what happens if women want careers; if sports become popular with new audiences; or if children feel powerless within the modern nuclear family? Mass media representations play out the possible answers to these questions, both documenting the moments of uncertainty and providing possible solutions, scenarios or imagined futures.

One might add a subcategory to that of unintended documentation, that of the new mass media and their use by ordinary people: cell phones and the internet in particular (see Liu in this volume). The ability of the modern subject to react immediately to events and news stories, allows us all not just to be critics, but also to actively, politically critique, ferment dissent and respond to the views of others. Part of what Latham's work (see his essay in this volume) on the Olympics indicates is that the new mass media have enormous potential to be used in a variety of ways: not just to keep in touch, but to put out alternative accounts; to comment on all versions of any incidents; to cement local and ethnic identities, as well as to debate the meaning of others' interpretations. Therefore, while the officials had a clear vision of what the Beijing Olympics would highlight about modern China and about the meanings that were intended to be conveyed, at the personal and local level there was room for different interpretations based on regional identity, for example.

Intended documentation is, of course, what news programmes and some documentary films attempt to do. To capture history on the hop we might say: to be there when it happened. Whatever *it* might be. News reporters make a living out of being there when it happened, the first to enter, the first to interview, the first to pay attention to, etc. Documentary films differ from the 'reality' of the news in that they often are meant to 'observe life' and if they capture a moment of change, then all the better, but this cannot be *demanded* of documentary film. It may be expected, such as in documentaries that follow a politician campaigning, for example, but if the film is truly observational, it cannot supply on demand a moment of change.

Film documentaries, the category into which we can put Olympic films, are somewhat related to news reporting and yet different. They are meant to observe and document an event while that event, as we have just seen with the Beijing Olympics, may be symbolically loaded with references to social and historical change. To film the Olympics, even the opening and closing ceremonies, is ostensibly to just document a spectacular event.[5] What the Olympics *means* for the home nation, however, might best be left to the news reporters and social commentators to discuss. As representations of representations, then, Olympic films perhaps seem to have an objective distance from the *politics* of change. However, the variety of responses to any documentation of the Olympics, particularly in the case of China, would indicate that objectivity is nearly impossible to achieve. Why is this the case?

Again, as the essays in this volume well demonstrate, there are two answers to this question. The first is simply that all representations are just that: re-presentations of a reality that has been packaged and is then presented to an audience – in this case a huge global audience. While the representation may bear a very specific intention on the part of its creators, the response of the audience to this representation is heterogeneous. For example, in relation to the Beijing Games, it is clear that representations of China often are read through Western Orientalist stereotyping; to which we can add a second influence, that of opposing political ideologies. Orientalism,[6] of course, has a political aspect, but the perceived oppositions between a Communist regime and that of the more 'Democratic' West, colour many of the contemporary Western readings of the representations of modern China. Nowhere was this more evident than in the ways in which various aspects of the Olympic Games were reported on: from the torch relay, to the issue of human rights in Tibet and Darfur, to every aspect of the opening and closing ceremonies – the foreign press' take on China was often critical. It was the earthquake on 12 May 2008 in the Sichuan province of China that helped to soften some of these critiques and led to the presentation of a more rounded view.

The contributions to this volume speak to the events and both the representations and their readings in a multiplicity of ways. We begin with an essay on Olympic representation in general: Hughson's survey of Olympic posters. This paper addresses the questions of representation, intention and the question of the nation-state's imagining. This is followed by Horne's and Whannel's assessment of the manner in which the Torch Relay was reported on in various newspapers and media; their paper clearly touches on the issues of Orientalist and political stereotyping. Jialing Luo's essay on the opening and closing ceremony reviews the intended meanings of these ceremonies; she considers the ways that China wanted to send a message about its new place in the global order. This is followed by Bladen's contribution in which he considers how the volunteers at the games were seen and reported on.

With Latham's essay we shift to a more Chinese-based context: his overview of the use of mass media during the Olympics is an important introduction to the five chapters that follow – all by Chinese scholars. Chen's essay gives us an examination of the Chinese primary intention in hosting the Olympics: he argues that this was an attempt to communicate with the broader global community. Liang continues this consideration of the Chinese intent by looking at the proposed meaning of the ceremonial surrounding the Olympics and of Western misunderstandings of it. Huang's looks at the internal diversity within China by considering how a Cantonese-speaking television station managed to work around CCTV's (China Central Television) monopoly of the Games' coverage. Liu's essay continues this theme by looking at the empirical data collected on the use of cell phones by migrant workers to keep in touch with the events and with family at home. Finally, Hwang's essay is one of three that considers the interplay between Western reporting and the events as seen by others; the theme of human rights raises its head here as it does in the essays on the Torch Relay. This marks a shift in theme back to the relationship between Chinese and Western perceptions of the games.

Finlay and Xin add a new dimension to this topic by looking at Japanese coverage and comparing it with the Western press, to give us a different view of events. Kidd returns to the problem of human rights and news coverage and raises questions that can well be applied to future games. Finally Majumdar's paper turns to look at the effect the Games had outside the Western world. The winning of a gold medal for India and what this means in terms of the nation's hopes to host a future Olympic Games, brings us back full circle to the idea that Beijing was just one of a sequence of Olympic Games. The lessons learned from hosting it are, at the moment, being considered in London, Madrid, Chicago, Tokyo and Delhi, as well as by the Olympic Committee itself. Our hope is that in some small way, this volume will contribute to this understanding of what happens when a nation decides to host the Olympic Games.

Notes

[1] My thanks to Jane Savoy, who organised and supported the conference at SOAS so brilliantly; the Centre of Chinese Studies at SOAS, who supported the young Chinese Scholars; and to Taylor and Francis for their support. My thanks also to D.N. Gellner, for commenting on the first draft of this.

[2] See Jarvie, Hwang and Brennan, *Sport, revolution and the Beijing Olympics*; US Congressional-Executive Commission on China, *The Beijing Olympics*; UN Environmental Programme, *Beijing 2008 Olympic Games*; Committee to Protect Journalists, *Falling Short*; Close, Askew and Xin, *The Beijing Olympiad*.

[3] For example, Brownell, *Beijing's Games*; Price and Dayan, eds, *Owning the Olympics*; Horne, *Sport, Revolution*.

[4] Martinez, 'Introduction'.

[5] MacAloon, 'Olympic Games'.

[6] Said, *Orientalism*.

References

Brownell, Susan. *Beijing's Games: What the Olympics Mean to China*. Lanham, MD: Rowman & Littlefield, 2008.

Close, Paul, David Askew, and Xu Xin. *The Beijing Olympiad: The Political Economy of a Sporting Mega-event*. Abingdon and New York: Routledge, 2006.

Committee to Protect Journalists. *Falling Short: As the 2008 Olympics Approach, China Falters on Press Freedom*. New York: Committee to Protect Journalists, 2007.

Horne, J. *Sport, Revolution and the Beijing Olympics*. Abingdon: Taylor & Francis, 2009.

Jarvie, Grant, Dong-Jhy Hwang, and Mel Brennan. *Sport, Revolution and the Beijing Olympics*. Oxford: Berg, 2005.

MacAloon, John J. 'Olympic Games and the Theory of Spectacle'. In *Rite, Drama, Festival, Spectacle*, edited by John L. MacAloon, 241–80. Philadelphia, PA: ISHI, 1984.

Martinez, D.P. 'Introduction: Gender, Shifting Boundaries and Global Cultures'. In *The Worlds of Japanese Popular Culture*, edited by D.P. Martinez, 1–18. Cambridge: Cambridge University Press, 1998.

Price, Monroe E., and Daniel Dayan, eds. *Owning the Olympics: Narratives of the New China*. Ann Arbor, MI: University of Michigan Press, 2008.

Said, Edward. *Orientalism: Western Conceptions of the Orient*. London: Penguin Books, 1978.

UN Environmental Programme. *Beijing 2008 Olympic Games: An Environmental Review*. Nairobi, Kenya: UNEP, 2007.

US Congressional-Executive Commission on China. *The Beijing Olympics and Human Rights: Roundtable before the Congressional-Executive Commission on China, One Hundred Seventh Congress, Second Session, November 18, 2002*. Washington, DC: US G.P.O., 2002.

The cultural legacy of Olympic posters

John Hughson

International Football Institute, University of Central Lancashire, Greenbank, Preston PR1 2HE, UK

By the time of the London Olympic Games in 2012, posters – officially commissioned in one way or another by host cities – will have been used to promote the forthcoming occasion for 100 years. But existing as more than material artefacts with a use value in advertising, these posters can be considered as artistic offerings with an intrinsic aesthetic value. To state this is not unproblematic, as posters can also be embroiled in the political controversies that accompany the holding of the Olympic Games in particular cities at particular points of those cities' histories. And in nearly all cases of Olympic celebration, posters may be seen to serve an ideological/nationalistic function. Yet, opportunity to view and appreciate a comprehensive range of Olympic posters and associated imagery from the time of the first modern Games in 1896 – afforded by a 2008 exhibition held in London – gives idea as to how posters may be used to reignite the prospect of the 'marriage of art and sport' desired by Pierre de Coubertin, founder of the modern Olympic Movement.

Introduction

This essay considers the cultural significance of Olympic posters. It was written during the Olympiad year of 2008, when the Games were celebrated in Beijing, China. The essay was inspired by the exhibition *A Century of Olympic Posters* displayed at the Victoria and Albert (V&A), Museum of Childhood at Bethnal Green, London, between the 17 May and 7 September. A book based on the exhibition was prepared by the curator Margaret Timmers, and subsequent references in this essay to posters from the exhibition are from copies of them in this accompanying volume.[1] The essay attempts to argue that through Olympic posters the 'marriage' between art and sport, the return of the Greek ideal envisioned by the key founder of the modern Olympic Games Pierre de Coubertin, can be approximated. This is not to say that posters per se will perform this role. The argument is made that only posters of intrinsic artistic value can re-establish de Coubertin's desired link. This is to be recognized as a highly subjective argument, a point made clear enough to the author during feedback discussion following oral presentations of versions of this essay on two occasions.[2] This important caveat notwithstanding, the essay goes on to argue for the return of art posters 'inspired by sport' as a means of re-establishing the ideal of sport and art in concert within the realm of culture.

The 'purpose' of Olympic posters

A promotional blurb for the *Olympic Posters* exhibition provides the following summary:

Since the early twentieth century, posters have heralded the Olympic Games, whetting our appetite and shaping our expectations of the event that is to come. With their broad popular appeal, and ability to project eye-catching and memorable imagery, posters have offered an ideal means of communication for the Games. Since the pioneering Stockholm Games of 1912[3] first exploited the full potential of an internationally-distributed Olympic poster, they have been a vital element in the planning process. They played a key role in publicity campaigns as interest in the event burgeoned in the post-war years, and became an essential part of sophisticated visual design programmes, as supremely exemplified by the posters generated for Mexico City 1968 and Munich 1972.[4]

As is the case with any effective promotional piece for an exhibition with an educational purpose, a number of questions arise from the brief definitional sketch. Here we are given the idea that the poster has a primarily utilitarian function – i.e. to advertise the forthcoming Olympic Games to be held in whichever city according to the four year cycle. But the mention of 'eye-catching and memorable imagery' suggests visual desirability and hence aesthetic appeal. In the poster, then, do we witness the utilitarian and aesthetic item being as one? This question pertains not only to Olympic posters, but to posters in general. Nor is this a matter of new enquiry. With the proliferation of posters in public spaces towards the end of the nineteenth century no less an artistic authority than John Ruskin quipped ironically: 'The fresco-painting of the bill-sticker is likely, so far as I see, to become the principal Fine Art of Modern Europe.' Pleased or otherwise, Ruskin was noting how posters were taking art beyond the exclusive confines of galleries and into public spaces such as the streetcar. This can be seen within related artwork, such as George William Joy's *The Bayswater Omnibus* (1895).[5]

Yet, the view has prevailed for some critics that advertising is the enemy of art and clearly, from this perspective, the aesthetic pretension of the poster is tenuous at best. But surely this is not the case for those Olympic posters that have been designed by recognized artists? The aforementioned poster for the Stockholm Olympic Games of 1912, designed by member of the Swedish Royal Academy, Olle Hjortzberg, provides an interesting example for such consideration. 'Hjortzberg was a decorative painter well known for his murals of church interiors.'[6] He was also a passionate believer in the poster as art form, being a member of the 'Artistic Posters' society. Hjortzberg's poster for Stockholm 1912 is described by Timmers as follows:

> His composition represented a parade of nations, each athlete bearing a billowing flag – with Sweden's at the forefront – and marching towards the common goal of the Olympic Games. It was also a celebration of the nude male body as an ideal, a symbol of athletic perfection in the classical tradition.[7]

However, the original design was altered from a totally observable naked male body to the version we see with the male subject's genitalia festooned with streamers. Within the traditions of western art, Hjortzberg's naked male body is uncontroversial, yet in the context of a poster heralding the modern Olympic Games it was regarded as beyond the pale. Even the amended version was challenged as indecent. For example, it was withdrawn from a railway station in Holland for being 'in the highest degree immoral'.[8] The Hjortzberg controversy indicates that the poster as art classification is not unproblematic. Hjortzberg worked within an artistic or cultural convention that he soon found to clash with social conventions of the early twentieth century.

The display of all art occurs, in one way or another, within sets of social relations. But art is traditionally regarded as existing above, if not beyond, the social realm. Thus the distinction, certainly within the German and English intellectual traditions, between culture and civilization or even more simply, as Raymond Williams put it, between culture and society.[9] In this western formulation, art should ultimately serve no utilitarian purpose and thus may we speak of 'art for art's sake'.[10] The poster, as already noted, serves a decidedly utilitarian purpose and in this sense exists primarily within the social realm. But may we stretch the parameters to speak of 'posters for art's sake'? This question is raised and answered in the affirmative by Dawn Ades in her essay appearing in Timmers's earlier edited collection *The Power of the Poster*.[11] Importantly, what are we getting at when we ask such a question? Being concerned with advertising an event, the poster might be seen as essentially ephemeral in character. Posters also give the impression of being insubstantial in physical quality. Appearing on billboards or walls on cheap paper they are readily damaged and disappear before too long. Unlike the items we usually regard as art they do not seem to stand the test of time, either in terms of aesthetic fascination or material existence. If we may speak of 'posters for art's sake', then surely posters must be able to be appreciated for purely aesthetic reasons. The *Century of Olympic Posters* exhibition helps our consideration in this regard.

Posters for art's sake?

The essay has already described the *Century of Olympic Posters* exhibition serving an educative role. Its very location within the V&A Museum of Childhood suggests the objective to provide an educational opportunity for young people to learn about the history of posters pertaining to the modern Olympic Games. This purposive role may be described as utilitarian but, it can be argued, this need not detract from the possibilities of artistic appreciation. In personal terms, I look back to my own visit to the exhibition as a highly rewarding educational experience and also one of artistic appreciation such as I may enjoy upon visiting other exhibitions more conventionally defined as involving a display of art. I have indicated in my introduction that I fully accept the adage – running from the Greeks through to Shakespeare and onto Hume – that 'beauty is in the eye of the beholder', this pertaining as much to the aesthetic appreciation of objects as it does to our opinion on the looks of fellow humans. With this declared I can draw attention to some of the posters I especially enjoyed looking at, without need of attempting an objective investigation or analysis as to why. Posters I remember being of aesthetic appeal upon the occasion of my visit include Hjortzberg's Stockholm poster, Martha Van Kuyck's poster for the Antwerp 1920 Games,[12] Jean Droit's poster for the Paris 1924 Games[13] and Ilimari Sysimetsa's poster for the 1952 Helsinki Games.[14] Each of these posters I looked at for several minutes and came back to observe at length on a second round through the exhibition.

Also amongst my favourites on the day were Franz Wurbel's poster for the 1936 Berlin Games and Ludwig Hohlwein's poster for the 1936 Winter Olympics, the latter sponsored by the German Railway Publicity Bureau.[15] A stated appreciation of the 1936 posters is perhaps provocative given the historical association of the respective Games with Hitler's National Socialist Regime. The artistic appreciation of Wurbel's and Hohlwein's posters is perhaps as problematic as an appreciation of Leni Riefenstahl's film *Olympia*. Writing in the 1970s, Susan Sontag declared *Olympia* to be an 'official production' of Hitler's regime rather than of the International Olympic Committee (IOC) and, therefore, not appreciable beyond its infamous political context.[16] Might the same be said for the posters by Wurbels and Hohlwein? As Timmers claims:

> the 1936 Berlin Games offered Hitler a supreme opportunity to promote his regime's prestige on a world stage … not only to invest the Third Reich with the pomp and glamour of the modern Games but, by appropriating and inventing images from antiquity, to associate it symbolically with the grandeur of the Roman Empire and the glories of the classical world.[17]

After an initial failure to find a suitable poster via an open competitive process that has become familiar in the lead-up to Olympic Games, Wurbel's design was selected from amongst a small group of drafts latterly commissioned directly by the publicity committee. Wurbel's image of a gigantic golden coloured athletic victor rising above the Brandenburg Gate was regarded as in keeping with the 'heroic realist' style favoured by Hitler.[18]

Hohlwein's poster is, perhaps, even more provocative in its possible promotion of Germanic superiority. As Timmer asks in her analysis of the poster featuring an apparently victorious Olympic skier, are we viewing 'the Aryan archetype of physical strength and perfection, his right arm raised as a Nazi salute'?[19] Hohlwein's association with the political powers of the day in Germany was longstanding. He had made a living by preparing propaganda posters for the German government during the First World War and from 1933 became a declared supporter of National Socialism, and was assumedly untroubled by his 1936 poster being used as a vehicle of political propaganda. Nevertheless, Hohlwein was widely regarded as a leading poster designer in the first half of the twentieth century and Timmers's description of his artistic significance is interestingly read in separation from the non-aesthetic judgements that intervene in an assessment of his character and political liaisons: 'Influenced by the distinguished British poster artists The Beggarstaffs and by contemporary art movements in France and England, he created a style characterised by asymmetry, block-like interlocking shapes, high tonal contrasts and bold lettering.'[20] As Bell-Villada suggests, attraction to artworks directly associable with Nazism pushes the 'Art for Art's Sake' belief to its limits.[21] A similar point was made by Walter Benjamin in the Epilogue to his famous paper 'The Work of Art in the Age of Mechanical Reproduction', first published in 1935/36. However, Benjamin is warning against the Italian Futurist Filippo Marinetti's aestheticizing of war, regarding this – prophetically given his time of writing – as the frightening logical endpoint of fascism's tendency to introduce 'aesthetics into political life'.[22] The posters of Wurbel and Hohlwein and, for that matter, Riefenstahl's *Olympia*, have more to do with the 'politicizing of art' that Benjamin explicitly associated with Communism.[23]

Posters and politics

The political usage of art posters by the Soviet Union has a significant history; several examples from the duration of the Soviet Union's lifespan as a nation are held in the Sergio Grigorian Collection.[24] Images displaying athleticism and sport began to appear in the mid to late 1940s and, gauging from the aforementioned collection, continued as a popular form of visual propaganda into the 1960s, alongside emerging images of popular enticement such as those of Soviet cosmonauts. The Soviet Union became the first communist nation to hold the summer Olympic Games, the XXIInd, in Moscow in 1980. These Games coincided with the final era of the Cold War and a particular period of heightened tension following the Soviet invasion of Afghanistan. Alan Tomlinson notes Olympic posters' move away from 'recourse to aggressively nationalist interests or human bodily stereotypes' following the Wurbel and Hohlwein posters of 1936.[25] This change is reflected in the posters for the Moscow 1980 Games. Despite the tendency for the post-Second World War Soviet poster to portray well muscled young male and female athletes, such imagery is largely missing from the posters of 1980. However, this is not to say imagery of Soviet nationhood is absent from the commissioned posters including the 'official poster'.[26] With regard to the latter, featuring the emblem for those Games designed by Russian artist Vladimir Arsentyev, Timmers comments: 'Arsentyev's concept of parallel lines above the Olympic symbol could be interpreted as five sports tracks and the unity of the sports movement, and also as the silhouette of one of Moscow's Kremlin towers topped by a red five-pointed star.'[27] This is a more subtle means of nationalist expression than the bold variant that reached its zenith with the 1936 posters, but nationalist expression all the same.

It would therefore be facile to accredit to the Germans the monopoly in using the Olympic poster as a vehicle for political propaganda. Given the involvement of national and regional governments and municipal councils in the bidding for, and hosting of, the Olympic Games, posters advertising the Games necessarily carry an ideological message. Olympic posters have always served such purpose to some extent. Having looked at the example from Moscow 1980 we do well to regard the example from the subsequent 1984 Olympic Games hosted by Los Angeles. The poster, designed by prominent artist Robert Rauschenburg (often associated with the pop-art movement)[28] came from a series of 'fine art posters' commissioned by the Los Angeles Olympics Organizing Committee (LAOOC). As described by Timmers, the central image draws upon the Los Angeles 'Star in Motion' emblem with 'interlocking stars crossed by horizontal stripes that appear to set the stars in motion'.[29] A collage of photographic images is inserted into the stars. Some of the images depict sporting activity, others random snaps of people that seem to give view to the diversity of American society. The overall image may be read as one of dynamism and progress – a positive statement, perhaps, on the American way. It is unlikely that Rauschenburg, an artist of some complexity, would have intended such a simple interpretation of his work. But then even rather apparent anti-nationalist cultural offerings, such as Bruce Springsteen's song 'Born in the USA' have been appropriated for flag waving glorification. By putting his poster design forward to the LAOOC Rauschenburg would have been aware of the usage to which it would be put. But again, we broach the issue of a distinction between aesthetic, political and utilitarian statuses.

The most deliberate political usage of posters in association with the Olympic Games occurs with what might be referred to as the anti-poster. In some cases this involves making mockery of the official Olympic posters, this is particularly so in circumstances where the Olympic Games are held in nations under human rights scrutiny for one reason or another. Perusal of the internet will readily reveal images drawing on the official poster for the 2008 Beijing Olympic Games to make a point of protest against those games being held in China. An earlier example of an anti-poster was that by Mexican militant artist Adolfo Mexiac.[30] In the lead up to the 1968 Games in Mexico City student protests against the high level of public spending on the Olympics in a relatively impoverished nation were heavy-handedly quashed by the police and the army. The message from Mexiac's striking poster featuring a gagged protester is clear enough, the inscription of USA on the padlock fastening the chain to the protesters mouth indicting the political influence of the USA along with Mexico's governmental authority.

In one case a poster has been used as a means of diffusing protest anticipated by the organizers prior to the staging of an Olympic Games. White Australia's terrible record of the treatment of its indigenous Aboriginal people was always likely to be raised as a point of protest from the time that nation's largest city Sydney was awarded the 2000 Games in 1993. The poster 'Peace Roo',[31] designed by David Lancashire, could hardly have been expected to quell criticism and protest, but it represented a clear attempt by the organizers to present a symbol of the Games as an occasion of racial reconciliation where white and black Australia come together and the olive branch is finally accepted. However, given that the Australian Prime Minister of the time continued to refuse to apologize to the Aboriginal people for the misdeeds since white settlement, any symbolic gesture such as that of the Lancashire poster rang hollow. And we remember other forms of symbolic protest such as the leading Australian rock band Midnight Oil – the lead singer of which is now a federal government minister – displaying the word 'sorry' on their clothing during their performance at the Games' closing ceremony.

Posters and the Cultural Olympiad

In the final section of this essay Olympic posters are discussed in relation to what has become known as the 'Cultural Olympiad'. My reflections on the Cultural Olympiad has benefited from reading essays by Beatriz Garcia and David Inglis, which appear in a recent edition of *The International Journal of Cultural Policy* on the theme of sport, cultural policy and urban regeneration.[32]

As is well-known, the word Olympism was used by Pierre de Coubertin to capture his sense of an eternal humanistic spirit. De Coubertin defined Olympism as a highpoint in the 'cult of humanity' where men strive to the limits of their imperfections. It is in this humanly based sense of excellence that they aspire to heroism. He, of course, drew this understanding from notions of how the Ancient Olympic Games in Greece had been conducted according to the Heroic ideal.[33] A book published in 1896 on the first modern Olympic Games shows on its front cover an image of the goddess Athena looking favourably towards the modern Athens of the day.[34] According to Inglis:

> when de Coubertin established the modern Olympics he was concerned not only to revive the games as a purely sporting event, but also to rekindle what he took to be the entirety of the ancient Olympic festival. Ancient Greek social structure and culture was, of course, nowhere near as differentiated and divided into autonomous realms as was the Europe in the latter part of the nineteenth century. The original Olympics had in fact begun in the sixth century BCE as a singing contest dedicated to the god Apollo; athletics competitions were only added at a later date. Thus the totality of the ancient Olympics in their heyday was characterised by a cultural complex of 'arts' and 'sports' (although these terms themselves are modern signifiers which point to differentiated social spheres the like of which did not exist at this time) ... Consequently, when de Coubertin sought to rekindle the 'Olympic spirit' in modernity, his aim was to 'take up the ethos of the panegyris from the classical festival – a festive assembly in which the entire people came together to participate in religious rites, sporting competitions and artistic performance'. On this vision, not only were the arts to be present at each Olympiad, they were the central means of expression of its core values, namely the pursuit of excellence (in a wide range of human endeavours) on the one hand, and a fostering of harmonious relations between nations on the other. In effect de Coubertin was proposing a form of Olympiad which was quintessentially 'modern' in that the values it promoted were secular, but which retained, against the powerful differentiating tendencies of modernity, key elements of the undifferentiated complex of sports and arts which had characterised ancient Greek experience. The modern Olympics were to be based upon an alliance of 'athletes, artists and spectators', the former two groups having come in modernity not only to be socially separated from each other, but also to be mutual antagonists, the one group championing the physical values of the body – sportive prowess, physical strength, and so on – and the other upholding the intellectual values of the mind and the soul. Ancient Greek culture had not made such a profound distinction between mind and body that modern culture did, and de Coubertin's attempt to resurrect the Olympics as a fusion of the sportive *and* the artistic was self-consciously an endeavour to heal what he, and many others of the time, thought of as a damaging rift in both human social organisation and the individual human being's sense of self.[35]

Yet, de Coubertin was more than a dewy-eyed romantic for ancient life. He knew that the cultural past of ancient times could not be replicated within the modern festival but, as suggested, believed that an increasingly industrialized world could benefit greatly from re-familiarization with, and aspiration to, the cultural spirit of the past. The problem, as Inglis notes, is that the 'structural differentiation' of the modern world had come to bear more rigidly on cultural life than de Coubertin had accounted for.

In short, the argument is that increasingly complex patterns of life in industrial times, including forms of culture, become differentiated and separate. Within this process cultural life is engulfed within the social realm and the differentiation that occurs is socially rather than culturally determined. Significantly, parallel historical trends impact upon how differentiation is played out. In regard to the arts and sport differentiation, the mind/body dichotomy became paramount. The mind/body dualism debate, of course, dates back to ancient times, but took a particularly sociological turn in industrial times with the increasing division between labour and other tasks. Activities within leisure life, as in work, were more than ever viewed as the mind and body differentiated. Accordingly, sport becomes seen as a primarily physical activity, art as a primarily mental activity. The social evaluation of these differentiated activities became inextricably linked to class – generally speaking and thus not exclusively – mental pursuits to the middle class, and physical pursuits to the working class. Furthermore, the tendency for the term culture to be associated with the arts and, hence, the bourgeoisie meant sport being demarcated outside the realm of culture.

The argument of Inglis, amongst others, is that the relationship between sport and the arts has suffered from this modern differentiation and this becomes most apparent when we recognize the disjuncture between the Games of the Olympiad and the Cultural Olympiad. To an extent, this view is supported by Garcia who, as a scholar actively involved in policy discussion, suggests that Games organizers need to return to a holistic humanism whereby Olympic sport and the cultural programme are seen as being an essentially united endeavour rather than two separate components needing to be yoked together. When the sport/culture nexus is looked at in this way the cultural core of the nexus goes unrecognized and the cultural or artistic programme tends to be regarded – whatever rhetoric might be bandied about – as primarily a corporate operation focussed on presenting the host city in what the organizers perceive to be the best possible light to an international audience, especially via the mass media. According to Garcia:

> Rather than separate identities that must be 'blended', sport, culture and education should be seen as dimensions of the very same principle. The sports and recreation science literature understands sport as a cultural manifestation and an activity through which education takes place. Thus, it is not possible to understand the concept of sport or Olympic sport, without reference to the concepts of culture and education. For this reason, the concept of a cultural programme separated from the sporting and educative programmes seems to be redundant. One would expect all of them to be integrated and perceived accordingly by everybody involved within the Olympic experience, from athletes to coaches, organisers and spectators. However, the lack of an integrated sporting cultural discourse perceived as such by average Olympic audiences and promoted as such by Olympic organisers, supporters and media, reveals that the idea of a perfect and evident integration of these concepts within people's minds is far from being a reality.[36]

Where Garcia diverges from Inglis is that she traces the disjuncture between the sport and cultural programmes of the Olympic occasion back to de Coubertin himself. She uses his phrase 'sport plus culture' to indicate that, despite his undoubted humanistic intentions, he must carry some responsibility for the way in which the cultural programme developed but grew apart from sport at the very outset.[37] The first major endeavour to bring art into the modern Olympic occasion was an Advisory Conference titled 'Incorporation of the Fine Arts in the Olympic Games and Everyday Life', held in Paris in 1906. The conference was largely de Coubertin's initiative and, even at this early stage, he met with resistance. Parisian sport writers ridiculed de Coubertin's talk of a grand marriage and reunification of mind and muscle, sport and art. His idea of a 'pentathlon of the muses' in the form of an Olympic competition for the arts, comprising music composition, literature, sculpture, painting and architecture, did not occur until the Olympics of 1912. But even then the organizers of the Stockholm Games were reputedly lukewarm about an arts competition.[38] Richard Stanton's book *The Forgotten Olympic Art Competitions* gives a detailed account of the correspondence between de Coubertin and the Stockholm organizers.[39] From this correspondence it is apparent that de Coubertin was of the view that the planned arts competition was not receiving the level of support he believed it warranted.

Posters 'inspired by sport'

Towards a conclusion, and in bringing the discussion explicitly back to Olympic posters, it is useful to note that de Coubertin's idea for an art competition involved awarding art works in the various fields that were directly 'inspired by sport'. Indeed, the emphasis on art inspired by sport was spelt out in invitations to the Art Competitions by organizing committees and was encoded in the Regulations of the Contests Literary and Artistic for 1912.[40] However, momentum gathered over the years for a shift from the holding of arts competitions to the arts festivals. This idea was strongly supported by Avery Brundage when he became President of the IOC in 1952.[41] In a 'circular' published in July 1953 Brundage set out the case as to why he believed that Olympic arts competitions had seen their day. One reason was that the arts awards tended to go to professional artists and Brundage saw this as being at odds with the amateur ethos of the Olympic Games. He further believed that the criteria for judging were necessarily arbitrary. To quote Brundage: 'even if the competition is limited to sport buildings, how can you compare the design for a stadium with that of a metropolitan athletic club ... or a swimming pool?' In regard to literature, Brundage noted that there was not just a problem in dealing with the assessment of different genres but also entries in various languages. To quote him, 'Who is there that understands all these languages and can compare the entries?'[42]

By the Melbourne Olympic Games of 1956 the arts competition was officially replaced by an 'Arts Festival' and related events were held at locations such as the Victorian National Gallery, the Melbourne Public Library, the Botanic Gardens and the Melbourne Town Hall.[43] In each category the displays had more to do with showcasing Australian art than with celebrating art 'inspired by sport' in the de Coubertin tradition. Indeed, the closest the Arts Festival seemed to come to this was a symphony concert held inside the architecturally praised Olympic Swimming Pool.[44] Although the cultural programming for subsequent Olympic Games has been significant, since Barcelona 1992 involving the staging of events over the four years in the lead up to the Olympics, the sport and art marriage promoted by the early arts competitions seems to be lost. It may well be the case that the games and the cultural programme of the Olympic occasion attract largely different audiences.

But, against pessimism and resignation, might Olympic posters hold something of an answer to the sport/art unification quandary. Competition has been used as the method to arrive at a decision for the selection of official posters, but my suggestion here is not for a poster competition in the manner of the old arts competition. Rather, it is for a poster festival in the manner of artists being invited to design posters specifically 'inspired by sport'. A memorable example along these lines was the series of posters published in conjunction with the Munich Games of 1972. Planned from the outset in 1967, the Munich organizing committee adopted the view that high-art could indeed be carried in poster form. They set out, 'to engage the best [international] artists' in a poster series that would 'relate artistic activity to the Olympic Games'.[45] Five series containing seven posters each were produced. Some versions of posters were produced on high quality paper – these were done by way of limited edition aiming at a collectors' market. The artists were selected by an appointed art commission and artists who would deliver avant-garde work were deliberately targeted. Artists contributing to this series included David Hockney, Tom Wesselmann, Jacob Lawrence, Horst Antes, Max Bill and Eduardo Chillida.[46] Artwork more accessible to a sports audience was presented in what was called the 'sports series' of posters that offered images of 21 different sport activities. Included in this series was the official poster for the Munich 1972 Games, featuring 'a photographic modification of the architectural model for the Munich Olympic Stadium'.[47]

The works in the Munich 1972 Olympic art poster series were clearly challenging but, as Timmers suggests, may be as good a material example of the art and sport marriage that we have in association with an Olympic Games.[48] I conclude by suggesting that this example be recalled to provide renewed inspiration for how the sport/art relationship may be reconciled. Specifically, then, it is proposed that commissioned artwork, 'inspired by sport', in the form of posters be commissioned by Olympic organizing committees or the cultural planning sub-committees thereof. This would be best done not just via the production and circulation of high quality prints but with the original poster artwork being put on display in a location in close proximity to, if not within, the main Olympic stadium. Beside each poster would be a short narrative by the artist giving some explanation of the work and its relationship to sport. Such a display, in keeping with the Munich example, would exhibit sport-inspired artistic posters as well as a series of individual 'sport' posters. This seems a promising way of getting the idea of the essential sport/art nexus (both art and sport as culture) across to a general audience. People may still end up not appreciating artwork such as Horst Antes' rather abstract offering in 1972, saying that it in no way reminds them of sport, but at least, in the context of the type of exhibition proposed, they may come some way to engaging with it and considering its aesthetic possibilities – art inspired by sport and a re-appreciation of the sport/art relationship inspired by posters.

Notes

[1] Timmers, *Century of Olympic Posters*. I am grateful to Margaret Timmers for taking the time to talk to me about the exhibition and for encouraging my presentation of this paper to the 'Documenting the Beijing Olympics' conference at SOAS, University of London, September 12–13, 2008.
[2] Another version of the paper, 'The Aesthetic Significance of Olympic Posters to the "Cultural Olympiad"', was presented in the Sport and Leisure Cultures seminar series at the University of Brighton, March 23, 2009. I am especially grateful to Professor Jonathan Woodham for his critically constructive comments made in discussion following this presentation.
[3] Timmers, *Century of Olympic Posters*, see poster on page 20.
[4] Ibid., see posters on pages 78 and 88.
[5] Timmers, 'Introduction', 8–10.
[6] Timmers, *Century of Olympic Posters*, 21.
[7] Ibid.
[8] Ibid.
[9] Williams, *Culture and Society*.
[10] The 'art for art's sake' ethos was expounded by the critic Walter Pater and developed rhetorically by Oscar Wilde. For a summary of their articulations see Bell-Villada, *Art For Art's Sake*, 73–96.
[11] Ades, 'Posters for Art's Sake'.
[12] Timmers, *Century of Olympic Posters*, 30.
[13] Ibid., 32.
[14] Ibid., 60. Sysimetsa's poster was originally prepared for the 1940 Olympic Games, which were scheduled for Helsinki. However, due to the disruption and delay caused by the Second World War, the Games did not come to Helsinki until 1952 and it was at this time that Sysimetsa's poster was officially used.

[15] Timmers, *Century of Olympic Posters*, 43, 46.
[16] Sontag, 'Fascinating Fascism'.
[17] Timmers, *Century of Olympic Posters*, 45.
[18] Ibid.
[19] Ibid.
[20] Ibid.
[21] Bell-Villada, *Art For Art's Sake*, 6.
[22] Benjamin, 'The Work of Art', 64.
[23] Ibid.
[24] Lafont, *Soviet Poster*.
[25] Tomlinson, 'Sport and Design', 121.
[26] Timmers, *Century of Olympic Posters*, 99.
[27] Ibid.
[28] Osterwold, *Pop Art*, 145–55.
[29] Timmers, *Century of Olympic Posters*, 102.
[30] Ibid., 77.
[31] Ibid., 122.
[32] Garcia, 'One Hundred Years'; Inglis, 'Cultural *agonistes*'.
[33] Hughson, 'The Global Triumph', 135.
[34] Timmers, *Century of Olympic Posters*, 14.
[35] Inglis, 'Cultural *agonistes*', 455–6.
[36] Garcia, 'One Hundred Years', 366.
[37] Ibid.
[38] Ibid., 368.
[39] Stanton, *Forgotten Olympic Art Competitions*, 30–49.
[40] Ibid., 34.
[41] Ibid., 241.
[42] Ibid., 244.
[43] *The Arts Festival of the Olympic Games Melbourne.*
[44] The prominent Australian architect and cultural critic Robin Boyd regarded the Melbourne Olympic Pool as being 'the first fairy story of Australian building'. See Serle, *Robin Boyd*, 148.
[45] Timmers, *Century of Olympic Posters*, 82. Another important poster project occurred in conjunction with the next Olympic Games, Montreal 1976. The Artists-Athletes Coalition for the Celebration of the 1976 Olympics, chaired by Olympic athlete and now leading sport scholar Bruce Kidd, sponsored the production of posters and related works intended to 'educate the Canadian public about de Coubertin's vision of bringing sport and art together' (Ibid., 95).
[46] Ibid., 84–7.
[47] Ibid., 88–9.
[48] Ibid., 83.

References

Ades, D. 'Posters for Art's Sake'. In *The Power of the Poster*, edited by M. Timmers, 72–99. London: V&A Publications, 1998.

Bell-Villada, G.H. *Art For Art's Sake and Literary Life: How Politics and Markets Helped Shape the Ideology & Culture of Aestheticism, 1790–1990*. Lincoln, NE: University of Nebraska Press, 1998.

Benjamin, W. 'The Work of Art in the Age of Mechanical Reproduction'. In *Media and Cultural Studies: Key Works*, edited by M.G. Durham and D. Kellner, 48–70. Oxford: Blackwell, 2001.

Garcia, B. 'One Hundred Years of Cultural Programming within the Olympic Games (1912–2012): Origins, Evolution and Projections'. *International Journal of Cultural Policy* 14, no. 4 (2008): 361–76.

Hughson, J. 'The Global Triumph of Sport'. *Sport in Society* 12, no. 1 (2009): 134–40.

Inglis, D. 'Cultural *agonistes*: Social Differentiation, Cultural Policy and Cultural Olympiads'. *International Journal of Cultural Policy* 14, no. 4 (2008): 463–77.

Lafont, M. *Soviet Poster: the Sergo Grigorian Collection*. Munich: Prestel, 2007.

Osterwold, T. *Pop Art*. Hong Kong: Taschen, 2007.

Serle, G. *Robin Boyd: a Life*. Melbourne: Melbourne University Press, 1995.

Sontag, S. 'Fascinating Fascism'. In *Under the Sign of Saturn* (Essays), 73–105. New York: Picador, 1980 [1975].

Stanton, R. *The Forgotten Olympic Art Competitions: the Story of the Olympic Art Competitions of the 20th Century*. Victoria, BC: Trafford, 2000.

The Arts Festival of the Olympic Games Melbourne. Melbourne: The Olympic Civic Committee of the Melbourne City Council, 1956.

Timmers, M. 'Introduction'. In *The Power of the Poster*, edited by M. Timmers, 7–25. London: V&A Publications, 1998.

Timmers, M. *A Century of Olympic Posters*. London: V&A Publishing, 2008.

Tomlinson, A. 'Sport and Design: Meanings, Values, Ideologies'. In *Image, Power and Space: Studies in Consumption and Identity*, edited by A. Tomlinson and J. Woodham, 115–35. Aachen: Meyer and Meyer, 2007.

Williams, R. *Culture and Society, 1780–1950*. London: Chatto and Windus, 1958.

The 'caged torch procession': celebrities, protesters and the 2008 Olympic torch relay in London, Paris and San Francisco[1]

John Horne[a] and Garry Whannel[b]

[a]School of Sport, Tourism and the Outdoors, University of Central Lancashire, Preston PR1 2HE, UK; [b]Department of Media Cultures, University of Bedfordshire, Luton, UK

Along with the opening and closing ceremonies, one of the major non-sports events associated with the modern Olympic Games is the torch relay. Although initiated in 1936, the relay has been subject to relatively little academic scrutiny. The events of April 2008 however will have cast a long shadow on the practice. This essay focuses primarily on one week (6–13 April) in the press coverage of the 2008 torch relay as the flame made its way from London to Paris in Europe and then to San Francisco in the USA. It discusses the interpretations offered in the mediated coverage about the relay, the Olympic Movement, the host city and the locations where the relay was taking place, and critically analyses the role of agencies, both for and against the Olympics, that framed the ensuing debate.

Introduction

Any discussion of how a sports mega-event has been represented – visually, aurally or in print – raises questions of selection, representation and meaning. As the Introduction to this volume suggests, certain questions – concerning the key stories, their dramatization, the construction of heroes and villains, the human interest angles and conflicts (political or otherwise) – are germane to an account that attempts to consider the ways in which a mega-event is inscribed into history. What was the impression produced and communicated by representations of aspects of the Beijing Summer Olympic Games? Here we focus on one of the key stories occupying media space for several months before the opening ceremony on the 8 August – the torch relay.

Along with the opening and closing ceremonies one of the main non-sports events associated with the modern Olympic Games is the torch relay. Although begun in 1936, the relay has been subject to little academic scrutiny. This essay focuses on one week in the press coverage of the 2008 torch relay as the flame made its way from London to Paris and then to San Francisco. It discusses the interpretations offered in the mediated coverage about the relay, the Olympic movement, the host city and the locations where the relay was taking place, and critically analyses the role of agencies, both those for and those against the Olympics, that framed the ensuing debate.

Between March and August 2008 the relay attracted clashes involving pro-Tibet and pro-Chinese government supporters, human rights activists and others wanting to demonstrate their support for or against the Beijing Olympic Games. The lighting of the Olympic cauldron by Li Ning on 8 August appeared to mark an end to the 'long running' political controversy surrounding the torch relay and, implicitly at least, could be seen as shifting attention away from politics to sporting and economic considerations – inaugurating as it did the sports events themselves and, for some commentators reflections on their likely impact on the relative economic fortunes of Adidas, Nike or Li Ning's own brand of sportswear and equipment.

It is possible to use many different theories to analyse the modern Olympic Games: as one of the chief vehicles of the 'society of the spectacle', as a 'pseudo event', or as a feature of the 'culture industry'. But these approaches have the tendency to formalize the properties of the events and rob them of specific content. As Whannel notes, they tend to open a gap 'between the multiple hybrid complexities of lived experience and the symbolic constructions of media representation'.[2] Hence it is useful to recall, as Roche suggests, that studying mega-events in the round requires at least two levels of analysis – structural (or formal) and phenomenological (or lived) considerations.[3] The torch relay and its representation also offer a case study through which to examine politics and media associated with the mega-event. If we consider, as Price and Dayan do,[4] that the Olympics are a 'media event', then we can approach the torch relay as a very good example of what happens when 'media events become marked by efforts by free riders or interlopers to seize the opportunity to perform in a global theatre of representation'.[5] What Price alerts us to is the political significance of the modern Olympic Games – the place they hold as a 'platform' – a 'mechanism that allows for the presentation of information and its transmission from a sender to a receiver'[6] – on a global scale. As Short suggests, the Summer Olympics are 'global spectacles, national campaigns and city enterprises'[7] at one and the same time. They are '"glocal" events of national significance'.[8]

The torch relay is no ancient Olympian ritual, but rather a classic example of the 'invention of tradition', devised in this instance by the Nazis for the 1936 Olympic Games to emphasize the supposed 'spiritual bond' between the German fatherland and the sacred places of Ancient Greece. A flame was lit in the stadium for the first time in the 1928 Olympic Games in Amsterdam, and again in 1932 in Los Angeles, but the first time the flame was lit at Olympia and conveyed by relay was 1936. The Ancient Greeks did have relays carrying torches, but there is no evidence that they ever did so in connection with the Olympic Games.

In short, the relay was invented in order to glorify the Nazi regime and assert its connection to Greek civilization as a sort of legitimating trope. Krupp, the German arms producer, created and sponsored the torches. While in Vienna, Austrian Nazis greeted the torch with cries of 'Heil Hitler' and demonstrated against Jewish members of the Austrian Olympic team, with a resultant 500 arrests; in Prague street fighting broke out between Sudetan Germans and Czechs. The Nazi anthem, the 'Horst Wessel Lied' was played in Ancient Olympia when the flame was lit. The song, which contains the line 'Already millions are looking to the swastika, full of hope' was also sung at the Opening Ceremony.[9]

The concept of the torch travelling around the world is another invention of tradition, but far more recent – it was only introduced at the 2004 Olympic Games. Prior to that the torch usually took the most direct route: while there were occasional ceremonies on route, the relay itself was largely restricted to Greece, the host country, and any other countries immediately en route. In 2004, for the first time, the torch took a more elaborate and circuitous route visiting countries around the world. While this all contributes to advance publicity for the Games, not always with perfect success, the main reason for the change is sponsorship. The Olympic Games is unique amongst major events in allowing no arena advertising. Consequently, despite paying huge sums to join the Olympic Sponsorship programme, the sponsoring companies get no access to the global television audience.

The global torch relay provides a set of mobile photo opportunities around the world, ensuring exposure of the brand name across media for a month or more.

As a global spectacle, consumed by audiences around the world, the Olympic Games become a focal point for political contestation. The hosts utilize the event to boost the image of their city and their nation; the sponsors to promote and enhance brand awareness and brand image, and campaigners use it to gain media coverage for their issues. The torch relay presents an opportunity for subversion or 'hijacking' by otherwise marginal actors. In this case 'piggybacking' or even 'piggyjacking'[10] might be considered more appropriate ways of referring to the situation where actors, 'finding a platform that has proven highly successful in establishing a major constituency for one purpose ... then convert that constituency to a different, unintended objective'.[11] Such associations between Olympic rituals and ceremonies can be deemed more or less legitimate. The recent commercialization of the relay – in 2008 heavily underpinned by the Chinese company Lenovo and other companies sponsoring the Games – can be seen as a contractually legitimate, as opposed to an 'ambush', form of marketing.

The torch took about a year to design to the specifications that would keep it burning on its varied journey around the world, said David Hill, vice-president of corporate identity and design for Lenovo, the computer manufacturing firm that designed the torch and a main sponsor of the torch relay.[12]

For the costs of the creation of the event to be borne by one group, and for the benefits (or at least mediation of a cause) to be obtained by others, is an example of platform 'hijacking'. The Olympic Games is a media platform with an assumed dominant narrative; the IOC, Games organizers, sponsors and athletic federations attempt to defend the narrative against counter narratives. Today this involves intense management of the narrative, although this does not guarantee success, as we will see. A problem for the Olympics is that there is some ambiguity over the ownership of the Olympic Games platform and the narrative. Who owns it? Is it the IOC, the organizing committee, the host city or nation, or the sponsors? There are complementary and competitive uses of the narrative, the former as in advertising by the Korean National Tourism Agency during the summer of 2008 attempting to persuade tourists to continue their stay in East Asia by visiting Seoul; the latter through the development of the alternate phrase 'The Genocide Games'. Some would see the division between the idealists, who are expressing internationalism, sentimentalism, global solidarity, and merchants, who are focussing on the event as a showcase for the global sports entertainment industry, as a major fault line in the contemporary Olympics. Yet 'promotionalism' in global civil society is unstable.[13] Hence the Olympic Games, as both a platform and a discourse, are unstable too.

The 2008 'journey of harmony'

'Human rights shadow over Beijing Games.'[14]
'Taiwan rejects China's planned route for Olympic torch.'[15]

From the start of the decision to award the Games to Beijing in 2001, and the commencement of the Beijing Olympiad in 2004, there was controversy, just as there had been in 1993 when the Beijing bid was marginally defeated by Sydney and behind which lay attempts to cast the Chinese bid in as bad a light as possible. In particular, regarding the torch relay, in 2008 there was disagreement over the route – involving the 'two Chinas' issue, Tibet and Mount Everest – for at least a year before it happened. Celebrities contributed to a call for a boycott of the Beijing Games on the basis of human rights abuses in China, and China's relations with Sudan and Darfur in particular. Prominent among these were the actors Richard Gere and Mia Farrow, the latter whose arguments led to the withdrawal of Steven Spielberg from producing the opening and closing ceremonies.[16] Archbishop Desmond Tutu later called for a boycott of the opening ceremony: 'Boycott opening of Olympics urges Tutu',[17] and appeared to receive some support from European political leaders such as Angela Merkel and Gordon Brown. On 24 March 2008 the torch was lit – and British TV covered the demonstration by members of Reporters without Borders at the ceremony in Olympia. The torch was then taken around Greece to Athens from where it was transferred to Beijing on 31 March.

London-Paris-San Francisco

The torch came to London 134 days before the Beijing Olympics opened. London's 31 mile route turned into a procession in which the torch was sometimes shielded by up to three ranks of guards – blue tracksuit wearing flame attendants (or 'flame retardants' as one wag renamed them), later to be revealed as members of the Chinese People's Armed Police – the London Metropolitan police on foot, and police as outriders on bicycles, horses and motorbikes.[18] It appeared, from the live coverage broadcast on TV, that anyone getting in the way or near the torch was either swatted aside by the police or arrested – there were 35 arrests by mid-afternoon. There were changes from the scheduled route – for example in Fleet Street the torch was transferred to a bus and taken to St Paul's. As Mihir Bose, the BBC's first sports news editor commented, instead of a view of the torch most people got a view of a police operation. By the time it was reaching its destination – the O2 Arena – Bose referred to it live on air as a 'caged torch procession'.[19]

As the relay made its way across London the BBC TV News 24 channel covered events as they unfolded. Occasionally athletes were called upon to comment on the situation. Olympic medal winner Duncan Goodhew stated that the Olympics was about excellence, equity and a force for good; the actions seen on the TV screen did not reflect well on the UK.[20] TV presenter and former tennis professional Sue Barker said that the event had been 'hijacked' by a series of pressure groups.[21] Lord Sebastian Coe, an Olympic champion, former conservative MP and director of LOCOG, said that most of the legs of the relay passed off without much incident. Athlete Kelly Holmes promoted a view very similar to the one put forward by Goodhew – which raised a suspicion that there was a prepared 'statement' for athletes and supporters to convey the preferred Olympic narrative about fellowship, internationalism and its general benefit to humanity.[22]

Print media coverage of the Torch Relay 6–13 April 2008

The agenda was set before the arrival of the torch in Europe in April by the television and print media coverage of the lighting ceremony and political developments in Tibet, which established the disruption of the torch relay as the main narrative theme: 'New Clashes in Tibet on Eve of Torch's Arrival in UK'.[23] Then when it arrived in London the torch relay stimulated the following headlines: 'Arrests, Fights, Jeering: Olympic Relay Sparks Anger and Chaos' and 'OLYMPIC SPIRIT COMES TO BRITAIN'.[24] Below the second of these headlines there were three pictures of police struggling with demonstrators with the words:

Faster! Officers rush to prevent protester from extinguishing the flame.
Higher! Additional security called in after man attempts to grab torch.
Stronger! Police get tough to keep the relay on course for Beijing.[25]

The general verdict of the British press was damning – the event was portrayed widely as a chaotic farce: 'The Event Descended into Chaos'; 'OLYMPIC MAYHEM' and

'Organisers hoped for a feelgood day of fun. Instead there was an atmosphere of tension, indecision and a siege mentality ... Celebrity torch bearers ran a gauntlet of abuse and threats ... Millions worldwide saw shocking scenes unfold'.[26] The comments continued: 'OLYMPIC RUN TURNS INTO FARCE: Angry demonstrators turned the Olympic torch procession into a farce yesterday as Britain's Olympic prestige was damaged by scuffles on its route through London.'[27] And: 'our Olympic showpiece ended in violence and farce ... a combination of sinister and slapstick ... bizarre scenes ... embarrassing fiasco ... was beamed around the world ... surreal circus ... Chinese goon army ... The burly minders'.[28]

The *Evening Standard* – then, the only paid-for daily London newspaper – linked events to a negative view of the UK and the capital city. The front page headline 'THE SHAMING OF LONDON' over a picture of a Malaysian family sleeping in a cardboard box in Heathrow Terminal 5 was above three sub headings which read:

> T5 travellers forced to spend night in cardboard boxes.
> Olympic torch fiasco descends into a war of words.
> No wonder these visitors swore: 'Bloody England'.[29]

In editorials the perspective varied, according to who was blamed for the events. The *Daily Mail* and the *Evening Standard* blamed the IOC for choosing China:

> When it awarded the Games to China it extracted a number of commitments from the Chinese government over human rights. It has done nothing like enough to make clear that, particularly in respect of Tibet, these commitments have not been honoured.[30]

> The real embarrassment is that the International Olympic Committee seems to have no moral compass in deciding who gets the Games. China's regime doesn't deserve this honour. Can the IOC be surprised when the public says so?[31]

The Sun, by contrast, regarded it as a victory for the tradition of protest and for the police:

> FREEDOM WINS

> We are lucky to live in a country that values its citizens' right to hold lawful peaceful protests. And police must be congratulated for their skill in allowing that to happen while preventing those with unlawful intentions from putting the flame out or injuring torch bearers.[32]

The role of the blue tracksuited torch guards was particularly controversial attracting headlines such as: 'Paramilitaries Guard Torch Relay'.[33]

The Greater London Authority, which co-organized the event, said: 'They were brought over by the Beijing organising committee. They were the responsibility of Beijing.' A spokesman insisted it was the British Olympic Association which was responsible for dealing with the Chinese. But the BOA's spokesman said: 'They were nothing to do with us. The relationship they had with the Met and the GLA was the responsibility of the GLA.' The Met Police said the Chinese guards had 'no executive powers' in Britain and were simply there to protect the torch. Privately, police were said to be furious as officers were made to look ridiculous, jogging along in cycle helmets and holding hands to form a chain around the bearers. MPs said the fiasco made Britain a laughing stock. But Olympics Minister Tessa Jowell said: 'I don't think it made us look bad. The police did the best job they could.'[34]

In general, the various implicated organizations did their best to deflect blame elsewhere. When the torch continued on its journey in Paris, amidst 'waves of chaos',[35] according to the headlines there was an almost tangible sense of relief in the manner in which the British press suggested the French had done no better and possibly worse in policing the protests:

SACRE BLEU

The Olympic torch was snuffed out four times yesterday as it was relayed through Paris – before eventually being put on a BUS to shield it from anti-Chinese mobs.[36]

Paris demonstrators force flame to be extinguished.[37]

MORE OLYMPIC CHAOS AS PROTESTS SNUFF OUT TORCH

The Olympic torch relay descended into French farce yesterday as protesters forced officials to abandon the Paris leg of the parade. Chinese minders extinguished the 'eternal flame' four times in as many hours so demonstrators could not get near it.[38]

Yesterday the mayhem continued in Paris. Security officials extinguished the torch four times before putting it in a bus for the final stages.[39]

The flame had to be extinguished three times amid safety concerns.[40]

The relay was now being subjected to ever enhanced security and growing restrictions in scale. By the time it arrived in San Francisco it had become a running story in the world's media, a soap opera in which the next episode was keenly anticipated. *The Guardian* reported that 'All police leave has been cancelled' and said: 'officials in San Francisco brace themselves for a repetition of the tumultuous scenes in Paris and London'.[41] The *New York Times* reported that a heavy law enforcement presence was expected, and that there would be a low-altitude, no-flight zone over the route.[42] Other papers reported: 'Olympic-Torch Protestors Given Slip in San Francisco' and 'Torch Relay Takes Detour'.[43] The events of 6–11 April 2008 were summed up by the *Guardian Weekly*: 'Torch's Journey Descends into Chaos'.[44]

Spin, counter-spin and fall-out from the 'Tour de Farce'

In the immediate wake of high profile media events, such as the 'caged torch procession' or 'Tour de Farce' as *The Guardian* named it,[45] key actors battled to establish their own frames and definitions of the situation as dominant. Famous names were reported as supporting the protests. Richard Gere attended a vigil in San Francisco and said that by parading the torch in Tibet, China was trying to give a false picture of peace and harmony there.[46] Celebrities were also participants in the torch relay and the British press emphasized their encounters with demonstrators:

> Stars are pounced on by protesters as London Olympic torch parade turns ugly. TV's Konnie Huq was set upon by a Free Tibet campaigner who tried to rip the torch from her hands. Olympic champ Denise Lewis was charged at by several activists while Sir Clive Woodward had his path blocked by a mob. Cricket star Kevin Pietersen had to be ushered away when campaigners threatened to swamp him … Amid endless booing and hissing, the stars – including Denise Van Outen, Paula Radcliffe, Arsenal's Theo Walcott and the Sugababes – were continually interrupted along the route.[47]

A BBC journalist based in China suggested that the normal response to difficult news in China was to delay, condemn and then deride. On this occasion there were other opportunities to counter the negative news: the foiling of a terrorist plot, the discovery of a heroine (Jin Jing), and concerns about Western media coverage of China by the ambassador to London as indicated by the headlines below:

China Foils Olympic Terror Plot.
Western Press Demonises China.
Chinese Ambassador Warns of Backlash.[48]

The Western media generally has long operated with a restricted and monolithic vision of China – overlooking tensions between progressives and reactionaries, liberalizing and conservative elements, central and local government. As a result an excessively static image of China is constructed, de-emphasizing the very rapid pace of change and adjustment that Chinese society is undergoing. The media in China, whilst subject to control and regulation, is also at times a resource for combating corruption.[49] Limited and stereotypical images and conceptions of East Asian (and other non-Western) societies is an identified feature of Western media coverage of sports mega-events, as much as political, economic and social issues. Wasserstrom identified the polarized vision of China routinely constructed in the US media – revolving between the nightmare and the dream of 'Big Bad China and the Good Chinese'.[50]

Celebrity involvement – featuring children's' writers and Hollywood actors – continued with the coincidence of 'Global Day for Darfur' on 13 April: 'Rowling demands action in Darfur'.[51] Another spin off was the concern that the protests might switch to sponsors of the relay, 'Olympic Torch Uproar Could Burn Lenovo' and 'Follow the Money: Olympic Protest Movement Turns its Sights on to Sponsors'.[52]

Conclusions

In the build up to any Olympic Games the media coverage is often focussed on two central questions: 'will it go over budget?' and 'will the facilities be ready in time?' The answer to both questions is usually 'yes'. Other newsworthy possibilities depend on the specific location and political developments at the time. In terms of news management by the organizing committee, the months leading up to the Games, are the most perilous period, in which negative stories can easily turn in to front page dramas, as occurred in 2008 during the torch relay. After the Games commence, by contrast, there is a massive turning inward of the media to events in the arenas and the stadia.

What does this account tell us about the coverage of the build up to the Beijing Olympic Games? Hosting the Olympic Games (and other mega-events) is a political act; public events and institutions involving decisions over the allocation of resources have political dimensions. They require consideration of the distribution of power, struggles and who gains from the situation. Narratives associated with hosting mega-events, and the Summer Olympic Games in particular, in East Asia have included the following: that it provides an opportunity to catch up or modernize, an opportunity to challenge (Western) modernity, and an opportunity to project distinctive forms of hybrid or hyper- modernity. Whether in the form of overt politics, protest or promotion, hosting a sports 'mega' provides an opportunity for power plays by states, civic authorities and groups for and against the event. Attempts to hijack the torch relay provoked a nationalist response, when previously the Olympics were being promoted as an internationalizing event. The Western media tended to portray the events of London, Paris and San Francisco as peaceful protests against a repressive regime and a military crackdown. The Chinese media eventually responded by considering the events as violent acts against innocent people (especially the disabled 'heroine' of Paris, Jin Jing) requiring the restoration of order and stability. In this way different actors sought to impose their frames of reference on the situation. Who has the power to define dominant narratives and frames remains a crucial question.

So what does this tell us about the politics of sports mega-events and the Olympic Games in particular? The Olympic Games attract attention globally for several months before the two-week event itself. Political issues get attached to it by virtue of it being a media event and platform. Nations, and since the late 1980s, cities as part of nations, put their power, competence and reputation on the line. Cities and nations can have alternative intentions. Olympic boosters and Olympic sceptics – politicians, sports, human rights and celebrities – have multiple interests when engaging in the politics of the Olympics. The Olympic Games deploys invented traditions – the oath, the village, the torch relay. The last serves to advertise and promote the Olympic Games, the host city, nation and the IOC. The expanded torch relay gave Olympic sponsors an opportunity to promote themselves away from the still-regulated stadia environment. The Olympics provides an opportunity to 'piggyjack' an event nonetheless.

What does this tell us about the media? Gatekeeping, agenda setting, framing and constructing news remain key aspects of the mediation of any event and mega-event. Power and influence to shape the agenda – and construct the story – remain tied to large media organizations despite the internet and the emergence of heterogeneous voices. Live coverage in key locations means the media agenda alters as the event develops. A person on the spot will not always be best informed about the progress of a news story.[53] Media representations are more central to contemporary politics than what happens in the street. Impression management is the new battleground. Hijacking or piggybacking will continue to pose problems for dominant narratives. The effect of vortextuality is dangerous for public relations, spin doctors and media managers.[54] The torch became a symbol of state power needing great protection. If the relay had been differently organized with different groups of people surrounding it (women, people of the world, children) a different image of it could have been constructed. Better image management and planning, based on a better understanding of the how the media works in specific instances might have averted or at least reduced the impact of the 2008 torch relay fiasco.[55]

All of this points out that the impact of the erosion of the public-private distinction, the declining powers of regulation and censorship, and the growth of celebrity culture, combined with the expansion of the media and the increase in the speed of circulation, have produced the phenomenon Whannel referred to as 'vortextuality'.[56] The various media constantly feed off each other in a process of self-referentiality and intertextuality. In an era of electronic and digital information exchange, the speed at which this happens has become very rapid. Certain super-major events come to dominate the headlines. It becomes temporarily difficult for columnists and commentators to discuss anything else. They are drawn in, as if by a vortex. There is a short term compression of the media agenda. Other topics either disappear or have to be connected to the vortextual event. In the midst of a vortextual moment, cartoons, radio phone-ins, celebrity columnists, news magazines, cultural commentators and letter pages are all drawn into the central topic. Among examples of this effect are funerals (the death of Princess Diana), trials (the verdict announcement in the Michael Jackson trial), and celebrity weddings (e.g. of David Beckham and Victoria Adams).

What does this tell us about the future? The Olympic Games are composed of diverse elements: modernity and tradition, festival and global spectacle, peace and internationalism, discipline and surveillance, youth, the IOC and commercial sponsors. It is difficult to keep opportunities for protest secure without risking poor image and depleting reputation further – like scandals – and maybe this is why no petitioners for protests were allowed in Beijing in 2008.[57] More, not less, difficult to predict is what will happen in the run up to London 2012 and beyond, but the spectacle is likely to become more closely monitored, policed and kept under surveillance, as the following newspaper headlines suggest:

> London May Forego 2012 Procession after Global Protests Against Beijing Games.
> IOC Set to Drop London's 2012 Torch Relay.
> No Olympic Torch Relay for London 2012.[58]

In the age of risk society where 'subpolitics' – motivated by ethical considerations, a decentered network form of organization and a pluralistic tactical focus – are more evident than institutionalized politics,[59] global social movements seek to develop new worlds and new sport and thus contribute to global civil society.[60] For authorities, including sports mega-event organizers, risk society raises questions about the calculation of spectacle and the need for enhanced impression management. In this context the Beijing Games and other Olympic Games will remain a field of contestation 'in which conflicting discourses, constituted by different regimes of truth produced by various interest groups, vie for global attention'.[61] Media events such as the Olympics are 'an exploited resource within a political economy of collective attention'.[62] A two-year cycle follows the pattern of the major sports mega-events. Just like the Olympic flame (as opposed to the torch) the global critical consciousness about social justice, social equity and social development cannot be extinguished when events come to an end. Sports mega-events 'have become strategic venues'[63] in political, as well as economic and sporting, terms.

Notes

1 This essay derives from a paper originally drafted for a symposium in London in September 2008 by John Horne and another presented by Garry Whannel in Beijing in August 2008.
2 Whannel, 'Caught in the Spotlight', 253.
3 Roche, *Mega-events*, 217–35.
4 Price, 'On Seizing the Olympic Platform'; Dayan, 'Beyond Media Events'.
5 Price, 'On Seizing the Olympic Platform', 86.
6 Ibid., 87.
7 Short, *Global Metropolitan*, 86.
8 Ibid.
9 For more on the 1936 Games, see Hart-Davis, *Hitler's Games*; Brohm, *Jeux Olympiques à Berlin*; Murray and Kruger, *The Nazi Olympics*; and Walters, *Berlin Games*.
10 Miah, Garcia and Zhihui, '"We are the Media"', 339; 343 n.10.
11 Price, 'On Seizing the Olympic Platform', 89.
12 *San Francisco Chronicle*, April 7, 2008.
13 Knight and Greenberg, 'Promotionalism and Subpolitics'.
14 *The Guardian*, August 30, 2004, 5.
15 *The Guardian*, April 27, 2007, 18.
16 See Price, 'On Seizing the Olympic Platform'.
17 Ibid. *The Guardian*, April 29, 2008, 18.
18 It was later stated that there were 2,060 Metropolitan police officers on duty on 6 April 2008 at a cost of £746,000. *The Guardian*, May 7, 2008, 7.
19 BBC News, 5.50 p.m.
20 BBC News 24, 3.50 p.m.
21 BBC News, 5.35 p.m.
22 Subsequently confirmed by journalist Richard Williams (*The Guardian*, April 8, 2008, Sport section, 7).
23 *The Guardian*, April 5, 2008, 1.
24 *The Guardian*, April 7, 2008, 1; and *The Independent*, April 7, 2008, 1.
25 *The Independent*, April 7, 2008, 1.
26 *Evening Standard*, April 7, 2008; *The Sun*, April 7, 2008; *The Sun*, April 7, 2008.
27 *Daily Express*, April 7, 2008.
28 *Daily Mail*, April 7, 2008.
29 *Evening Standard*, April 7, 2008.
30 Ibid.
31 *Daily Mail*, Editorial, April 7, 2008.
32 *The Sun*, April 7, 2008.
33 *Financial Times*, April 9, 2008, 10.
34 *Daily Mail*, April 8, 2008.
35 *International Herald Tribune*, April 8, 2008.
36 *The Sun*, April 8, 2008.
37 Ibid., 3. Note that it was the torch and not the flame that was extinguished according to other reports.

38 *Daily Express*, April 8, 2008.
39 *Daily Mail*, April 8, 2008.
40 BBC News, April 11, 2008. www.bbc.co.uk.
41 *The Guardian*, April 9, 2008.
42 *New York Times*, April 8, 2008.
43 *Wall Street Journal*, April 8, 2008, A7; *USA Today*, April 8, 2008, A1.
44 *Guardian Weekly*, April 11, 2008, 12.
45 *Guardian Weekly*, April 11, 2008, 2.
46 BBC News, April 9, 2008. www.bbc.co.uk.
47 *Daily Mirror*, April 7, 2008.
48 BBC News Online, April 10, 2008; BBC News Online, April 13, 2008; *The Guardian*, April 14, 2008, 11.
49 Whannel, 'Caught in the Spotlight'.
50 Wasserstrom, 'Dreams and Nightmares', 179.
51 BBC News Online, April 11, 2008.
52 *Wall Street Journal*, April 20, 2008, B1; *The Guardian*, April 20, 2008, 3.
53 On the day of the London leg of the torch relay, GW in London, observing and taking pictures of the torch relay, called JH in Edinburgh to find out what was happening via the BBC TV broadcast. As is often the case it is possible to be too close to an event to fully understand it. The significance lies in what images and words are utilized to narrate the events in the media.
54 Whannel, *Media Sport Stars*.
55 Whannel, 'Caught in the Spotlight'.
56 Whannel, *Media Sport Stars*.
57 Although we have to avoid the double-bind identified by Wasserstrom, 'Dreams and Nightmares', 179, protests against a regime can be considered as an indication of the repressive nature of a regime; the absence of such protests can equally be interpreted as evidence of just how repressive a regime is!
58 *The Guardian*, April 9, 2008, 3; *The Guardian*, August 6, 2008, 'Sport section', 1; *The Times*, August 6, 2008.
59 Knight and Greenberg, 'Promotionalism and Subpolitics'; see also Beck, *Risk Society*.
60 Harvey, Horne and Safa, 'From "One World, One Dream"'; Price, 'On Seizing the Olympic Platform'.
61 De Kloet, Chong and Liu, 'The Beijing Olympics', 9.
62 Dayan, 'Beyond Media Events', 397.
63 Ibid.

References

Beck, U. *Risk Society: Towards a New Modernity*. London: Sage, 1992.
Brohm, Jean-Marie. *Jeux Olympiques à Berlin*. Paris: Editions Complexe, 1980.
Dayan, D. 'Beyond Media Events: Disenchantment, Derailment, Disruption'. In *Owning the Olympics: Narratives of the New China*, ed. M. Price and D. Dayan, 391–401. Ann Arbor, MI: University of Michigan Press, 2008.
Hart-Davis, Duff. *Hitler's Games*. London: Century, 1986.
Harvey, J., J. Horne, and P. Safa. 'From "One World, One Dream" to "Another Sport is Possible": Alter-Globalization, New Social Movements and Sport'. Paper presented at conference 'To Remember is to Resist: 40 years of Sport and Social Change', Toronto, May 20–22 2008.
De Kloet, J., G.P.L. Chong, and W. Liu. 'The Beijing Olympics and the Art of Nation-State Maintenance'. *China aktuell* 2 (2008): 5–35.
Knight, G., and J. Greenberg. 'Promotionalism and Subpolitics'. *Management Communication Quarterly* 15, no. 4 (2002): 541–70.
Miah, A., B. Garcia, and T. Zhihui. '"We are the Media": Nonaccredited Media and Citizen Journalists at the Olympic Games'. In *Owning the Olympics: Narratives of the New China*, ed. M. Price and D. Dayan, 320–45. Ann Arbor, MI: University of Michigan Press, 2008.
Murray, William and Kruger, Arnd, eds. *The Nazi Olympics*. Urbana and Chicago, IL: University of Illinois Press, 2003.
Price, M. 'On Seizing the Olympic Platform'. In *Owning the Olympics: Narratives of the New China*, ed. M. Price and D. Dayan, 86–114. Ann Arbor, MI: University of Michigan Press, 2008.
Roche, M. *Mega-events and Modernity*. London: Routledge, 2000.

Short, J.R. *Global Metropolitan: Globalizing Cities in a Capitalist World*. London: Routledge, 2004.

Walters, Guy. *Berlin Games: How Hitler Stole the Olympic Dream*. London: John Murray, 2006.

Wasserstrom, J. 'Dreams and Nightmares: History and U.S. Visions of the Beijing Games'. In *Owning the Olympics: Narratives of the New China*, ed. M. Price and D. Dayan, 163–84. Ann Arbor, MI: University of Michigan Press, 2008.

Whannel, G. *Media Sport Stars: Masculinities and moralities*. London: Routledge, 2002.

Whannel, Garry. 'Caught in the Spotlight: Media Themes in the Build-up to the Beijing Olympic Games'. In *Pathways: Critiques and Discourse in Olympic Research*, ed. Robert K. Barney, Michael K. Heine, Kevin B. Wamsley, and Gordon H. MacDonald. Ninth International Symposium for Olympic Research. Alberta: International Centre for Olympic Studies, 2008.

'Betwixt and between': reflections on the ritual aspects of the opening and closing ceremonies of the Beijing Olympics

Jialing Luo

Department of Social Anthropology, Darwin College, University of Cambridge, Silver Street, Cambridge CB3 9EU, UK

Taking as its point of departure the traditions associated with the Olympic Games, this essay discusses the sentiments and aspirations of a nation 'betwixt and between'; one that is recovering from a traumatic modern history; is promulgating the ideology of *harmony* as part of the formation of an intangible social structure; and is experiencing uncertainties in the government about how to fulfil its political vision of establishing a 'harmonious society'. Specifically, drawing on both anthropological theories of ritual and data collected in Beijing as part of long-term multi-sited fieldwork, the essay looks at three displays of cultural performance during the 2008 Olympics opening and closing ceremonies: *'Footprints and Five Rings'*, *'Harmony'* and *'The Memory Tower'*. Through analysing how China attempted to use the opening and closing ceremonies as public rituals for realizing its dream of reinventing itself as a nation, and how this ambition has been frustrated and promoted, the essay hopes to demystify China's coming-of-age rite of passage from an anthropological perspective, and to bring a new dimension to the development of concepts of ritual by using Beijing as a case study.

The Olympics as phenomena of ritual and symbolism

The Olympics originated in Greece in 776 BCE as a celebration involving sacrifices and ceremonies worshiping Zeus and continued until they were banned on the basis of violating the spirit of Christianity in 393 CE. Revived as a secular festival in the late nineteenth century, the Games have appeared to continue this entanglement between sport and religious or quasi-religious forms embracing the 'ethos of the *panegyris*',[1] conditioning to a great extent the multi-dimensional symbolism of modern times and of the modern nation state. Officially endorsed by the International Olympic Committee, the sacredness of the Olympics that 'owed their purity and importance to religion'[2] manifests itself in an array of symbolic practices ranging from the collective rituals of the Games' large-scale opening and closing ceremonies to the specially designed emblems and mascots loaded with meanings. These differentiate the Olympics from other gatherings, while making symbolic connections with the ancient festivals.

Unlike many religious tribal rituals, observed by anthropologists such as Victor Turner[3] and Max Gluckman,[4] during which spirits were invoked or God made present to mediate in rites of initiation, conflict and the like, the modern Olympics opening and closing ceremonies blur the boundaries between the sacred and the secular. Here, the secular shares in the fundamental 'unquestionability' of the sacred in the sense that 'unquestionable tenets' exist in 'secular political ideologies' as in religion.[5] That is to say, without involving any supernatural beings, the secular ceremonies are equally capable of staging social discourses and producing 'unquestionable doctrines',[6] based on what one imagines. These secular rituals are just as functional and communicative, if not more so, as the religious ones.

Thus, the attention-grabbing Olympic opening and closing ceremonies are public rituals, whose cosmopolitan and unique nature means that no host country could pass up the opportunity to communicate the core cultural values of the nation state in which it was held. With the sacred associations to the ancient Greek Games in the background, the modern secular ceremonies are meticulously arranged to generate dramatic attempts to fulfil the host country's ambitions. Therefore, while verbally emphasizing Olympism as a philosophy of life, promoting an internationally understood physical and spiritual strength, peace, friendship, equality, fairness, success and joy, the Olympics have been put to a variety of often political or commercial purposes. Hitler used the Berlin 1936 Games to assert his racial superiority theories, while the Los Angeles 1984 Olympics introduced 'named sponsorship' and 'private finance'.[7] The pragmatism and the increasing complexity of the Games and their symbolism sometimes go beyond what the Olympics were intended to mean in the first instance.

Since winning its bid in 2001 to host the 2008 Olympics, Beijing underwent unprecedented changes at a stunning speed to prepare itself for the Games. Thomas Friedman[8] has termed this transformation a Biblical-like seven years of nation-building. In contrast to the Atlanta 1996 Games, an apparently local event, and the Athens 2004 Games, situated between the local and national, the Beijing Olympics was national in every sense. Simply put, there were seven host cities throughout China, and the Olympic torch was carried through 113 cities in 31 provinces, autonomous regions and *zhixiashi* (municipalities directly under the Central Government of China): a journey totalling 40,000 kilometres. Attaching great national pride to its role as host, the state mobilized enormous resources to make the Games a historic success. Amongst other things, a huge budget of £21 billion was invested.

China seemed to be showcasing its economic achievements and claiming international status through the medium of the Olympics. Following a decade-long period of stable double-digit economic growth, the country had anticipated a grand liminal phase, in which it would separate itself from its past as a neglected child while incorporating itself into the established international family as a fully-fledged and significant member. The Olympics offered China a chance to come of age through initiation via a symbolic, global ritual. However, due to its varied meanings potentially bearing contradictory interpretations, ritual is always risky. In the following discussion, three cultural performances, '*Footprints and Five Rings*', '*Harmony*' and '*The Memory Tower*' will be analysed in order to shed light on how China, influenced by an entrenched culture deeply rooted in history, attempted to use the opening and closing ceremonies as public rituals for realizing its dream of reinventing itself, and how this ambition was both symbolically promoted and frustrated within its ritualistic context.

Intended meanings: *Footprints and Five Rings*

Performed on a huge 147-metre-long and 22-metre-wide LED screen in the shape of an ancient Chinese painted scroll, through a designed conjunction of tradition and modern technology, the opening ceremony of the Beijing Olympics was intended to unfold a romanticized 5,000-year history, highlighted by cultural presentations such as the playing of Taiji,[9] a display of movable printing characters and the depiction of Zheng He's voyage to the West during the Ming Dynasty (1368–1644). The ceremony was widely acclaimed as an indisputably impressive visual experience; however, some of my interviewees, especially the non-Chinese, questioned the lack of clarity and the way in which some of its messages were delivered.

A review of the prologue of *Footprints and Five Rings* puts the controversy into perspective. Leading up to the formal start of the opening night was a sequence of 29 giant footprints, fireworks in the shape of footsteps, across the sky of Beijing, signifying the passing of the Olympics to China as the 29th host country. However, there exists an underlying symbolism in the use of the footprints travelling a distance of 15km along the ancient south-north axis of the imperial city of Beijing, from Yongdingmen (the Gate of Permanent Stability), and through a string of other historical sites: Tiananmen (the Gate of Heavenly Peace), the Forbidden City, Jingshan (Coal Hill), the Drum Tower and the Bell Tower, all the way up to the modern Bird's Nest Olympic stadium, in which the opening ceremony took place. This can also be seen to reflect the path of history that Beijing and China have travelled, and to bring the past into the present.

It is difficult to understand the symbolism of the footprints and the subtlety of the choice of route for the fireworks' display if one is not familiar with the cultural and historical backgrounds that transformed the social and physical landscapes of Beijing. Chinese society, for centuries primarily existing only inside its walls and towers,[10] was reluctant to proactively communicate with the rest of the world until 1978 when the 'reform and openness' policy was initiated, but still remains a mystery to many outsiders. To understand China, one must first and foremost comprehend its culture in its own terms. According to structuralists such as Edmund Leach and Claude Lévi-Strauss, culture, the 'most complex whole',[11] needs to be interpreted by decoding the messages rooted in symbolism.[12] Leach states that: 'to understand symbolism is to explore in detail a specific ethnographic context'.[13]

Any cultural analysis of Beijing cannot separate itself from the unique history of the city, dating back to the Dynasty of Western Zhou (1046 BC–771 BCE). However, Beijing did not become the national capital until the Yuan Dynasty, the reign of the Mongols when the Old Beijing was built by Kublai Khan (1215–94), founder of the Yuan. It was established according to the Rites of Zhou,[14] part of the Confucian classics written more than 2,000 years ago, detailing the principles of how to set up an imperial city. Old Beijing was constructed with the imperial buildings at the front, the market area at the back, on an underlying grid structure of square courtyard residences lining up to form small alleys, called *hutongs* (a Mongol word meaning 'water well'). The entire city was divided into two symmetrical parts by an axis running from north to south with the Ancestral Temple to the east and the Altar of Land and Grain to the west.

These concepts of spatial arrangement, underpinned by Confucian ideology, work towards creating an ordered, harmonious and stable society that the state must maintain. They continued to play a role in the following Ming (1368–1644) and Qing (1644–1912) Dynasties, when Beijing remained the capital of all China, and was rebuilt and extended southwards during the Ming Emperor Yongle (1360–1474). This was an important idea that the opening ceremonies were intended to convey; however it was impossible to put most of the audience, who had no prior knowledge, into the frame necessary to understand this historical depth and complexity: the opening ceremony, overloaded with meanings, rendered itself opaque.

The intention was also to reveal the line of history through the fireworks lighting up the previously mentioned reminders of the nation's vicissitudes along a particular axis, for instance at Jingshan, where the last emperor of the Ming Dynasty hanged himself during a crisis of internal uprisings and external Manchu threats, thus marking the end of one empire and the beginning of another. Jingshan was also called Fengshui Hill. Fengshui – literally translated to mean 'wind and water'[15] – is a traditional system of beliefs in the causal relationship between spatial arrangements and (mis)fortune. According to this concept, it is auspicious for buildings to be situated to the south of a hill or mountain, which is large enough to be considered 'protection' to the buildings. The Forbidden City stands to the South of Jingshan.

Passing the old centre of Beijing, the last footprint stepped into the sky above the Bird's Nest, where it burst into scattering twinkling stars that fell to the ground of the stadium to form the shining Five Rings of the Olympics. Celestial beings, whose images were derived from the ancient murals in the Dunhuang caves, then gracefully lifted up the Five Rings into the sky. However, the spectator merely saw a pleasing aesthetic display, not understanding a deeper cultural meaning.

Immediately following this beautiful scenario was the formal ceremony of raising the Chinese National Flag to the sound of the National Anthem of China. Fireworks, the national flag and national anthem are symbols repeatedly used during important, massively-participated Chinese ceremonial occasions. As part of ritual, a 'mechanism' that 'converts the obligatory into the desirable', a symbol 'encapsulates the major properties of the total ritual process which brings about this transmutation'.[16] Take the symbolism of the fireworks in the opening ceremony. As discussed, it was meant to unveil the underlying social and ideological structures from a historical perspective, as well as to link the past to the present and other parts of the world to China. This homogeneous functionality of symbol and ritual contributes to a Geertzian 'deep play' within a sustaining social and cultural context, albeit with varied interpretations, where 'thick description' is both necessary and significant thanks to the richness and complexity emerging from the interweaving of the symbols and ritual. The flow of symbols, arranged in a way that a ritual would take its course, prescribed and phased and intended to channel the audience's emotions and fulfil the organizers' objectives, was designed to condition the ceremony as a status-rising ritual through celebrating the culture and civilization of the host country.

As the fireworks went off in the distance and people cheered, a message was meant to be delivered: history led China to the glory of the Olympics, and China was embracing the world. This grand-scale cultural presentation, through creating a shared reality via the story-telling nature of ritual, distinguished itself as an ideal medium for mass education about the sense of community. Overwhelmed by a distinctively Chinese feel, and by the 'cinema in real time',[17] both Chinese and non-Chinese audiences were, at least temporarily, captivated by a sense of history, identity, friendship and openness, as well as by the ambitious Chinese Olympic vision of '*One World One Dream*' that the government meant to communicate. To a great extent, China wished to present itself as an evolving and open nation.

Considering ritual to be essentially a form of communication, as a 'text' with meanings between the lines,[18] Geertz[19] notes the strong power and huge impact of public rituals, whether religious or secular, and terms them 'culture performances' following Singer, in which a variety of individuals' 'moods and motivations' as well as 'metaphysical conceptions' are captured to 'shape the spiritual consciousness of a people'. It is through fusing 'ethos and world view' that a ritual combines the real world with the imaginary one and leads to 'idiosyncratic transformation in one's sense of reality'.[20]

What Geertz does not write about is the possible fleeting and superficial experiences of such sensational ritual effects, perhaps caused by insufficient understanding of the cultural and historical context of the ritual-performing people. Thus, remaining in the background of the opening ceremony was a deeper ideal that had shaped a people and a nation; what they had lived through and the vocabulary they would use to describe themselves are important. 'Thick description' remains the task of the anthropologists. Unaware of any 'deep play', the spectators were conveniently exposed to what the ritual apparently said, not what it alluded to. In this sense, ritual can mask what lies behind it, or can fail to communicate complex ideas, especially when it is a one-off occasion such as the Olympic ceremonies with no opportunity to make things clearer through future repetition.

On top of this, the episode of *Footprints and Five Rings* turned out to be an inspired arrangement that almost resulted in failure when the story of the computer-generated 'footprints' exploded in the Western media. To achieve a better visual effect on television, the organizers substituted fake fireworks for the real ones. This was seen in the West as manipulation of symbols, whose meanings turned from being an unclear cultural representation to propaganda.

Performance and risk: the Harmony scene

Returning to the display of Chinese characters at the Beijing opening ceremony, these characters were created in an original way through the alteration of a matrix of movable-type printing, one of the four great inventions of ancient China. A total of 897 performers acted as the 897 blocks of Chinese characters, creating images of pictographs and other patterns. They bounced up and down, and spelled out three versions, ancient and modern, of the Chinese character 'harmony' ('He' in Chinese) or 'peace', meant to demonstrate the evolution of Chinese characters as well as of Confucian philosophy which emphasizes harmony. Subsequently, the characters were transformed into an image of the Great Wall.

Harmony has been a deeply ingrained value in Chinese culture and tradition. It is both explicitly and subtly expressed in various temporal-spatial, tangible and intangible forms, ranging from the ancient conception of Yin and Yang in Taiji,[21] to the original checkerboard layout of Beijing and the old courtyard residences where people used to live their everyday lives. From the round altars and square foundations of the Temple of Heaven, where the Emperors of the Ming and Qing Dynasties worshipped Heaven and prayed for a good harvest, to the Chinese stance of handling things through the 'middle way', the ancient cosmology of harmony has always been an unwritten rule guiding almost all aspects of social and personal life. It is the 'one character that holds the clues of everything'.[22]

There is no exception to this ideal, even in modern architectural creations, no matter how alien they may appear at first sight. Respectively located next to each other to the east and west of the central axis of Beijing, the world-class avant-garde designs of the Bird's Nest and the Water Cube (the National Aquatics Centre) in fact originated from the basis of the harmonious balance of Yin and Yang and 'round heaven, square earth'. In his presentation at the 6th International Forum on the Beijing 2008 Olympic Games, John Bilmon, one of the major architects for the Water Cube, revealed the mystery surrounding the relationship between the two seemingly incompatible architectures. He describes the Bird's Nest as 'fire, radiating, yang, masculine and exciting' and the Water Cube as 'water, absorbing, yin, feminine and poetic'.[23] It is the philosophical and sophisticated combination of these contrasting elements that produces aesthetic beauty in Chinese cultural and social constructions, where peace finds its way in reconciling opposing and conflicting ideas. According to Bilmon, the Water Cube won fierce international bidding as the National Aquatics Centre due to its observance on traditions as a good yin complement to the Bird's Nest. In addition, its 'squareness' reinforces the distinctive 'roundness' of the Bird's Nest.

However, it is always extremely difficult to maintain the delicate balance of different components and factors. Each of the 897 dancers was said to have had their own sequence of movements, and to have practised it for almost one year. The situation is generally the same with any other cultural display, both at the Beijing ceremonies or on any other occasion, albeit on a different scale. Precision, discipline and harmony seem to be internalized in individuals, whose worldviews, officially shaped by Confucianism and its variants, have gone through years of instability, normalization and modernization, and have sometimes become distorted.

Dressed in Qin (221BC–206 BCE) costumes, the performers enacted the Confucian lines 'Harmony is precious' in extreme uniformity, as in real life they have to meticulously embody the symbolism of harmony. The idea of harmony was introduced in the first chapter of the *Analects*, a collection of Confucius' words and acts, as the underpinning of the practice of Li (which can be roughly translated as 'propriety'), a principle that had been adopted as a virtue and strategy by the ancient kings in coping with a wide range of matters, both state-making and mundane. The *Analects*, together with works of the subsequent Confucian thinkers such as Mencius, forming Confucianism, lie at the core of the Chinese culture.

Some people whom I have interviewed, especially the non-Chinese, found the way that harmony was exhibited was disquieting. It was spoken of as a powerful reminder of Zhang Yimou's (Chief Director of the opening and closing ceremonies) martial art film *Hero*. Despite its beautiful cinematography, *Hero* has been criticized for its political motives, taking a positive stance on the King of Qin, the First Emperor who unified China through the violent extinction of six other small countries to establish his hegemony. One of the most notorious facts about him is perhaps his burning of books and burying intellectuals whom he deemed threatening (fenshu kengru, 焚书坑儒). He created a unified Chinese writing system and built the Great Wall, both represented in the performance, and built a centralized authority, a system that many non-Chinese scholars think still functions today.

There could be many different ways of understanding the presentation of harmony against the backdrop of the Olympics' public ritual. The multi-facetedness of ritual makes it an ever-intriguing topic, drawing the attention of anthropologists no matter which culture they study. Following his identification of the problems of ritual in general and the 'complexity and uncertainty about a ritual's meaning'[24] in particular, Gilbert Lewis proposes that ritual be treated as a performance, more concerned with the mechanics and details of the way in which it is conducted, allowing individuals freedom to 'search out, interpret and discover'[25] the messages that it carries. This is similar to Geertz's cultural analysis, 'guessing at meanings, assessing the guesses, and drawing explanatory conclusions from the better guesses'.[26] In other words, the meanings of a ritual, a significant component of culture to which Geertz's theory safely applies, primarily emerge out of a good guess. A guess is usually a conditioned reflex, drawing on the individual's previous experiences with the subject matter, way of thinking, 'learning', 'degree of attention'[27] they give to it and the like. In this sense, according to Lewis and Geertz, the ambiguity of the ritual's meanings is not viewed as a deficiency, but as a source of inspiration inviting various responses.

To put it another way, consciously or subconsciously performed, any ritual inevitably entails different levels of exegesis, adding to its abstruseness. Conscious rites are conveniently understood to reflect the culture and social structure. Subconscious rites are sometimes barely perceptible and thus can be deceptive; stimulating the search for explicitness either from a fixed system of knowledge or from individuals' imaginations. The different images and experiences that a ritual is likely to produce in individuals or groups may well result in bewilderment, though even this may possibly be intentional, so the ritual conveners could continue to play a controlling role in and out of the ritual.

In an indefinable way, some of my interviewees mentioned that a hint of ritualized violence could be subtly felt from the artistic fonts of the Chinese character harmony. The subtext that harmony and peace are actually based on force and violence also could be read. A *Guardian* editorial[28] that found the opening generally 'magnificent and unsettling' was concerned over the politics of the 'fearsomely disciplined dancing or the precision kitsch'. If not well managed, harmony could collapse into a series of extremes, as the Chinese aesthetic of duality implies.

Therefore, ritual performance can be highly risky, in the sense that they may may lead to an understanding completely different from that of the ritual performers. For instance, Geertz argues through his 'thick description' of the ritual of the Balinese cockfight that it 'makes nothing happen',[29] and matters only to the cocks. Also Leo Howe[30] finds in Bali that cockfights are more concerned with social function rather than meaning by asserting that the inner intention of the ritual is of paramount importance; he perceives that the 'centre' bet is more about status than money.

Combined with Mary Douglas' interpretation of ritual as 'essentially a symbolic replication of the social order',[31] what is at risk in the public ritual of the opening and closing ceremonies is the well-being of a social and political mechanism, betwixt and between various conflicting and competing factors. Ritual will not make 'all the participants pass to the winning side', as Lévi-Strauss might anticipate.[32] However, Alan Macfarlane possibly suggests an alternative. In his paradigm-shifting book *The Origins of English Individualism* Macfarlane sees the rise of English liberty from a balance of clashing interests between different power groups.[33] There are conditions under which balanced chaos and conflicts may give birth to equilibrium and harmony. For contemporary China, as it always has been, only an original and genuine harmony of peace between nature and human beings, between round heaven and square earth, and between Yin and Yang, free from manufactured contamination, can presage the development of a harmonious society.

Rite of passage: the Memory Tower

In many indigenous cultures described by anthropologists, girls become women through puberty rites and boys become men through circumcision rites. Arnold van Gennep[34] conceived of a tripartite structure and analysed the functional significance and ceremonial patterns of the sequence of rituals that mark each turning-point that an individual experiences during their lives. According to him, similar arrangements underlie transition rituals such as birth, puberty, marriage and death. These comprise three phases: the pre-liminal, the liminal and post-liminal, representing the conditions of separation, transition and incorporation respectively.

Victor Turner[35] advanced van Gennep's theory further to focus on liminality, the transitional state or 'interstructural situation', and conceptualized the states of 'betwixt and between' and *communitas*. Turner thought that the ritual subjects are 'betwixt and between' all the defined social systems and fixed states during the indeterminate liminal period of ambiguity and paradox in ritual, which is 'accompanied by processes of growth, transformation, and the reformulation of old elements in new patterns'.[36] On the other hand, *communitas*, a Latin word for community, also typical of liminality, emphasizes the equal relationship among the initiates in which social status and rank are dismantled and fairness, progress, unity and friendship are encouraged. This homogeneous and egalitarian state of existence as 'Each for all, and all for each'[37] is understood as togetherness of the ritual subjects responding to the Olympic slogan of 'One World One Dream'.

Particularly, Turner discussed rituals of status elevation, in which the ritual subject is 'conveyed irreversibly from a lower to a higher position in an institutionalized system of such positions'.[38] This theoretical paradigm was found to go beyond religion and permeate through secular life,[39] which Turner himself confirmed in saying that rites of passage could be found in all societies. 'In complex large-scale societies', he noticed, 'liminality itself ... has tended to re-enter structure and acquire a full complement of structural roles and positions'.[40]

Rituals seem to exist in all modern societies, as well as in the contemporary nation state of China, which traditionally had been a heavily ritualized society. Caroline Humphrey and James Laidlaw argue: 'Ritual is still assumed to be efficacious, in the sense that nothing more than performing it brings about a desired transformation'.[41] Here, 'desired transformation' is key to understanding ritual for the very simple reason that rituals are performed to 'make something happen'.[42]

At the closing ceremony, as the Olympic flame was extinguished, a 23-metre high Memory Tower was created. Inspired by a ritual found amongst the ethnic minority Miao, the performative creation of this tower by acrobats, who displayed extreme strength and power, symbolized the eternity of the Olympic flame and spirit. The acrobats impressed the audience by climbing all the way to the top of the tower, with ease, within 12 seconds. Three hundred and ninety-six bodies formed the shapes of the Olympic flame and Dancing Beijing, emblem of the Beijing Olympics, on the tower. The scene was intended to reflect the Olympic motto 'higher, faster and stronger' and was highly memorable. Moreover, the strength of life was glorified through the challenge to the limits of the human body in this performance, where the Chinese anthropologist[43] saw the symbolism of reproduction representing the power of sex, as well as the vitality of a nation and the might of the state.

Some foreign journalists raised questions about why some episodes of China's modern history were omitted from the ceremonies. Zhang Yimou responded that it was difficult to represent these. My interviews, conducted both inside and outside the Bird's Nest during the Olympics, revealed that many ordinary Chinese people could actually sense the subtle way in which modern history was embedded in the ceremonies. They spoke of a traumatized past marked by foreign invasion and domestic turmoil, especially stressing the Hundred Year Humiliation – the period of time from the Opium War in the 1840s, marking China's semi-colonization by Western countries, to the foundation of the New China by Mao in 1949 – which has been constantly referred to by the state media as an unforgettable and traumatic collective memory. Fairbank[44] would have been strongly criticized for his comments on part of the 'treaty century',[45] – as he termed it; the Hundred Year Humiliation in a Chinese sense – as the culmination of 'cultural interchange' remarkable in world history.

Viewed from inside China, this period of time was an exclusively dark era associated with negative words such as 'feudal', 'corrupt', 'backward' and 'sick'. Amongst many traditional stereotypical images of old China, men's pigtails and the practice of women's foot-binding were highlighted as two of the most disgraceful cultural signs that should be substituted with fresh and stunning icons such as the Bird's Nest and the Water Cube. These were intended to be symbols of a new culture and identity. In particular, many interviewees talked about the aggression of the Eight-power Allied Force in 1900 as a painful memory for generations of Chinese who lived during the era when the country was known as the 'Sick Man of Asia'. They had always been reluctant to show how powerless they felt about the past.

The following story may explain the tradition in Chinese culture of important things being represented indirectly. A group of competitors were asked to do a painting of an ancient temple hidden in the forests of a mountain. The award-winner turned out to be the painting without a temple at all. Instead, there was a monk carrying water among the trees. The parallels between the ceremonies' reference to painful events and the painting are obvious. The pain of this era was highlighted more so for the avoidance of expression, as in the absence of the temple in the painting. When absence is conspicuous, silence can be symbolically powerful.

The Chinese people whom I interviewed usually generalized about the domestic misfortunes since 1949, referring to them all as 'domestic turmoils' without further commenting on each of them. When asked why, they replied that the Olympics are more internationally concerned, while home affairs should be discussed on a different occasion. From the perspective of the majority of the Chinese interviewees, the dream of the Olympics was primarily a dream of becoming able-bodied and powerful. The ceremonies were viewed as if they were a curative cult, helping China to live with its past, to remember, forget and forgive the experiences of the Hundred Year Humiliation. This was 'efficacious' with the presence of former 'attackers',[46] now returning as guests, celebrating together this extravagant carnival.

Stunningly choreographed, the initiation of a nation 'betwixt and between', attempting to overcome growing pains and anticipating a desired transformation of its international status, helped regain national confidence and release tension. Rather than a sporting festival, the Beijing Olympics were intended to be the rite of passage for China's coming of age, a state-mediated symbolism that, to some extent, succeeded in encouraging and uniting its people. In this sense, it could be understood as a ritual largely performed for the people themselves rather than for the visitors, who found it difficult to read the underlying meanings, some of which were hard to comprehend even for some Chinese viewers. Comprising two sections of the *Brilliant Civilisation* and *Glorious Era* performances, all cultural presentations, especially at the opening ceremony, fittingly contributed to a Chinese reading of the Chinese experience, 'a story they tell themselves about themselves'.[47]

Therefore, in contrast to the many commentators who think that the major purpose of the lavish ceremonies was to advertise the might of the government of China and to impress the non-Chinese as a superpower, I would argue that there also existed the motif of self-entertainment for the nation and its people, celebrating the regaining of China's position in the international community as one of the oldest civilizations that had lagged behind for centuries. It portrayed the nation as sharing success and happiness – a nation that needs approval from others before they approve of themselves.

After the Games

Many issues surrounding the ceremonies are equally thought-provoking. Both the artificial fireworks, mentioned earlier in this paper, and the lip-synched *Ode to the Motherland* created quite a stir. The official response to them is that they happened for the sake of national interest. Authenticity had to give way to a flawless Olympics, preserving the face of the state. It was said one whole year was needed in order to design and produce the special effects of the fireworks display lasting merely 55 seconds each explosion. Also, the beautiful girl had to move her lips without actually singing in order to impress the world with both a perfect appearance and a perfect, though unreal, voice. More surprising might be the weather modification on both the opening and closing days, as well as the traffic prohibition and the closing down of thousands of factories in the neighbouring provinces to improve air quality. This obsession with perfection is pathological, deeply associated with an inferiority complex and insecurity, typical of a nation suffering and recovering from a traumatic experience. While they knew it was manipulative to arrange the afore-mentioned occurrences, they simply did them and then informed the media when asked. It was the chance of the century that 'the world takes the same stage at the same time'[48] when their 'hundred-year Olympic dream' was to come true. This eagerness and radicalism to show the very best of China, without taking into consideration what were not appropriate, resulted in suspicion that 'we saw and heard only what the Chinese wanted us to see and hear'.[49]

However, the image of a rising yet immature superpower was both impressive and disturbing at the same time. There have been many hypotheses about the future of China, including the one that the twenty-first century belongs to this country. The question of whether the Beijing Olympics will be a watershed in Chinese history has been raised. The 1960 Olympics in Rome was thought to have changed the world. For example, the political and athletic threat that Soviet Russia posed to the United States was seen to signal 'an old order dying and a new one being born'.[50] China now appears to be the factor that challenges the world's current socioeconomic landscape. In particular, the Beijing Olympics was viewed as a metaphor for China's catching up with the United States. China's success was deemed to be troubling on the basis of evidence.[51] Rivalry between the two countries was simply shown by the way they tried to top the medals' chart, China ranking the competing countries according to the gold medal count and the States the total medal count instead; China won the most gold medals, while the States won the most medals overall.

On the other hand, the resurgence of China could be perceived as the return to the 'normal state' of world order, since China, together with India, used to be world leaders before the fifteenth century.[52] Where China is going remains to be seen. In the end, it is largely in the hands of the state, an actor with great capacity for determining and implementing national goals and controlling and coordinating various sectors at all levels. Oksenberg discerned in the Chinese leaders a lack of an 'overarching vision of the nation's political future that guides their incremental responses to the institutional challenges that confront them'.[53] Uncertainty exists among the leaders, as well as in the state, who may find it hard to envisage a nation 'betwixt and between'. What is happening in China has not occurred elsewhere on this planet. Without sufficient experience to learn from, it is an experiment to transform China, where the government has been trying to manage the state as a project, as demonstrated by the Beijing Olympics.

The 'nearly perfect' Beijing Olympics was a short-lived event. Approximately 16,400 couples in Beijing and about 100,000 couples throughout China got married on the opening day of 8 August 2008,[54] a most auspicious day with several occurrences of the lucky number eight. As the marvel of the ceremonies fades away, the newly-married couples, as well as the nation as a whole, face a reality fraught with problems. According to a recent NetEase online news report,[55] a number of these couples divorced shortly after the Olympics.

During an interview, Zhang Yimou was asked to summarize his understanding of the Opening Ceremony. The word he used surprised the whole world. 'Romance', he said. 'We Chinese people have always been romantic since ancient times, our painting, poetry and music all articulate a romantic turn of mind. Romance is deep in our blood and mind, and we do not need to show it on the surface'.[56] Politics was not even worth mentioning.

However, the symbolism of the Beijing Olympics goes beyond romanticism. As has been discussed in this essay, there were intentions about how cultural displays, such as the *Footprints and Five Rings*, *Harmony* and *Memory Tower*, should be understood. Indeed, most viewers were convinced of the intended meanings through being exposed to the emotionally-charged moments of ritual performance that, to a great extent, successfully created an 'imagined community'. On the other hand, since rituals are multivocal and risky, the messages were not always interpreted in the same way by all people and especially not by non-Chinese participants. Interviews conducted in the UK interestingly involved mention of 'a strong, almost exaggerated idealism'[57] in the ceremonies.

Through exploring deeper historical and social contexts and by analysing possible interpretations, this essay has attempted to emphasize the self-affirming and status-rising characteristics of the curative rite that aimed to help China and its people overcome its past, and look into a future free from the perceived historical burdens that emerged from the Hundred Year Humiliation as well as the ambiguity of harmony. China is trying to evolve and establish its position in an international arena through celebrating a rich cultural heritage that has defined a people. However, since such a complex culture had been cut off from the world at large, the intended symbolism was ambiguous and sometimes even contradictory when viewed from outside China.

Notes

[1] Gold and Revill, 'The Cultural Olympiads', 59. *Panegyris* is a Greek word, meaning gathering. Specifically, as Gold and Revill put, it was a 'festive assembly in which the entire people came together to participate in religious sites, sporting and artistic performance.

[2] From the International Olympic Committee website: http://www.olympic.org/uk/games/ancient/history_uk.asp.

[3] Turner, *The Forest of Symbols*; Turner, *The Ritual Process*.

[4] Gluckman, *Order and Rebellion*, 110–36.

[5] Moore and Myerhoff, 'Secular Ritual', 3.

[6] Ibid.

[7] Gold and Gold, 'Athens to Athens', 39.

[8] Thomas L. Friedman, 'A Biblical Seven Years', *International Herald Tribune*, August 27, 2008. http://www.nytimes.com/2008/08/27/opinion/27friedman.html?_r=1.

[9] Here Taiji means Taijiquan, a form of Chinese martial art.

[10] There were intermittent international contacts in the Tang Dynasty (618–907) and the Yuan Dynasty (1271–1368), etc. The Qing Dynasty (1644–1912) experienced a massive foreign invasion.

[11] Geertz, *The Interpretation of Cultures*, quotes Tylor, 4.

[12] Morris, *Anthropological Studies of Religion*, 222.

[13] Leach, *Culture and Communication*, 49, 55; Morris, *Anthropological Studies of Religion*, 222–3.

[14] Sit, *Beijing*, 25.

[15] Fengshui, a system of beliefs about the nature of Heaven and Earth capable of providing benign Qi, energy of life force, that would turn ill luck into good. Fengshui considers it important and auspicious that an imperial palace should be located to the south of a hill, which explains the situation of the Forbidden City to the South of Jingshan.

[16] Turner, *The Forest of Symbols*, 30.

[17] Comments made during the NBC broadcast of the opening ceremony of the Beijing Olympics 2008.

[18] Howe, 'Risk, Ritual and Performance' discusses Geertz.

[19] Geertz, *The Interpretation of Cultures*, 113; and Geertz quotes Singer, *The Great Tradition*, 140–182.

[20] Geertz, *The Interpretation of Cultures*, 112–13.

[21] *Taiji* means 'Supreme Ultimate', a state that reconciles *yin* and *yang*, two elements that contradict and complement each other in a natural world, such as with heaven and earth and male and female.

[22] BBC live broadcasting of the opening ceremony of the Beijing Olympics.

[23] Bilmon, 'The Olympic Movement'.

[24] Lewis, *Day of Shining Red*, 8.

[25] Ibid., 38.

[26] Geertz, *The Interpretation of Cultures*, 20.
[27] Lewis, *Days of Shining Red*, 7.
[28] 'The Torch Passes'. *The Guardian*, August 9, 2008.
[29] Geertz, *The Interpretation of Cultures*, 443.
[30] Howe, 'Risk, Ritual and Performance'.
[31] Morris, *Anthropological Studies of Religion*, 231.
[32] Howe, 'Risk, Ritual and Performance', 76; Lévi-Strauss, *The Savage Mind*, 32.
[33] Simon Carr has also commented on this. *The Independent*, 10 November 2007.
[34] Van Gennep, *The Rites of Passage*.
[35] Turner, *The Forest of Symbols*; Turner, *The Ritual Process*.
[36] Turner, *The Forest of Symbols*, 99.
[37] Ibid., 101.
[38] Turner, *The Ritual Process*, 167.
[39] Morris, *Anthropological Studies of Religion*, 253.
[40] Turner, *The Forest of Symbols*, 167.
[41] Humphrey and Laidlaw, *The Archetypal Actions*, 1.
[42] Feuchtwang, 'On Religious Ritual', 57.
[43] Interview with Professor Wang Mingming from Peking University in Beijing on 27 August 2008.
[44] Fairbank and Goldman, *China*, 205.
[45] Fairbank called it a 'treaty century', since many treaties had been signed between Western and Chinese governments for the foreign governments to benefit from winning in the battles.
[46] This is a term used by several interviewees.
[47] Geertz, *The Interpretation of Cultures*, 448.
[48] Maraniss, *Rome 1960*, xii.
[49] Ralph Routon, 'Olympics: Almost Perfect, But Not Quite'. *Colorado Springs Independent*, August 14, 2008. http://www.csindy.com/gyrobase/Content?oid=oid%3A28534.
[50] Maraniss, *Rome 1960*, xi.
[51] Robert J. Samuelson, 'The Real China Threat'. *Washington Post*, August 20, 2008, A15.
[52] Nicholas D. Kristof, 'China's Rise Goes Beyond Gold Medals'. *The New York Times*, August 21, 2008). http://www.spiegel.de/international/0,1518,573436,00.html.
[53] Oksenberg, 'China's Political System', 201.
[54] Tania Branigan, 'Olympic Weddings: Chinese Couples Queue to Get Married on Lucky Day'. *The Guardian*, August 8, 2008. http://www.guardian.co.uk/world/2008/aug/08/china.olympics20082.
[55] NetEase (October 16, 2008), also called news.163.com, one of the leading internet news websites in China. http://news.163.com/08/1016/14/4OCOOMT9000120GU.html.
[56] Zhang Yimou in an interview with the *Xinhua News Agency*, China, August 8, 2008, reported by Wang Yong. http://news.xinhuanet.com/olympics/2008-08/08/content_9060804.htm.
[57] This has been discussed with several informants in the UK.

References

Bilmon, John. 'The Olympic Movement and Urban Development'. Paper presented at the International Forum on the Beijing 2008 Olympic Games, July 2008, Beijing.

Carr, Simon. 'Brown claims to know where our values lie. But has he located back to the Middle Ages?'. *The Independent*, 10 November, 2007.

Fairbank, Johan King, and Merle Goldman. *China: A New History*. Enlarged edn. Cambridge, MA; London: The Belknap Press of Harvard University Press, 1998.

Feuchtwang, Stephan. 'On Religious Ritual as Deference and Communicative Excess'. *Journal of the Royal Anthropological Institute* 13, no. 1 (2007): 57–72.

Geertz, Clifford. *The Interpretation of Cultures*. New York: Basic Books, 1973.

Gluckman, Max. *Order and Rebellion in Tribal Africa*. New York: The Free Press of Glencoe, 1954.

Gold, John R. and Margaret Gold. *Olympic Cities: City Agendas, Planning and the World's Games, 1898–2012*. Oxford: Routledge, 2007.

Howe, Leo. 'Risk, Ritual and Performance'. *The Journal of the Royal Anthropological Institute* 6, no. 1 (2000): 63–79.

Humphrey, Caroline, and James Laidlaw. *The Archetypal Actions of Ritual: A Theory of Ritual Illustrated by the Jain Rite of Worship*. Oxford: Clarendon Press, 1994.

Leach, Edmund. *Culture and Communication*. Cambridge: Cambridge University Press, 1976.

Lévi-Strauss, Claude. *The Savage Mind.* 1972.

Lewis, Gilbert. *Day of Shining Red.* Cambridge: Cambridge University Press, 1980.

Macfarlane, Alan. *The Origins of English Individualism: The Family, Property and Social Transition.* Oxford: Blackwell, 1978.

Maraniss, David. *Rome 1960: The Olympics that Changed the World.* New York: Simon & Schuster, 2008.

Moore, Sally F., and Barbara G. Myerhoff. 'Secular Ritual: Forms and Meaning'. In *Secular Ritual,* edited by Sally F. Moore and Barbara G. Myerhoff, 3–24. Vangorcum, Assen; Amsterdam: Van Gorcum & Comp. B.V., 1977, 193–208.

Morris, Brian. *Anthropological Studies of Religion: An Introductory Text.* Cambridge: Cambridge University Press, 1987.

Oksenberg, Michel. 'China's Political System: Challenges of the Twenty-First Century'. In *The Nature of Chinese Politics: From Mao to Jiang,* edited by Jonathan Unger. London: Weidenfeld & Nicholson; Armonk, NY: M.E. Sharpe, 2002.

Singer, M. 'The Great Tradition in a Metropolitan Center: Madras'. In *Traditional India,* edited by M. Singer, 140–182. Philadelphia: The American Folklore Society, 1958.

Sit, Victor F.S. *Beijing: The Nature and Planning of a Chinese Capital City.* New York; Brisbane; Toronto; Singapore: John Wiley & Sons, 1995.

Turner, Victor. *The Forest of Symbols: Aspects of Ndembu Ritual.* Ithaca, NY: Cornell University Press, 1967.

Turner, Victor. *The Ritual Process: Structure and Anti-structure.* New York: Aldine de Gruyter, 1969.

Van Gennep, Arnold. *The Rites of Passage.* London: Routledge and Kegan Paul, 1960.

Media representation of volunteers at the Beijing Olympic Games

Charles Richard Bladen

The Business School, University of Greenwich, Park Row, Greenwich, London SE10 9LS, UK

The specifics of Olympic Games' volunteering are currently unclear, as more needs to be understood about who volunteers, why, what they do and what they gain from it. Hence media coverage of volunteering at the 2008 Beijing Olympics potentially offered insights into these important questions for the continued staffing of future mega-events and the possible achievement of their promised legacies. However, a comparison of English language, domestic and foreign press reports revealed acute differences in the discourses used in the representation of volunteering at the Games. This essay explores these distinctions and their implications and presents results which clearly relate to two different hegemonic discourses.

Introduction

The specifics of Olympic Games' volunteering are currently unclear, as more needs to be understood about who volunteers, why, what they do and what they gain from it. Hence media coverage of volunteering at the 2008 Beijing Olympics potentially offered insights into these important questions for the continued staffing of future mega-events and the possible achievement of their promised legacies. However, a comparison of English language, domestic and foreign press reports revealed acute differences in the discourses used in the representation of volunteering at the Games. This essay, in three sections, reviews literature relevant to this type of volunteering and media representation, the method used to analyse domestic and foreign press discourses, and a discussion of their distinctions and their implications.

Volunteering

Wilson states that: 'Volunteering means any activity in which time is given freely to benefit another person, group, or organization'.[1] Though this definition does not preclude the volunteer receiving benefits from their work, a helpful development is provided by referring to Cnaan *et al.*'s continuum which attempts to distinguish between narrowly and broadly defined volunteering by dividing volunteers into groups according to levels of free-choice, remuneration, structure and intended beneficiaries of their activities.[2]

Stebbins classifies volunteering as a leisure pursuit. However, as Wilson and Musick observe, the general classifications of volunteering as leisure or tourism activities are convenient due to their unpaid nature and belie the fact that they are generally productive. This view is supported by Liao-Troth who asserts that the volunteer's relationship with the organization with whom they are working is governed by a psychological contract as much as any paid employment.[3]

Though the primary implication of the role of volunteer assumes no monetary payment in return for their service, Olympic volunteers commonly receive formal benefits in kind, and informal satisfactions derived as a result of their involvement. Such satisfactions have been identified by researchers[4] as altruism and egoism, the key to understanding volunteers' motivations to work in sports events.

Mega-events, which are defined as 'short-term events with long-term consequences',[5] are unfeasible without the involvement of large numbers of volunteers to provide various services to organizing committees and attendees. The official target for the Beijing 2008 Olympic Games was set beforehand at 70,000 mid-games volunteers. Several official reports claimed that this figure reached an excess as high as one million at the peak period of the Games.[6]

The importance of volunteers to the design and delivery of mega events such as the Olympic Games is expanded by Cuskelly *et al.*:

> Volunteers are fundamental to the success of international multi-sport events such as the Olympic, Paralympic and Commonwealth Games as well as sport events at the local, state/provincial and national level. Sport event organizers rely on the knowledge and skills of event volunteers to administer competitions, liaise with visiting teams, work with media and security organizations, manage hospitality and catering services, and provide services for athletes, sponsors, spectators and other event stakeholders.[7]

The 2012 London Organizing Committee of the Olympic Games' bid focussed on the role of volunteers as a way to achieve greater levels of community involvement in the Games in order to make contact with 'hard to reach' social groups, which can be considered as a 'soft' legacy factor, as described by Preuss.[8]

Various attempts in the event literature to explain volunteer motivations assist organizers little with the Olympic model. For example, McCurley and Lynch emphasize the non-event volunteer's commitment to the advancement of a cause or organization.[9] Other explanations, mainly based on generic, human-resource motivation theories, in the absence of further supporting research, have failed to provide practical explanations for Olympic volunteers' motivation. Event-specific studies tended to link the motivations of event volunteers to altruism. However, they generally found more of a relationship between altruism and *initial* volunteer attraction than the action of *repeat* volunteering. Conversely, Stebbins found that 'career' volunteers were not altruistic, but continued volunteering due to the intrinsic rewards associated with the volunteering experience itself.[10]

Authors can find little reason for the trend that sports-event volunteers seem increasingly unwilling to commit for longer periods, preferring to restrict their support of events to the short-term.[11] If this is not addressed at the planning stage, it is possible that the benefits of volunteers' training and experience will be lost by the events industry as a result of either an unwillingness to re-volunteer, or if their previously acquired skills are sold to employers. This would in turn impair the effective creation of a future event-volunteer pool or the development of its skills' availability for future events.

Two main groups found to be most likely to volunteer are students and the elderly, due to time-availability. Students have a greater tendency to volunteer than other groups for reasons such as institutional encouragement to do so, and associated improvements in academic performance.[12] As Wilson and Musick found, the higher educated are more likely to volunteer and to repeatedly volunteer due to attachment factors, and once established these do not diminish due to the physical impairment often brought about by old age. In fact, although some researchers argue that due to various social changes the tendency to volunteer is declining overall, Wilson argues that a new category of healthy, elderly volunteers is expanding.[13]

The breadth and scope of volunteering roles have been identified.[14] Baum and Lockstone, supported by their extensive literature review, clearly delineate the following broad research questions for investigation related to volunteering on the extensive scale of a mega-event context, such as the Beijing Olympic Games:

- What do volunteers do at the Olympics?
- Who are they?
- What motivates them?
- How does volunteering affect them?
- What else do they do at the event apart from volunteer?
- Is volunteering recidivistic?[15]

It is hoped that the media representations of volunteers examined in this study will partly help to answer these questions.

Media representation

Representation, from the perspective of semiotics, involves the production of symbols based upon what has been socially accepted and agreed upon. It is through these simpler symbols that the more complex, mediated 'real' can be communicated by the media to its audience. Such representations have been divided into those of the world, people's social relations, and their social and personal identities.[16] Harvey Brown demonstrated how cultural representation could be used as a tool of domination through its potential to extend labelling to particular cultural categories.[17] His focus was on how classifications were used to create moral hierarchies through which those they pretended to describe could be controlled. He argued that cultural representations were related to the establishment and maintenance of moral and political orders, supported by the ideology of their producers. The basis of these orders relied on the effective categorization of members of groups using lists of prescribed attributes by which outsiders' perceptions and knowledge about them could be conveyed. This process can then be used to contrast one group with another in order to reinforce distinctions.

This role of the media with respect to ethnic representation is highlighted by La Ferle and Lee:

> The issue of ethnic representation is important because in a media-dominated society, such as the United States, people often rely on the media to portray and define those things they have not experienced for themselves. To provide an efficient path to cultural understanding, mass media employ stereotypes as a convenient categorization tool.[18]

As an important sub-section of the mass media, newspaper representation is widely recognized as a major influence on national, public opinion. This influence is controlled by journalists and their editors. However, Cotter observes 'journalists write stories, and consequently, research into story structure or narrative becomes relevant to account for their motivations'.[19] Media representations have been researched in a variety of diverse contexts including not only cultural and ethnic groups, but also gender, business roles, consumers and inhabitants of 'third world' countries.[20]

There has been limited academic work published on the representation of sport volunteers by the media. Sport research into media representation to date has tended to focus on the sportspeople engaged in sport competitions, including, among others, sport celebrity, particular sports, sport's fans, the representation of athletes' gender, national sports culture, representation of disabled athletes, indigenous athletes and race.[21]

Method

In light of the issues raised above, this study intended to analyse the main discourses surrounding the representation by the media of Chinese nationals who volunteered as part of the Beijing 2008 Olympic Games' official BOCOG volunteering programme. In accordance with the 'tradition' of such an approach, little structure to the study or its prescribed outcomes was pre-determined, other than the obvious restrictions resulting from sample choice. It was hoped that such a study would not only provide social insight into the role of the media and its representation of Chinese volunteers, their activities and motivations at the Olympic Games, but also possible indications to further assist effective future workforce and media management at mega-events of this kind.

According to Potter, discourse analysis 'has an analytic commitment to studying discourses as texts and talk in social practices ... it is the medium for interaction; analysis of discourse becomes, then, analysis of what people do'.[22] As with similar media-discourse studies, a modified approach to Potter and Wetherell's method was used.[23] Various search terms were used in order to establish the widest possible number of articles. The main focus was English-language Olympic-volunteering articles published during August 2008, as this was the main period of relevance for this type of publication. Any articles related to the involvement of foreign volunteers were excluded from the sample. This resulted in the collection of 82 articles which were categorized according to their source, with 22 being from Chinese news agencies and 60 from English-speaking, foreign newspapers. The articles analysed from 'foreign' countries were mainly from Britain and the USA, but also included articles from South Africa, Spain, Singapore, Australia, New Zealand, Canada, Finland, India, Qatar and one article by the United Nations was included. The articles were sorted according to their main themes into a coding frame. The form and effects of the discourses presented were then analysed, using Gee's seven key aspects for the analysis of discourse, which are: its significance; the activities that are being enacted; the identities that are being recognized as operative; the relationships the language used was trying to enact; the politics as a perspective on social goods that were being conveyed; the connections or disconnections that were being made; and finally the signs, systems and knowledge that were being privileged or disprivileged.[24]

There are many limitations to this methodology. It is recognized that to focus solely on those articles published in the English language is to ignore much of the grassroots Chinese-speaking viewpoint, as well as most of the domestic readership of the Olympic Games' coverage. However, the main objective of this study in the context of this event was to examine the representation of volunteers to the international community outside China. It would have also proved informative to have included media other than newspaper articles, but it was decided for such a study of language in text, as well as consistency of comparison and ease of acquisition, to restrict analysis in this way. This consideration also mitigated the obvious impact of the use of second-language English by Chinese news organizations, versus the ease of communication by newspapers in English-speaking countries.

Critical analysis

The first main theme that emerged from the analysis of domestic Chinese online press reports was of friendly, altruistic, Chinese Olympic volunteers who had overcome intense competition to be appointed and who provided services essential to a successful Olympic event, and the effective representation of their country and culture. The competing theme from foreign, online press reports was of Chinese Olympic volunteers who lacked the adequate skills required for this type of event and who functioned covertly as a tool of the Chinese state to promote fakery at the event.

These two themes could be divided into supporting sub-themes in the discourses related to the main elements of representation which accorded with Baum and Lockstone's main research questions, which included their identity as volunteers, their roles at the event, their motivations, how volunteering affected them, and what else they did at the Olympics apart from volunteer.[25] The main critical incidents in which these sub-themes were illustrated included stories related to the use of volunteers as security personnel for the Olympic Games, use of them to fill empty stadia seating at sporting competitions, and the specific use of elderly volunteers.

The sub-themes that supported the viewpoint of the Chinese press were that the chosen Chinese volunteers had overcome intense competition in order to be selected, they were proud to represent their country and their culture, and had done so successfully as the largely unrecognized 'heroes' of the games. Chinese volunteers had to learn new skills to function as effective volunteers, and had paid a high price to serve at the games, particularly the elderly. Chinese volunteers were motivated by a desire to help others, and had gained many benefits and skills from the experience of volunteering, and though they sometimes lacked the necessary skills, they were trying and learning as best as they could.

The sub-themes that supported the viewpoint of the foreign, English-speaking press were the use of volunteers as security personnel as a covert tool of government control. This had involved the close control of volunteers by the state. They had worked long hours for little benefit against their wills, and in particular the elderly were abused, were dissatisfied with their duties and derived little from the volunteering experience. The volunteers possessed poor language skills, were disingenuous, and were too many in number.

Both categories of press frequently quoted excerpts from the personal narratives of volunteers. The Chinese press supplemented these viewpoints with quotes from government officials associated with volunteering at the Games. Overall, the Chinese press adopted a tone, written generally in the third person, which tended to sound more official and objective. The foreign press tended to rely more on the first person narratives of journalists, lending a more subjective tone. All reports that mentioned actual volunteers focussed on either the young or the elderly.

Representation of volunteers' identities

The most striking representation by the majority of Chinese and foreign online press reports was the sheer size of the volunteering force. Chinese reports tended to quote figures in excess of a million and often referred to volunteers as being 'unsung heroes' of the event, suggesting that without them it would not have taken place.[26] Some foreign reports detracted from this impression with negative references to there being too many volunteers. References were made to problems such as 'giddy volunteers clog the sidewalks'.[27]

The view that there were too many volunteers was developed by *The Guardian* newspaper, which highlighted a response from a renowned sporting coach:

> At the weekend the notoriously mannerly Brazilian football coach Dunga managed to find fault with the sheer attentiveness of the service, as though he were a fine diner complaining of an over-zealous waiting staff. 'We could do with fewer volunteers', he sniffed. 'There are too many of them round the team.'[28]

One report emphasized the excessive number of volunteers by suggesting '[o]ne barely takes two steps without bumping into an Olympic volunteer', and possibly implied that there was too little for them to do by adding '[t]hey are all kind, they all offer help and they all walk with you a couple of steps before passing you off like the Olympic torch itself to another smiling volunteer'.[29]

Chinese reports tended to portray the identity of the average volunteer as friendly, enthusiastic, skilled, willing to help and willing to learn, as well as willing to endure hardship and inconvenience to ensure the Olympic Games were a success for all. Both sets of reports made reference to volunteers' smiles, manners and the positive demeanour with which they executed their tasks. One Chinese report described them as 'a group of smiling, pretty, youthful college-age individuals who are helpful beyond belief'.[30] They impressed Tokyo Governor Shintaro Ishihara, who was 'especially moved' by their enthusiasm and good manners,[31] and Achim Steiner, executive director of the United Nations Environment Programme, who claimed that volunteers would 'win the hearts and minds of visitors to Beijing'.[32] Whilst volunteers' smiles were included in foreign reports, they often included symbolic language which trivialized their appearances with descriptions related to volunteers' 'relentless chirpiness',[33] and their 'garrulous, giggling enthusiasm'.[34] Chinese portrayals of individuals, such as the young female volunteer who had held the head of a visitor who had fainted, were used to illustrate a sort of nobility of character. This story was described as 'a great sensation', and she was described as 'so beautiful when you extend your helping hands. You are the embodiment of the traditional virtues of the Chinese – hospitable and caring'.[35]

However, many foreign reports alluded to volunteers being disingenuous. One *New York Times* article emphasized volunteer sloganeering by quoting them as saying '[w]e waited 100 years for this moment, so we will sacrifice and endure any hardship', and the journalist added, '[b]ut poke a bit deeper (and put down the reporter's notebook) and the sloganeering can give way to grumbling'.[36] In similarly unsubstantiated fashion, one report accused volunteers of wearing 'perma-smiles' which were wearing thin.[37]

Representation of volunteers' roles at the event

The significance of volunteering was emphasized mainly by domestic press reports which linked the indispensability of their activities to the successful delivery of the event. This crucial influence of the volunteers was often accompanied by emphasis of the range, importance and effort required to complete their volunteering duties. For example, one report claimed they had been '[c]harged with being the cornerstone of the modern Olympic movement', and '[w]ith an ever-present smile, they're involved in many different matters, such as information, translation, transport, security, and any call for help'.[38] One report spoke about volunteers being trained to provide AIDS prevention advice to visitors.[39] Foreign press reports tended to acknowledge the same roles and duties, but described them as boring or tedious, and emphasized that the volunteers missed most of the actual sporting events coverage.[40] Whilst realistic admissions were made by the Chinese press about the shortfalls in many of the volunteers' English and problem solving skills, they stated that they were 'doing their best' and would 'enrich their experience' and future employability from volunteering.[41]

Representation of volunteers' motivations

Chinese reports alluded to volunteer motivation by emphasizing what they did at the Olympics in contrast to their normal or preferred activities. There were even accounts of people spending their honeymoons away from their spouses, and some link between volunteers leaving earthquake relief efforts in order to travel to Beijing to honour their volunteering duties. Elderly volunteers were represented in terms of their old age and the physical hardships they had overcome to volunteer. The theme of long hours, tiredness and hard work applied to volunteers of all ages in terms of early starts, number of passengers helped or journeys made. These observations were linked by Chinese reports to volunteer happiness, or the types of services provided to visitors. One *Guardian* report framed this service provision in terms of monitored performance, suggesting volunteers had to complete personal activity log-books for later inspection by their supervisors.[42]

Representation of how volunteering affected them

Volunteers' enthusiasm that was expressed in domestic reports was commonly linked to their pride at being able to present their country and their culture to the world through the media and to the international visitors and athletes at such a historic event. This pride was usually expressed in relation to other aspects of the volunteer's perceptions of themselves or their role. For example, one volunteer remarked '[i]t is a pity we missed the live broadcast, but we are proud to have worked for the ceremony's success'.[43]

One similar report focused on an elderly 'security' volunteer born in 1905 and emphasized his character attributes, stating that he was 'quite strict about his work', and that he was 'so proud … to be part of hosting the Games'.[44] Gratitude for their participation was generally expressed by volunteers as 'being happy'.[45] The skills learned as a result of volunteering were often articulated, such as by the student who observed 'when I graduate from school, I guess I won't be afraid of any tough job (with this experience)'.[46] This report also added that other rewards had come in the form of 'heartfelt' thanks and 'compliments in return' from Olympic visitors the volunteers had helped.[47] Foreign media reports, emphasized hardships, poor benefits and work in the form of long hours, working in high temperatures, poor food, tedious tasks and boredom, and little tangible reward. One volunteer was quoted as saying that dealing with an Olympic visitor was 'like a small glimmer of fun in this ocean of tedium'.[48]

There was suggestion by *The Times* that these conditions had led to negativity among volunteers and that 'after weeks of hard slog and only a T-shirt to show for it … there are signs of a revolt'. The same article quoted one volunteer referring to 'getting very tired' three times in two sentences. It seems obvious that following at least one month of long hours and hard work these attitudes are more likely to be expressed because of feelings of fatigue rather than intentions to rebel. As with previous cases in the foreign press, there seemed no evidence offered to support such a claim of impending revolt. Similarly, elderly volunteers were reported to be not 'showing up for their shifts or are pulling out of being a volunteer', by an elderly lady who was said to have 'tutted, but even she admitted she was struggling to enjoy her duties'.[49]

There was a general pattern observed throughout this Olympic coverage which saw 'spin' by one party, which was subjected to 'counter-spin' by the other, resulting 'counter-counter-spin'. The ways in which volunteers were affected by volunteering is a possible case in point. Probably, as a result of the negative representations already described, towards the end of the Olympics, domestic news reports about volunteers began to focus on their positive experiences. One report quoted narratives of a single volunteer who referred to lifelong lessons she had gained in teamwork, endurance, handling difficult situations, holding her temper, becoming more mature, and making new friends as a result of volunteering.[50] Such reports also alluded to the idea of an event legacy, rare in relation to event volunteering.

Representation of what else volunteers did at the Olympics apart from volunteer

Two press stories on both sides of the divide focussed on the use of volunteers for purposes that were argued by the foreign press to be unsuitable for allocation to Olympic volunteers; their use for political purposes, mainly related to security duties, and event fakery, mainly related to artificially-created 'cheering squads' used to fill empty stadia seats.

Several Chinese press portrayals were of elderly 'security volunteers' who carried out security duties. At least one publication mentioned the 103-year-old resident that had patrolled the neighbourhood for 30 years and took pride in making the area safe.[51] This type of representation was developed by several of the foreign newspapers who insinuated, yet did not substantiate, that this type of activity had a sinister connection with the Chinese security forces and that volunteers were being used by them to work on covert, government political agendas. These connections were mainly implied either through vague, personal observations of the journalist, or by association of volunteers with other, more official parts of the state mechanism. For example, a journalist for one newspaper remarked about volunteers that '[o]n the surface, it's incredible courtesy. A layer deeper, it's another vehicle of control, guiding each visitor down a path with no room for detour.'[52] However, it is not surprising that following loss of life at the Atlanta Olympics through terrorism and the resulting, negative publicity, everyone associated with subsequent mega-events would be required to be vigilant with respect to security, including volunteers in particular due to their size and breadth of presence. This historical factor was impacted by a reported terrorist threat. Additionally, crowd control, following high profile disasters at sporting events, would also require management by the planning committee through volunteers. Both motivations would provide a justification for not only the practical management steps associated with such a large-scale event, but also the utilization of surveillance as a practical technique of control.[53]

The suggestion that volunteers might just be tools of the political state was made by the foreign media through inferred relationships between volunteers and police, or government security officials which were made repeatedly by inclusion of the word 'volunteer' together in sentences with 'police', 'security guards' or references to 'communist'. These were often placed in paragraphs emphasizing government political controls in the city as a result of the Games. The following account implies a negative association and a suggestion that 'the people's Olympics' could only be viewed by local people from a relative distance due to the heightened security situation:

> 'The torch has gone out!' said a young student volunteer. ... A couple of minutes later, the flame of the official torch was visible above the lines of security guards, volunteers and police ... A few thousand non-approved Beijing residents were also allowed to watch the heavily guarded relay from behind barriers about three metres further back from the road.[54]

However, although specific discussion of torch relay disruption by pro-Tibet protestors is beyond the scope of this paper, it would seem relatively logical that heightened security would be present at this scene. It also follows that volunteers would be present in their usual capacities. This apparent inconsistency may be explained by Wasserstrom's argument,[55] which focuses on an emerging Western thought that the path to the successful future democratization of China would be found via the good people of the country (the Good Chinese), rather than its political leadership (Big, Bad China). This case of media representation possibly demonstrates the fear observed by Wasserstrom generated by a Western suspicion that despite the adoption of some Olympic values by good Beijing volunteers, they might be used as the face of a bad regime. It appears that the foreign media, understandably perhaps in view of their own interests and role, still consider the Olympic Games to be more of a media-event than a mega-event. The latter view would likely prompt a greater emphasis of the complexity involved in the planning and execution of an event of this kind and therefore the relative success displayed by the Beijing Planning Committee at this Olympic Games. However, according to the former view, journalists would be more likely to place importance on any discussion of China's perceived progress towards (as opposed to perfection of) democratization and the adoption of international (i.e. primarily Western) Olympic values. This bias and emphasis is likely to be exacerbated due to the customary training of journalists for the Western media profession who are less likely to possess the necessary knowledge and experiences to effectively shape a discourse about the features of a successful mega-event, than are to be able to discuss a media-event. It should not be forgotten that in the midst of Western media discussions about torch-relay protests, human rights and political controls, the Olympic Games is a sporting event as well as a cultural event.

This distinction perhaps also helps to explain the reports regarding the use of Chinese volunteers to fill stadia seating, which resulted in charges of fakery by the Western media. By early August, Chinese and foreign news reports began discussing the reasons for the large numbers of empty seats in Olympic stadia at competitions. Though the reasons for this are not within the scope of this study, the foreign newspapers focussed on this absence of spectators.[56] Both domestic and foreign reports highlighted that this was the first event of its kind that had successfully sold out and the *China Daily* had preceded the Games with a promise that all seats would be filled.[57] However it was clear from television broadcasts of events that large numbers of ticket holders had failed to attend. Neither press group mentioned that empty seats had been a major criticism of both the 2004 Athens Olympic Games and the 1988 Calgary Winter Olympics.[58]

Foreign reports tended to emphasize the International Organising Committee's urging to solve the problem.[59] Both Chinese and foreign press reports represented the use of volunteers to fill the empty seats in different ways, with Chinese reports openly admitting that the Olympic organizers had used volunteers to fill seats in arenas to maintain spectator atmosphere, and foreign reports used terms such as 'dispatching' and statements such as 'officials are bussing in teams of state-trained "cheer squads" identifiable by their bright yellow T-shirts to help fill the empty seats and improve the atmosphere'.[60] *The Daily Telegraph* ridiculed the approach taken by the organizers to encourage the volunteers to cheer in the stands for both competing teams. They used this as a symbol of China's long journey ahead to adopt Western values and practices.[61] There is no previous record of Olympic volunteers being used in this capacity. However, event design and staging requires the management of crowd dynamics and numbers in order to avoid, as the *Boston Globe* put it in the title of one report, 'Empty Seats, Lack of Buzz'.[62] This incident led to recent reports from the IOC that it planned to specifically address steps to avoid similar problems in this area at future events of this kind.[63]

Conclusion

It is likely that subsequent mega-event volunteers will, at least in part, be products of the types of discourses developed here. However, potential London 2012 Olympic volunteers might be forgiven, in the light of such conflicting Beijing press coverage, for remaining uncertain about their future Olympic image, role and benefits. The importance of volunteers to the effective staffing of mega-events will undoubtedly continue as an emphasis of future planning committees. In the meantime, the media discourse of Beijing 2008 has provided a new picture of Olympic volunteering in its provision of the representation of volunteers' identities, the tasks they perform, their motivations and perceived benefits in the context of 'Good Chinese' volunteers. However, as this foregoing discussion of the exchange of hegemonic discourses demonstrates, not only did China execute one of the most successful mega-events in mass-media history, partly through the volunteering efforts of the good Chinese volunteers, but in the process invited more traditional foreign media representations of 'Big, Bad China'.

Notes

1. Wilson, 'Volunteering', 215.
2. Cnaan, Handy and Wadsworth, 'Defining Who is a Volunteer', 365.
3. Stebbins, 'Volunteering'; Wilson and Musick, 'Attachment to Volunteering'; Liao-Troth, 'Are They Here'.
4. Cuskelly, Hoye and Auld, *Working with Volunteers.*
5. Roche, 'Mega-events', 1.
6. Baum and Lockstone, 'Volunteers'; Volunteering England, 'Volunteering England Statement'; BOCOG, *Facts and Figures.* See, for example, 'Smiling Volunteers Win Another Olympic Gold for Beijing', *China Daily*, August 14, 2008.
7. Cuskelly, Hoye and Auld, *Working with Volunteers*, 145.
8. Preuss, 'The Conceptualisation and Measurement of Mega Sport'.
9. McCurley and Lynch, *Essential Volunteer Management.*
10. For example, see Bowdin *et al.*, *Events Management*; Van der Wagen, *Human Resource Management*; see Elstad, 'Continuance Commitment'; Coyne and Coyne, 'Getting, Keeping'; Cuskelly, Hoye and Auld, *Working with Volunteers*; Flashman and Quick, 'Altruism is Not Dead.
11. Stebbins, 'Volunteering'.
12. For example, see Cuskelly, Hoye and Auld, *Working with Volunteers*; Sundeen and Raskoff, 'Volunteering Among Teenagers'; Sax and Astin, 'The Benefits of Service'.
13. For example, see Wilson and Musick, 'Attachment to Volunteering'; Nichols, 'Pressures on the UK sports sector'; Wilson, 'Volunteering'.
14. Gladden, McDonald and Barr, 'Event Management'.
15. Adapted from Baum and Lockstone, 'Volunteers'.
16. Mitchell, 'Representation'; Fairclough and Wodak, 'Critical Discourse Analysis'.
17. Harvey Brown, 'Cultural Representation'.
18. La Ferle and Lee, 'Can English Language Media', 142.
19. Cotter, 'Discourse in the Media', 425.
20. For example, see La Ferle and Lee, 'Can English Language Media'; Harvey Brown, 'Cultural Representation'; George, Hartley and Paris, 'The Representation of Female Athletes'; Cuneen and Spencer, 'Gender representations related to sport celebrity'; Hartman, 'Television and Movie Representations'; Mitissus and Elliott, 'Representations, Text and Practice'; Gilkes, 'Caring at a Distance'.
21. For example, see Rahman, 'David Beckham'; Neo and Savage, 'Shades of Green'; Crabbe, 'THE PUBLIC GETS'; Crolley and Teso, 'Gendered Narratives'; Pederson, 'Examining equity in newspaper photographs'; Marschik, 'Mitropa'; Poulton, 'Mediated Patriot Games'; Howe, 'From Inside the Newsroom'; Staurowsky, 'Getting Beyond Imagery'; Bruce, 'Marking the Boundaries.
22. Potter, 'Discourse Analysis', 146.
23. For example, see Potter and Wetherell, *Discourse and Social Psychology.*
24. Gee, *Situated language and learning.*
25. Baum and Lockstone, 'Volunteers'.
26. 'Smiling Volunteers', *China Daily* August 14, 2008.
27. 'Worrying about Traffic, Not Who Wins the Gold', *New York Times*, August 5, 2008.
28. 'Olympics: London will Struggle to Match this Army on Volunteer Frontline', *The Guardian*, August 19, 2008.
29. 'Art of Deception', *The Baltimore Sun*, August 7, 2008.
30. 'Beijing *huang yin nin*: A Volunteer's Story', *Twin Cities Daily Planet*, August 14, 2008.
31. 'Smiling Volunteers', *China Daily*, August 14, 2008.
32. Ibid.
33. 'Weary Beijing Volunteers Verging on Mutiny', *Timesonline*, August 22, 2008.
34. 'Olympics', *The Guardian*, August 19, 2008.
35. 'Smiling Volunteers', *China Daily*, August 14, 2008.

36 'Worrying about Traffic, Not Who Wins the Gold', *New York Times*, August 5, 2008.
37 'Weary Beijing Volunteers Verging on Mutiny', *Timesonline*, August 22, 2008.
38 '2008 and Beyond – Olympic Volunteer: My Part in the Games', CCTV, August 7, 2008.
39 '80,000 Condoms in Beijing Olympic Village all Taken Away During Games', *China View*, September 5, 2008.
40 'Olympics', *The Guardian,* August 19, 2008.
41 'Smiling Volunteers', *China Daily*, August 14, 2008.
42 '2008 and Beyond', CCTV, August 7, 2008; 'Pointing the Way to Olympic Glory', *China Daily*, September 8, 2008; 'Olympics', *The Guardian*, August 19, 2008.
43 'Pointing the Way to Olympic Glory', *China Daily*, September 8, 2008.
44 'Centenarian Olympic Volunteer Proud to See Games', CCTV, August 6, 2008.
45 '2008 and Beyond', CCTV, August 7, 2008.
46 'Smiling Volunteers', *China Daily*, August 14, 2008.
47 Ibid.
48 'Weary Beijing Volunteers Verging on Mutiny', *Timesonline*, August 22, 2008.
49 Ibid.
50 'Volunteering: The Influence is Subtle, but Lifelong', *China Daily*, September 12, 2008.
51 'Smiling Volunteers', *China Daily*, August 14, 2008.
52 'Art of Deception', *The Baltimore Sun,* August 7, 2008; Foucault, *Discipline and Punish*.
53 Foucault, *Discipline and Punish*.
54 'Crowds Flock to Torch Parade in Olympic City', *The Earth Times*, August 6, 2008.
55 Wasserstrom, 'The year of living anxiously'.
56 'BEIJING BEAT: Empty Seats, Lack of Buzz', *Boston Globe*, August 12, 2008.
57 'Empty Seats Unlikely in Beijing Olympics', *China Daily*, May 15, 2008.
58 ''88 WINTER OLYMPICS: NOTEBOOK; Empty Seats Upset Residents', *New York Times*, February 19, 1988.
59 'BEIJING BEAT: Empty Seats, Lack of Buzz', *Boston Globe*, August 12, 2008.
60 'Beijing Is All Dressed Up, But No One Is Going', *Washington Post*, August 13, 1988.
61 'Beijing Olympics: China Confused in the Art of Chanting', *The Daily Telegraph*, August 21, 2008.
62 'BEIJING BEAT: Empty Seats, Lack of Buzz', *Boston Globe*, August 12, 2008.
63 'Olympics-IOC to Learn Lessons from Empty Seats in Beijing', Reuters, November 27, 2008.

References

Baum, T., and L. Lockstone. 'Volunteers and Mega Sporting Events: Developing a Research Framework'. *International Journal of Event Management Research* 3, no. 1 (2007): 29–41.

Beijing Organizing Committee for the Games of the XXIX Olympiad (BOCOG). *Facts and Figures of Beijing Olympic Games.* 2008.

Bowdin, G.J., J. Allen, W. O'Toole, R. Harris, and I. McDonnell. *Events Management.* 2nd ed. Oxford: Elsevier, 2006.

Bruce, T. 'Marking the Boundaries of the 'Normal' in Televised Sports: The Play-by-play of Race'. *Media Culture Society* 26 (2004): 861–79.

Cnaan, R.A., F. Handy, and M. Wadsworth. 'Defining Who is a Volunteer: Conceptual and Empirical Considerations'. *Nonprofit and Voluntary Sector Quarterly* 25, no. 3 (1996): 364–83.

Cotter, C. 'Discourse in the Media'. In *Handbook of Discourse Analysis*, edited by Deborah Schiffrin, Deborah Tannen and Heidi E. Hamilton, 416–436. Oxford: Blackwell, 2003.

Coyne, B., and E. Coyne. 'Getting, Keeping and Caring for Unpaid Volunteers for Professional Golf Tournament Events'. *Human Resource Development International* 4, no. 2 (2001): 199–216.

Crabbe, T. 'THE PUBLIC GETS WHAT THE PUBLIC WANTS: England Football Fans, "Truth" Claims and Mediated Realities'. *International Review for the Sociology of Sport* 38, no. 4 (2003): 413–25.

Crolley, E., and E. Teso. 'Gendered Narratives in Spain: The Representation of Female Athletes in Marca and El Pais'. *International Review for the Sociology of Sport* 42, no. 2 (2007): 149–66.

Cuneen, J., and N. Spencer. 'Gender representations related to Sport celebrity portrayals in the Milk Mustache advertising campaign'. *Sport Marketing Quarterly* 12, no. 3 (2003): 140–150.

Cuskelly, G., R. Hoye, and C. Auld. *Working with Volunteers in Sport: Theory and Practice.* London: Routledge, 2006.

Elstad, B. 'Continuance Commitment and Reasons to Quit: A Study of Volunteers at a Jazz Festival'. *Event Management* 8, no. 2 (2003): 99–108.

Fairclough, N., and R. Wodak. 'Critical Discourse Analysis'. In *Discourse as Social Action*, edited by TA van Dijk, 258–84. London: Sage, 1997.

Flashman, R., and S. Quick. 'Altruism is Not Dead: A Specific Analysis of Volunteer Motivation'. In *Motivating Volunteers*, edited by L. Moore, 154–70. Vancouver: Vancouver Volunteer Centre, 1985.

Foucault, M. *Discipline and Punish: The Birth of the Prison*. London: Penguin, 1991.

Gee, J.P. *Situated language and learning: A critique of traditional schooling*. London: Routledge, 2004.

George, C., A. Hartley, and J. Paris. 'The Representation of Female Athletes in Textual and Visual Media'. *Corporate Communications: An International Journal* 6, no. 2 (2001): 94–101.

Gilkes, P. 'Caring at a Distance: (Im)partiality, Moral Motivation and the Ethics of Representation – Manipulation and Exploitation? Western Media and the Third World'. *Ethics, Place & Environment* 15, no. 3 (2000): 317–9.

Gladden, J.M., M.A. McDonald, and C.A. Barr. 'Event Management'. In *Principles and Practice of Sport Management*, edited by L.P. Masteralexis, C.A. Barr, and M.A. Hums, 42–59. Gaithersburg, MD: Aspen, 1998.

Hartman, K.B. 'Television and Movie Representations of salespeople: Beyond Willy Loman'. *Journal of Personal Selling & Sales Management* 25, no. 3 (2006): 283–92.

Harvey Brown, R. 'Cultural Representation and Ideological Domination'. *Social Forces* 71, no. 3 (March 1993): 657–76.

Howe, D.P. 'From Inside the Newsroom: Paralympic Media and the "Production" of Elite Disability'. *International Review for the Sociology of Sport* 43, no. 2 (2008): 135–50.

La Ferle, C., and W.N. Lee. 'Can English Language Media Connect with Ethnic Audiences? Ethnic Minorities' Media Use and Representation Perceptions'. *Journal of Advertising Research* March (2005): 140–53.

Liao-Troth, M.A. 'Are They Here for the Long Haul? The Effects of Functional Motives and Personality Factors on the Psychological Contracts of Volunteers'. *Nonprofit and Voluntary Sector Quarterly* 34, no. 4 (2005): 510–30.

Marschik, M. 'Mitropa: Representations of "Central Europe" in Football'. *International Review for the Sociology of Sport* 36, no. 1 (2001): 7–23.

McCurley, S., and R. Lynch. *Essential Volunteer Management*. 2nd ed. London: Directory of Social Change, 1998.

Mitchell, W. 'Representation'. In *Critical Terms for Literary Study*, edited by F. Lentricchia and T. McLaughlin, 11–122. Chicago, IL: University of Chicago Press, 1990.

Mitissus, D., and R. Elliott. 'Representations, Text and Practice: A Discourse-Analytic Model of the Consumer'. *Advances in Consumer Research* 26 (1999): 312–9.

Neo, H., and V.R. Savage. 'Shades of Green, Fields of Gold: Representations, Discourse and the Politics of Golf in Singapore'. *Landscape Research* 27, no. 4 (2002): 397–411.

Nichols, G., P. Taylor, M. James, K. Holmes, L. King, and R. Garrett. 'Pressures on the UK sports sector'. *Voluntas* 16, no. 1 (2005): 33–50.

Pederson, M.P. 'Examining equity in newspaper photographs: A content analysis of the print media coverage of interscholastic athletics'. *International Review for the Sociology of Sport* 37, no. 3–4 (2002): 303–318.

Potter, J. 'Discourse Analysis as a Way of Analysing Naturally Occurring Talk'. In *Qualitative Research*, edited by D. Silverman, 144–60. London: Sage, 1997.

Potter, J., and M. Wetherell. *Discourse and Social Psychology: Beyond Attitudes and Behaviour*. London: Sage, 1987.

Poulton, E. 'Mediated Patriot Games: The Construction and Representation of National Identities in the British Television Production of Euro '96'. *International Review for the Sociology of Sport* 39, no. 4 (2004): 437–55.

Preuss, H. 'The Conceptualisation and Measurement of Mega Sport Event Legacies'. *Journal of Sport amd Tourism* 12, no. 3–4 (2007): 227.

Rahman, M. 'David Beckham as a Historical Moment in the Representation of Masculinity'. *Labour History Review* 69, no. 2 (2004): 219–33.

Roche, M. 'Mega-events and Urban Policy'. *Annals of Tourism Research* 21 (1994): 1–19.

Sax, L.J., and A. Astin. 'The Benefits of Service: Evidence from Undergraduates'. *Education Record* 78 (1997): 25–32.

Staurowsky, E.J. 'Getting Beyond Imagery: The Challenges of Reading Narratives about American Indian Athletes'. *International Journal of the History of Sport* 23, no. 2 (2006): 190–212.

Stebbins, R.A. 'Volunteering, A Serious Leisure Perspective'. *Non-Profit and Voluntary Sector Quarterly* 25, no. 2 (1996): 211–24.

Sundeen, R., and S. Raskoff. 'Volunteering Among Teenagers in the United States'. *Nonprofit Voluntary Sector* 23 (1994): 383–403.

Van der Wagen, L. *Human Resource Management for Events: Managing the Event Workforce.* Oxford: Elsevier, 2007.

Volunteering England. 'Volunteering England Statement – London 2012 Olympic and Paralympic Games Legacy'. http://www.volunteering.org.uk/WhatWeDo/Policy/Whatwearesaying/Volunteering+England+Statement+London+2012+Olympic+and+Paralympic+Games+legacy.

Wasserstrom, J.N. 'The year of living anxiously: China's 1999'. In *Twentieth Century China, New Approaches*, edited by J.N. Wasserstrom, 256–265. London: Routledge, 2003.

Wilson, J. 'Volunteering'. *Annual Review of Sociology* 26 (2000): 215–40.

Wilson, J., and M.A. Musick. 'Attachment to Volunteering'. *Sociological Forum* 14, no. 2 (1999): 243–72.

China's media viewed through the prism of the Beijing Olympics

Kevin Latham

Department of Anthropology and Sociology, School of Oriental and African Studies, Russell Square, London WC1H 0XG, UK

The Beijing Olympics made visible, through various media practices and events associated with them, a range of different component parts of the constantly and rapidly changing Chinese media landscape. By following the Chinese, and to some degree foreign, media coverage of the Olympics this paper presents a range of clear examples that draw our attention to some of the key ways in which Chinese media work and some of the important changes and developments that are currently taking place in this area of Chinese social life. The paper identifies the more important of these developments treating them under three broad interrelated headings. The first is the relationship of the media to the government and the paper argues that this relationship requires reconceptualisation in ways that avoid the stereotypical polarities of state control and resistance. The second area for discussion relates to the relationship between Chinese and foreign media. I will argue that coverage of Olympics-related events in both Chinese and foreign media reveal important transformations in this relationship. The third issue relates to the rapid growth of new media use in contemporary China. To understand contemporary developments in Chinese media it is impossible to ignore the emergence of new media and new technologies – the Internet, mobile phones, digital television and mobile television in particular. However, the emphasis will not only be on what is new. It is also important to consider how old media habits continue to shape new media agendas and transformations. The paper argues that these developments require us to reconceptualise the Chinese media landscape in ways that break with the established frames of reference.

A prism refracts white light in such a way as to make visible its different component colours that are otherwise not generally perceptible by the human eye. This makes it possible both to break down light and understand its make up, but also to understand each component which is thrown into a relief of its own, in terms of its own characteristics. We might view the Olympics as having a similar effect in relation to understanding different aspects of contemporary Chinese society. The metaphor is a little crude and pushed too far would surely break down, but as a starting point for this essay and for thinking about the relationship between the Olympics and Chinese media, it is helpful. The Beijing Olympics have to some degree acted as a prism for the white light of Chinese media. They have made visible, through various media practices and events associated with them, a range of different component parts of the Chinese media landscape. That is not to say that these components can only be viewed or understood through the Olympics, nor is it to say that the Olympics somehow magically unveil secret hidden practices, but it is fair to say that by following the Chinese, and to some degree foreign, media coverage of the Olympics a range of clear examples present themselves that draw our attention to some of the key ways in which Chinese media work and some of the important changes and developments that are currently taking place in this area of Chinese social life. In this essay, I shall point to some of the more important of these aspects of, and changes in, Chinese media practices that may help us better understand the trajectories of recent developments in the Chinese media landscape.

For convenience of analysis and discussion, these developments can be considered under several key headings, even if they are all ultimately interrelated. The first is the relationship of the media to the government, which has long been a key defining feature of Chinese media practices and remains of crucial importance today. However, I will argue that this relationship requires reconceptualisation in ways that avoid the stereotypical polarities of state-control and resistance. The second area for discussion relates to the relationship between the Chinese and foreign media. I will argue that coverage of Olympics-related events in both the Chinese and foreign media reveal important transformations in this relationship. Whereas once the Chinese authorities tended to try to ignore and deny access to foreign media representations of China, now Chinese media often engage directly with foreign media output in critical and analytical ways that aim more at discrediting them and limiting their impact within China than preventing their circulation. To understand contemporary developments in Chinese media it is impossible to ignore the emergence of new media and new technologies – the Internet, mobile phones, digital television and mobile television in particular – and this will constitute the focus of discussion for the third issue identified in this essay. However, the emphasis will be not only on what is new. It is also important to consider how old media habits continue to shape new media agendas and transformations.

These three areas of discussion do not offer a comprehensive overview of changes in China's media. However, they do raise enough key issues and point to enough of the important transformations in Chinese media sectors for us to start to see important ways in which we might reconceptualise the Chinese media landscape and this will be the task of the latter stages of this essay.

The relationship of the media to government

Perhaps one of the most common adjectives used to describe the Chinese media, particularly popular with western journalists, is 'state-controlled', conjuring up images of centralized censorship, dictatorial regimes of propaganda production and shackled journalists forced to succumb to the will of the central authorities.[1] This perception of the Chinese media goes hand-in-hand with the range of ideas from democratization to dissidence that sees any kind of chink in the armour of this propaganda machine as a site of resistance with the potential to bring down the regime, lead to social unrest, if not complete chaos, and the liberation of Chinese people denied the freedoms of thought and speech.

There is some truth in such accounts. For example, decisions are taken about the censorship of media content at a central level on a regular basis; media organizations are ordered daily to print or broadcast specific news content and journalists have to sacrifice their personal opinions in favour of those of the party in order to cling onto their jobs.[2] However, true though that may be, it is as inadequate a representation of the daily practices of Chinese media production as would be an alternative that said all media are now driven predominantly by market principles. Understanding how the Chinese media work requires us to be far more subtle, far more complex and far more sensitive to a diverse range of practices that include censorship and dissidence, but also self-censorship, complicity, the circumvention of regulations, give and take between journalists and media watchdogs as well as the daily production of huge quantities of media content considered by almost everyone to be completely apolitical.[3]

Aside from offering a useful piece of shorthand for a range of practices otherwise too complex to summarize, in relation to Chinese media the notion of 'control' is therefore potentially misleading and unhelpful. For this reason it is useful to consider an alternative vocabulary such as that of 'direction', 'instruction', 'influence', 'reaction', 'pressure', 'negotiation' or 'contestation'. The Beijing Olympics offered many opportunities to talk about direction, pressure, instruction and influence, for instance in relation to the significance of the Games for China, their ability to demonstrate the country's economic, technological and social achievements over three decades of reform and the welcome extended to the rest of the world.[4] There were clear efforts to direct key media messages from the centre and one could identify many instances where such directions were obediently followed. Over the period immediately before and during the Games there was an almost complete marginalization of any other news, domestic or international, in the mainstream broadcast media. Government attempts to silence internal dissident voices through threats, force, persuasion or various other means were also largely successful. However, that is not the whole story. There are other instances where we need to think in other terms such as negotiation, contestation, influence, reaction or engagement.

Consider, for instance, images that circulated widely on the internet in China in June and July 2008 showing street scenes in Weng'an, Guizhou Province, just weeks before the opening ceremony of the Beijing Olympics. On 28 June 2008 thousands of protesters attacked and ransacked the local offices of the public security bureau in the town in response to rumours of a police cover-up relating to the death of a school girl who fell from a bridge in the city shortly before the protests. Typical images, many taken with mobile phone handsets, depicted huge crowds with thousands of people cramming the streets of Weng'an near the headquarters of the public security bureau. They show smoke billowing from burning buildings and people standing on overturned police vehicles. Some showed protestors using their raised vantage points on top of such vehicles to get a better view with their cameras and cellphones.[5]

Such images, which circulated on the Internet, along with many others of the same incidents, both within China and overseas, do not show the 'harmonious' society ('hexie shehui') of official propaganda which underpinned central motifs in Zhang Yimou's extravagant display of Chinese cultural history at the opening ceremony of the Games in August. On the contrary they show social unrest, vandalism, street violence and disrespect for the law and its representatives. Some such images even index their own significance in terms of transformations in China's media landscape by clearly showing participants in the disturbances taking films or photos with cameras and their mobile phones. Such photos index precisely the kind of uncontrolled, decentralized, uncensored personal media production and consumption that they themselves – probably captured on a similar device and uploaded onto the Internet – represent.

However, the complexities of Chinese media are not revealed simply by the appearance of images like these on the Internet. Rather, one has to consider the trail of mediated interactions that these demonstrations set in train in the summer of 2008 and their relation to the final outcome of the case. The demonstrations, like others in recent years in China, were themselves organized to some degree using mobile phones for communication.[6] Subsequently, the news of the disturbances spread by mobile phone and the Internet around the country, with 'netizens', as Chinese Internet users are known, around the country thriving on the case for the next couple of weeks. The rapid, initially uncontrolled circulation of images, stories, eye-witness accounts, rumours, jokes and commentary ensured that Weng'an became a national news story over the next couple of weeks, whereas in the past – say 10 years earlier – it would have been fairly easily contained as a local news story. After the initial circulation of these reports, China's Internet police started trying to close it down. Key words, such as Weng'An, the names of key players in the story and ultimately even key phrases like 'doing push-ups', which took on its own satirical significance in the case, were blocked in search engines and webpages started being blocked or taken down from the Internet.[7] However, these efforts at censorship only triggered a second round of interest in the story that saw the more dedicated and technically-minded Internet users finding all sorts of ways to circumvent Internet filters and controls to continue posting comments, images and jokes related to the story.[8]

A few weeks after the disturbances in Weng'an and once new media activity related to the case had calmed down to some considerable degree, the story took another intriguing turn with senior party and government officials in Weng'An county being sacked, high ranking provincial officials being shipped in to sort out the situation, a public criticism of the inadequacies of the original handling and reporting of the case and a new semi-official version of events being circulated in China's mediasphere through prominent newspapers including those often considered to take a more critical stance towards authority, such as the *Southern Metropolitan Daily*.[9] This semi-official version of events included interviews with the young people on the bridge back in June and attempts to directly clarify issues – such as suggestions that one of the young men involved was related to party officials – that had fuelled rumours of corruption and injustice on the Internet. In this case it is possible to see the heavy hand of the state clamping down on dissident opinion – the filtering and blocking of the Internet for instance – but the full progression of events suggests that in many ways the authorities were not directing the story, but reacting to it. They may have *tried* to control accounts of what happened and public understanding of the issue, but they constantly found themselves trying to rein in unruly versions of events rather than simply promoting their own. What happened in Weng'an – including the sacking of senior party officials – and how it came to be understood in the public domain around the country have to be understood in relation to two key factors. Such an understanding is inseparable from the complex process of underdetermined media practices that ensued over these few weeks in the summer of 2008 and the fact that the Olympics were due to start little more than a month later.

Had it not been for the Olympics and the massive national and international media attention on China that they inevitably entailed, the events in Weng'an would not have been dealt with anywhere near as quickly, decisively and some might say sympathetically, as they were. With the Olympics on the horizon there was no time for delay. A resolution to the situation had to be found, public discontent had to be answered and dealt with and dissident media voices needed to be silenced, not by censorship but by engagement. Consequently, this case offers a clear example of how the prism of the Olympics highlighted the transformation of the relationship between media and government in China in recent years. The old party-centred structures of propaganda, censorship and self-censorship so familiar from the Maoist past, are still in place, but the context of their operation has changed and they have been supplemented by an array of more complicated media practices.[10] The old formulae of control and resistance do not offer an adequate understanding of what is going on. Indeed, in a case like that of Weng'an, it is difficult to pin down just who was calling the tune as events unfurled.[11]

The relationship of Chinese to foreign media

The Beijing Olympics offered many opportunities to ponder the relationship between the Chinese and foreign media and highlighted the increasing importance of this relationship. China's official attitude to foreign media has become ever more double-edged. There is an inherited tendency from the past to consider all foreign media with caution and suspicion. However, what the Olympics revealed on many occasions is that the Chinese media increasingly find themselves in dialogue with foreign journalists, particularly their China-related media representations.[12] Up until the end of the 1990s, the default approach to foreign media in China was exclusion. The basic principle was to prevent foreign media from circulating in China unless they did so under strictly circumscribed conditions.[13] Combined with the conceptualization of Chinese media production, which has for decades assumed a hermetically sealed Chinese population receiving only messages produced under strictly controlled conditions,[14] this principle has meant that foreign media – particularly political news – representations have generally been excluded, ignored and denied an existence in the Chinese media landscape. In many instances this principle is still operative today and can be seen in everyday Chinese media practices from the clumsy censorship of Hong Kong television relays in Guangdong Province, through the blocking of foreign websites to import quotas for foreign films.[15] However, such practices now sit alongside efforts to engage with foreign media reporting in ways that do not attempt to deny their existence so much as to limit and, if necessary, undermine their credibility.[16]

These new practices of engagement take various forms and are found across different media sectors including radio, television, the internet, newspapers and magazines. A prominent example is the popular *Global Times* ('huanqiu shibao 环球时报') newspaper which offers a daily digest of foreign media reporting on Chinese and international affairs. Importantly, the format includes not only carefully selected content from foreign media sources but also direct or indirect guidance as to how to read and understand that content. The *Global Times* came into its own at various times in the run up to the Olympics with the protests in Tibet and the disrupted international Olympic torch relay offering numerous opportunities to comment. This commentary, moreover, comes to constitute a kind of dialogue with foreign – predominantly, but not exclusively, western – journalism.

For instance, following the widely acclaimed opening ceremony of the Beijing Olympics on 8 August 2008, foreign media latched onto a Chinese press report revealing that the televised footage of the spectacular firework footprint that featured in the opening ceremony was not filmed live, but was in large part prepared in advance using computer animation and footage from previous rehearsals. This stimulated widespread accusations in foreign media about the 'falsity' of the Beijing Olympics which were only strengthened a few days later when it turned out that a young girl singer in the same ceremony was lip-synching to another girl's voice. On 13 August 2008, just after the barrage of negative foreign press reporting about falsity, however, the *Global Times* led with a full-page story entitled 'The Real China Brings the World Closer' ('zhenshi zhongguo ling shijie qinqie 真实中国令世界亲切'). This article opened with the following statement, which can be seen as a clear riposte to foreign reporting about the opening ceremony: 'With more than 30,000 foreign journalists all reporting at the same time from Olympic China, the China that the world sees cannot possibly be false.'[17] The text went on to explain to readers how foreign media consumers had been informed about the problems in Xinjiang and other negative news about China including the death of two US citizens linked to the Olympic volleyball team. It also closed the opening paragraph with the following: 'Even if there are still now some western media spreading lies about Beijing, like describing the city of Beijing as a military city, there are nonetheless very few people in the west who believe such talk.'[18]

Once the games were over, in a prominent article entitled 'The Olympics Enhance China's Communication with the World' ('aoyun shi zhongguo yu shijie goutong') and subtitled 'According to experts, if there are still people in the west who criticise China without reason, the propaganda effect will greatly be diminished' ('zhuanjia cheng ruguo xifang zai you ren huluan zhize zhongguo, xuanchuan xiaoguo jiang da zhekou'), the newspaper returned to this familiar theme:

> Even if there are some anti-China journalists in the west who are starting again to write provocative articles on China and a US White House spokesman criticised China for 'not having taken the opportunity of the Olympics to improve its human rights record', nonetheless a poll reported on the website of US magazine *Sports Illustrated* showed ordinary western people's approval of the Beijing Olympics.[19]

The article continues to report that 66% of US-based online respondents to the poll thought that the Beijing Games had been the best out of the last four sets of games, which included the Atlanta Games (voted for by 15% of respondents). However, in keeping with the general style and character of the *Global Times* the article also goes on to quote a range of positive comments culled from newspapers or news media websites in the United Kingdom, Japan, France, Germany, the US and India.

Another example of this kind of engagement with foreign media reporting around the Olympics came in the middle of July 2008, in the final run-up to the Games. Many foreign media reports were focused on the security build up in the city with journalists focusing on the training and deployment of specialist anti-terrorist swat teams, the increasing military and police presence on the streets in the capital and other manifestations of the ever more visible mobilization of security forces in the run-up to the Games. Much of this reporting asked critical questions about whether the build-up represented the exaggerated response of an authoritarian regime and focused on its implications for the rights of ordinary Beijing citizens and expelled migrant workers. However, within days the *Global Times* was fighting back with a front page article (on 14 July 2008) condemning this kind of churlish criticism and asking what foreign journalists would say if there were some kind of terrorist atrocity in the city during the Games or the safety of world leaders were somehow jeopardized?[20] The significance, for this analysis, of these kinds of reports is not however in their specific content, but in the fact that they represent a new kind of dialogue and critical interaction with western reporting of China with which its citizens are assumed to be at least in part familiar. The assumption, once a mainstay of Chinese journalism, that Chinese people would not be aware of what western media were saying, is no longer considered feasible by either the Chinese authorities or media professionals. Indeed, quite on the contrary, mainstream news media now increasingly see the importance of acknowledging and engaging with such reporting.

This kind of strategic engagement with western media reporting on China can be usefully seen as a kind of 'inoculation' in Barthes'[21] terms referring to the convention in news of 'allowing radical voices a controlled moment of speech that is nominated and inserted into the narrative in such a way as to ensure that the social body is strengthened and not threatened by the contrast between it and the radical'.[22] In this way at least some critical foreign media reports are no longer ignored, hidden and avoided but are, on the contrary, acknowledged, discussed and interpreted in a way that makes them 'safe'. Their criticisms of China are carefully addressed and answered while also being undermined by association with unfair anti-China bias in foreign media.[23] This represents a significant change from Chinese approaches to foreign media even as little as 10 years ago when foreign criticism was still, with only rare exceptions, censored, avoided or ignored in the domestic media.

China's emerging new media landscape

The Beijing Olympics were dubbed the 'high tech' Olympics by its organizers and they were clearly expected to demonstrate to the world a level of technological development and competence comparable with the world's leading economies.[24] China's array of new technologies was intended to play a key role in conveying the message at home and overseas that China is worthy of its increasingly important and prominent position on the world stage. Some of the most visible and high profile features of this high-tech China were associated with new media and the Games were also expected to give a boost to the country's new media sectors.[25]

China Mobile, the country's largest and most profitable telecoms operator and a very high profile sponsor of the Games, was running Olympics-related advertising campaigns years prior to their launch. The company also launched the country's first commercial trial of third generation (3G) mobile phone technologies just a few months before the opening ceremony and timed to coincide with the Games. This was widely reported by national and local news sources. The new 3G service was also based on the home-grown Chinese TD-SCDMA platform which provides the only technological alternative to the established European (WCDMA) and North American (CDMA2000) platforms.[26] In actual fact the launch of TD-SCDMA came too late to be widely used during the Olympics. Nonetheless, there was high-profile advertising both for the phones and the services available to their users particularly at the time of the Games when much was made of the ability to watch both live and archived events on 3G handsets.

The Beijing Games were also seen as offering a breakthrough in the online coverage of major sporting events as well as major news stories more generally. CCTV coverage of the Games was available online to those with broadband connections, which now means most Internet users in China.[27] The top Internet portals such as Sohu.com and Sina.com had high profile sites dedicated to Olympics coverage including results, news reports, on-demand video of recent competitions and Olympics events as well as some live relays of CCTV coverage. These sites offered a comprehensive range of Internet services including bulletin boards (BBS), blogs, news, photos, streaming video and clips, profiles of top sports stars and much more. New media also featured prominently within the mainstream CCTV coverage of the Games.[28] For instance, one daily afternoon show on the main CCTV news channel – which was one of the channels fully devoted to Olympics coverage for the period of the Games – involved young studio presenters discussing the latest results and events of the day with constant reference to incoming text messages (SMS) and emails. New media were drawn fully into the mainstream to add highly visible interactivity and a lively, youthful and contemporary feel to the coverage.

New media coverage of the Games in Beijing also included digital mobile television coverage on some lines of the city's light rail network. Even if this included only limited live coverage of sports events during the Games, digital mobile television on the public transport networks – including buses and some taxis – in the city had been covering many aspects of the Games and the build up to them for more than a year beforehand. This included educational programming on the Beijing Games and Olympic history as well as introductions to the rules and technical aspects of different sports. News bulletins covered all the latest developments in the preparations for the games while reporting results and medals tallies throughout the Games. Travelling spaces in the capital were transformed into Olympics-consuming arenas.

These new media aspects of the organization and presentation of the Games – the relation to mobile media, the Internet and the transformation of public spaces – draw our attention to the massive transformations that new media have made to China's media landscape over the last decade. Many of them were not specifically new for the Olympics – many television shows have used email, telephone hotlines and SMS to enhance interactivity for several years now. Yet, with an eye on the Olympics as a show case for China's technological development and sophistication, new media were particularly prominent and evident in the preparation, organization and media coverage of the Games.

Nonetheless, as shown by the example of social unrest in Weng'an discussed above, the emergence of new media practices in the Chinese media landscape is not simply a technological transformation, but has to be associated with other shifting relationships of power between key players in this landscape including media users, professionals, party cadres of different kinds at different levels of the political structure and in some cases also foreign journalists. The supplementarity, interrelatedness and interactive nature of new media in relation to traditional print and broadcast mass media should awaken us to the need to see Chinese media as no longer easily segmented according to media type (i.e. television, radio, Internet, newspapers etc.).[29] Rather, as Olympics coverage showed clearly, there are new emerging forms of interdependability between different media platforms. CCTV proudly drew attention to its online broadcasting, just as the portals used their video coverage of the Games as a prominent part of their self-promotion. Newspapers, television and radio reports all reported online activity in bulletin boards and other Internet discussion forums as an indication of public opinion and reaction in relation to key Olympics events and news stories such as sprinter Liu Xiang's withdrawal from the 110m hurdles or Chen Zhong's controversial exit from the Taekwondo competition.[30] Chinese media are increasingly interdependent and interrelated.

An example from the Olympic Torch relay in Guangzhou points to how this kind of media interrelatedness can play out in ordinary people's lives. A key informant in my research explained how he had been attending the torch relay in the city with his daughter. By chance he had been caught on camera by Guangdong Television's live coverage of the event. Shortly afterwards his image was relayed on the mobile television service broadcasting on the city's underground light railway where a good friend of his saw him and his daughter cheering right in front of the camera. His friend called him on his mobile phone and they arranged to meet at the rally identifying a meeting place with reference to the images that had been on television. This case shows not only how media practices are multiply interrelated, but also the extent to which people's engagement with Olympic events – the Torch relay in this case – could be a complex and highly mediated experience even for those participating 'live' in the event.[31]

However, interrelatedness does not mean homogeneity. Indeed, the two events mentioned above – Liu Xiang's withdrawal and Chen Zhong's defeat – and how they were covered by different media reveal the need to differentiate carefully between the relationships between media, government and populace for television and the Internet, for instance. In both cases, CCTV, Xinhua and other prominent national media organizations quickly conveyed a 'standard' position that was repeated on news bulletins, discussion programmes, chat shows, sports reports and elsewhere, almost certainly broadly formulated by higher authorities. On this reading Liu Xiang was not to be criticized personally. He was to be supported and sympathized with. Meanwhile the judges' decision in Chen Zhong's case, although disappointing, should be respected for its impartiality. However, in both cases, BBS and blogs revealed a wide array of divergent views and opinions. In relation to Liu's case, for instance, views ranged from conspiracy theories through to deep personal depression, anger, sneering and indifference. While Chen Zhong's exit from the Games prompted detailed discussions about the rules of Taekwondo, why or whether the judges were right or wrong as well as the personal disappointment, frustration or for that matter happiness and satisfaction, that netizens felt in relation to the case as well as a host of other opinions and comments.

Old habits die hard

Chen Zhong's exit from the Beijing Olympics Taekwondo competition was also revealing in another way. In particular the live television coverage of the events surrounding her defeat and departure from the competition showed ways in which old originally politically-driven anxieties about the relation between content and audiences are easily aroused. On 23 August 2008 at around 17.30, CCTV's Olympics Channel was broadcasting live from the venue of the women's 67kg Taekwondo competition. A fixed camera was focused on the area where the semi-final of the competition was due to take place between China's Chen Zhong and Mexico's Maria del Rosario Espinoza while a CCTV commentator made occasional comments to pass the time and set the scene. However, the competitors were late to emerge and after a short while in their place came an IOC official who made an announcement in English saying that after analysis of video footage of Chen Zhong's bout with Britain Sarah Stevenson following a British appeal on the outcome, the judges had no alternative but to change their original decision on the match and award victory to the British competitor. The announcement was greeted by cheers from presumably the British camp, but otherwise there was little reaction from the crowd, the majority of which was probably awaiting a translation that was not forthcoming. Meanwhile two young Chinese translators seated immediately behind the IOC official showed shock and concern on their faces, one covering her mouth with both hands.

The announcement was, however, welcomed with some incredulity on the part of the CCTV commentator, his first reaction as he absorbed what had been said being, 'It's not possible!' ('bu hui ba!'). After a couple of minutes in which the commentator speculated on what would happen next and whether there would be a Chinese counter-appeal, CCTV's footage switched back to the studio. The studio presenters expressed disappointment and repeated briefly what had happened. A few minutes later the coverage returned to the gymnasium to get an update from their reporter, but with only an audio link and no images. He reported that there had been mixed reactions from the crowd including some strong protestations. However, instead of continuing to show the rest of the competition, the channel switched to other coverage including updates on the day's medal winners and progress in other competitions. Revealingly this also included two updates on the weather within the space of ten minutes while the semi-final of the Taekwondo, now between Stevenson and Espinoza, was entirely ignored.[32]

In this case, clearly a decision was taken by television producers not to show the semi-final and to cut live images from the gymnasium. What was at issue was not simply the fact that Chen Zhong was out of the competition, but the uncertainty of what might happen as a result. Discussions of these events with Chinese journalists and television professionals in following weeks and months suggested that there were likely to have been two main concerns that led to this course of action by CCTV. One was that the crowd at the stadium might behave badly in some way and that would look bad for China and the organizers. The other was that paying too much attention to the issue might provoke angry reactions among ordinary Chinese viewers. Consequently, the safest course of action was to switch the coverage to other things. This case is a reflection of how self-censoring anxieties among television producers about upsetting their professional and/or political superiors could easily lead to conservative, 'play-safe' options being selected to override the 'disorderly'[33] potential of a live broadcast situation.

More strategically planned examples of this kind of attitude in Chinese news circles are indicated by the fact that in the build-up to the Games over the preceding year, journalists quite widely reported a tightening of editorial grip on daily news reporting. Television, newspaper and radio journalists were all working in environments where reporting of more positive and less negative news was strongly encouraged, where they were constantly reminded to avoid sensitive issues, where excitement about the Olympic Games looming on the horizon was to be maintained and where the list of topics not to be reported was generally growing longer rather than shorter.[34]

The speed with which Chinese media sources and politicians moved to mobilize sympathetic support for Liu Xiang on his exit from the Games was an indication of another old Chinese media habit that persists from the past: didacticism. The propaganda function of Chinese mass media is still written into their operational constitutions and whatever changes and developments may have occurred in Chinese media over the last two to three decades,[35] the need for Chinese media producers to tell their imagined viewers, readers or listeners the appropriate way to understand news and current affairs is still easily identified in much media output.

Olympics didacticism, telling media consumers how they should understand the Games and Games-related events and occurrences, was clearly visible on a daily basis in China. Apart from reactions to particular events like the withdrawal of Liu Xiang from the 110m hurdles, there had been repeated messages in different forms and across all Chinese media from newspapers and radio to the Internet and SMS news bulletins, stressing particular ways to understand the games. These included its importance as recognition of China on the international stage as well as cautious warning at the end of the games that China's record-breaking medal haul does not mean that China was now a sporting 'superpower'.[36]

The important point to draw from these examples, is that although China's media landscape has been transforming itself for decades and is now populated by new technologies that offer a far more complex array of communicative possibilities than could even have been imagined 20 years ago, there are nonetheless many media production practices, particularly in news, that owe their rationale and prevalence to older structures and procedures of media production. These older practices are often cited by foreign journalists as examples of 'state-control' of the media in China. However, although they might loosely be seen in such a light, they need to be understood alongside and as part of the more complex array of media practices that now constitute media consumption and production in contemporary China.

Through the prism of the Olympics: reconceptualising China's media landscape

The discussion above is inevitably limited in scope given the length of this essay. However, the issues and examples covered do help us to identify a number of key features of China's media landscape that should encourage those trying better to understand China's media to reconceptualise key practices and relationships that constitute them.

First, as Olympics coverage made abundantly clear, there is now a much greater interdependence between different media. In many cases new media practices, and those relating to the Internet in particular (though not exclusively), play a key role in forging these new kinds of relationships. There was intense competition between China's leading Internet portals to attract netizens to their Olympics coverage, which was only made possible through collaboration with other media organizations – television stations and other broadcasters, newspapers, news agencies and other website operators. Similarly, CCTV was very keen to highlight its own live online coverage (through streaming television and video-on-demand) of the Games, while the station's television coverage used mobile phone services and the Internet to enhance interactivity, liveliness and to maximize a sense of participatory viewing.

Related to this first point, it is now also increasingly problematic to compartmentalize Chinese media practices according to media type. Television, radio, Internet and newspapers are increasingly difficult to separate out from one another even if each has its own sets of particular circumstances and characteristics. We might consider, for instance, some of the top news stories in Chinese and foreign media from the period of the Games and how they developed. The 'fake' fireworks story relating to the opening ceremony emerged from a few lines in a short, relatively insignificant article in a local Beijing newspaper on the day after the opening ceremony. A seemingly innocent comment from one of the organizers about how the fireworks spectacle had been achieved was picked up upon by Chinese journalists and Internet users, subsequently drew the attention of foreign scholars and journalists and found its way within a day or two to prominent positions in leading daily newspapers, television news bulletins and other news sources throughout the world. Once it became such a prominent international story, it was inevitable that it would be picked up on, revisited and (by some) responded to in China. If it had not become a prominent foreign news story it is hard to imagine it would have received so much attention in China even if it originated in Beijing in a Chinese report.

Again related to the opening ceremony, we might think of how comments from another organizer in a broadcast radio interview led to the other prominent 'fakery' story of the games relating to the dubbing of another girl's voice over that of the girl chosen to sing in the stadium.[37] It was not so much the radio as a medium that enabled this story to develop so quickly, but the Internet. The interview was available for a time online and it is there that most people subsequently came to hear it in China, either directly through the radio station's website or through copies being posted on YouTube-like video-sharing websites.[38] After that it was reported upon and discussed across all kinds of media both within China and overseas.

The example above of my informant participating in the Olympic Torch relay in Guangzhou pushes this discussion of cross-media interdependence and interactivity in another direction. What that case revealed was the extent to which everyday practices in China's large cities at least can be heavily mediated. There was not simply the event, with its 'live' audience and then separate media coverage of it. Rather, the media coverage was a fundamental and constituting aspect of the 'live' experience itself. Distinguishing and differentiating the two would be highly problematic. This mediation of everyday experience also relates to the transformation of experiences of space and place through mobile telephony (including data and media services), the Internet, outdoor public television screens, mobile television in public transport and personal digital video cameras. The mediatization of everyday life and sociality is multi-faceted and involves diverse sources of information, modes of interaction and modes of experience.

The opening ceremony and the furore surrounding the fireworks display is a good example of how the lines between live events and mediated events have been blurred. The fireworks display was conceptualised, organized and executed with a television audience in mind. For instance, it effectively had no central location from which it could be appreciated in person and the only way to see it as conceptualised by the organizers was on a television screen, where, as we have seen, digital technologies made it entirely possible to blur the boundaries between live footage and enhanced digital imagery of past events. As anyone trying to enjoy the fireworks display on the night would have found, the immediate 'live' experience was heavily compromised in favour of the television spectacle and effectively displaced by the mediated digital experience.[39]

In all of this, digital imagery and communication is also increasingly important and requires us to formulate new understandings of how Chinese media operate from the conceptualisation of media product and audiences through to the relationship between government, media and the general populace. Relationships of 'control' and propaganda are not best understood in terms of top-down hierarchical structures of ideologizing. Nor are they best understood, for that matter, in terms of resistive strategies. Rather, it is necessary to consider the limitations and possibilities of the digital portability of images and messages, the transformation of the Chinese authorities' ability to dictate and shape news agendas, the complex array of old, new, more, less and not at all sophisticated strategies and practices they adopt to deal with this shift in the mobilisability of power and the complex configurations of innovation, challenge and complicity that characterize contemporary journalistic practices.[40] Consequently the narrow focus on political control and ideology in understandings of Chinese media starts to appear increasingly inadequate and anachronistic. Chinese lives are heavily mediated in diverse and complex ways. Media imagery and representations are increasingly contested and contestable. Government messages increasingly (though far from always) have to compete and negotiate for their position in a media environment that is increasingly crowded, is open to new forms of intervention by a widening range of people and is characterized by changing relationships of power.

Notes

[1] Cases are too numerous to mention in detail. For a random sample from respected media organizations in the UK and USA see, Michael Bristow, 'China Criticises Western Media'. *BBC News*, http://news.bbc.co.uk/1/hi/world/asia-pacific/7312376.stm, 25 March 2008; Phelim Kine, 'Censorship isn't Good for China's Health'. *Wall Street Journal*, http://online.wsj.com/article/SB122368041325124731.html, 11 October 2008; David Barboza, 'Pressed Over Tibet, China Berates Foreign Media'. *New York Times*, http://www.nytimes.com/2008/03/25/world/asia/25tibet.html, March 25, 2008; and for a more recent example see Chris Hogg, 'How the Chinese Reported Tiananmen'. *BBC News*, http://news.bbc.co.uk/1/hi/world/asia-pacific/8069940.stm, 4 April 2009.

[2] For an overview of Chinese journalism see Burgh, *The Chinese Journalist*. For a detailed example of the kind of practical negotiation of personal and institutional values that journalists engage in on a daily basis see Latham, 'Media and the Limits of Cynicism in Postsocialist China' (2009). For a consideration of the unstable 'liminal' climate in which journalists operate in China and the contradications and tensions this creates with dominant Olympics narratives see Smith, 'Journalism and the Beijing Olympics'.

[3] See e.g. Latham, 'Nothing But the Truth'; Latham, 'SMS, Communication and Citizenship'; Latham, *Pop Culture China!*; Latham, 'Media and the Limits of Cynicism in Postsocialist China' (2009); Hemelryk, Keane and Liu, eds., *Media in China*; Zhao, *Media, Market, and Democracy*; Lee *et al.*, *Power, money and media* (2000).

[4] For exploration of these kinds of messages see also Brownell, *Beijing's Games*; Price and Dayan, eds., *Owning the Olympics*; Cha, *Beyond the Final Score*; Close, Askew and Xu, *The Beijing Olympiad*.

[5] To view some such images go to, for example, http://www.zonaeuropa.com/20080701_1.htm (last accessed June 14, 2010).

[6] Cf. also for example, Rafaele, 'The Cell Phone'.

[7] One of the young men who was with the girl on the bridge the night she died was reported in official versions of events as saying he was doing push-ups on the bridge when his friend fell.

[8] For an account of some of the cat and mouse uses of technology that Chinese netizens deploy see Chase, Mulvenon and Hachigian, 'Comrade to Comrade Networks'.

[9] For example, 'Weng'an County Party Secretary and County Head Forced to Resign' ('weng'an xianwei shuji xianzhang bei mianzhi') and 'We Did Not Have Sexual Relations' ('women mei fasheng guo xing guanxi'). *Nanfang Dushibao*, July 5, 2008, A10. http://epaper.nddaily.com/A/html/2008-07/05/node_523.htm.

[10] See Latham, 'SMS, Communication and Citizenship', Latham, 'Media and the Limits of Cynicism in Postsocialist China' (2009); Latham, 'Nothing But the Truth'; Lynch, *After the Propaganda State* (1999).

[11] Indeed, the Chinese authorities already openly acknowledge this changing relationship between government, media and the general population. A recent article in the *People's Daily* commenting on social unrest in Shishou, Hubei Province, images and news of which circulated rapidly on the Internet, pointed out: 'In the Internet age, anyone can become a source of information and all can become subjects expressing their opinions. To draw an analogy, it is as if everyone has a microphone in front of them. This makes even greater demands for the guidance of public opinion. Facing up to spontaneous events, the government and mainstream media can no longer simply issue information. They also have to understand and grasp the pulse of all kinds of online information sources and rapidly respond to public suspicions. This requires the government and particularly the propaganda departments to have sharp, precise public opinion gathering and assessment capabilities.' 人民日报人民时评：突发敏感事件，政府如何避免缺语、失语、妄语' (Lu, 2009, my translation).

[12] See Xia, '国外媒体如何报道08奥运' (2008).

[13] Hence the existence of foreign film import quotas and strict licensing arrangements for a limited number of foreign television channels, for instance.

[14] See Latham 'Nothing But the Truth' (2000), 646.

[15] Theory and practice do often differ. For instance, film quotas do not prevent the general circulation of pirated foreign movies on illegal DVDs and there are numerous ways of circumventing Internet filters and accessing blocked websites, for example. See Chase, Mulvenon and Hachigian, 'Comrade to Comrade Networks'.

[16] See Barboza, 'Pressed Over Tibet, China Berates Foreign Media'. Bristow, 'China Criticises Western Media'.

[17] Feng *et al.*, 'The Real China Brings the World Closer'.

[18] Ibid.

[19] Ji *et al.*, 'The Olympics Enhance China's Communication with the World: According to Experts, if there are still People in the West who Criticise China Without Reason, the Propaganda Effect will greatly be Diminished'.

[20] Miao *et al.*, 'Dirty water sprinkled on Olympic security'.

[21] Barthes, *Mythologies*.

[22] Fiske, *Television Culture* (1989), 291.

[23] For further discussion of widespread discourses of anti-China bias in foreign media reporting of the Olympic torch relay see Latham, 'Media and the Limits of Cynicism in Postsocialist China' (2009), 5. Shortly before this at the end of March 2008, western media reporting of the unrest in Tibet often characterized by fundamental factual errors, mistranslations and the imposition of pre-conceived journalistic narrative frames provided much of the evidence used by Chinese critics to undermine the authority of even the most reputable of western media organizations when it came to reporting of the torch relay. In the Tibetan case, the anti-cnn.com website provided a central focus for this kind of criticism and itself became a topic of discussion in other media reporting. For instance CCTV broadcast a half-hour news analysis programme on western media bias in China reporting with a particular focus on the disturbances in Tibet and drawing upon anti-cnn.com analysis and materials (see CCTV's News Channel's *Xinwen 1+1* [新闻1+1] (*News 1+1*) broadcast March 28, 2008.

[24] See, for example, Humphreys and Finlay, 'New Technologies'; BOCOG, 'Concepts of the Beijing Olympic Games: Green Olympics, Hi-tech Olympics, Peoples' Olympics'. 5 August, 2004. http://en.beijing2008.cn/32/87/article211928732.shtml.

[25] See for instance Wang, 'New Media and the 2008 Olympic Games'; Xu, 'New Media Should Rely on the Olympics to Reach the Heavens'; Ma '新媒体影响媒介生态环境'; *People's Post and Telecoms Post*, 'The Beijing 2008 Olympic Games will Open Up an Era of New Media'.

26 Time division synchronous code division multiple access (TD-SCDMA) has been developed with some collaboration from foreign technology companies such as Siemens and it is a development of US technology company Qualcomm's CDMA technology, but it is generally seen as offering Chinese telecoms equipment makers the chance to pay lower intellectual property rights fees than they do for the two established rival technologies.

27 According to official statistics at the time of the Games there were 253 million Internet users in China with 84.7% of these enjoying broadband access. CNNIC (China Internet Network Information Centre), 'Statistical Report on the Development Situation of China's Internet' ('zhongguo hulian wangluo fazhan zhuangkuang tongji baogao'). 2008. www.cnnic.cn.

28 On CCTV's new media Olympics see Zhang, 'CCTV: The Realisation of the New Media Olympics'.

29 See, for example, He and Zhu, 'The Ecology of Online Newspapers', on the relationship between newspapers and the Internet.

30 Liu Xiang, probably China's best known track and field athlete and one of the country's most widely anticipated gold medal winners, withdrew at the last minute from his first heat of the 110m hurdles with a leg injury. Due to massive build up since Liu's victory in the same event in Athens four years earlier, the nation was shocked by this dramatic and unexpected exit. Chen Zhong meanwhile, another Athens gold medal winner, saw her victory against Britain's Sarah Stevenson in the 67kg Taekwondo competition controversially reversed after an appeal from the British team. Although to a lesser degree, this produced a flurry of media attention and online discussion (discussed further below).

31 Incidentally, in this case the same informant and his daughter were photographed by a leading daily newspaper in the city, something he then followed up by looking for other images online on the newspaper's website.

32 Weather updates usually came around once every four or five hours.

33 See Latham, *Pop Culture China!*

34 This is a summary of observations made to me in interviews, discussions and personal communications by journalists and news editors in Beijing and Guangzhou over a period stretching from November 2007 through to August 2008. Immediately before the Games, foreign newspapers and other news agencies widely reported a list of 21 points supposedly circulated to journalists as a guide for how to cover the Games (see, for example, 'The 21 Edicts from the Chinese Governments Propaganda Unit', *Sydney Morning Herald*, August 14, 2008. http://www.smh.com.au/news/world/the-21-edicts-from-the-chinese-governments-propaganda-unit/2008/08/14/1218307016317.html; 'The 21 Edicts of Chinese Coverage', *The Guardian*, August 15, 2008. http://www.guardian.co.uk/news/blog/2008/aug/15/the21edictsofchineseolymp). I discussed this list quite extensively with different Chinese journalists, none of whom said that they had ever seen this list, but many agreed that it summarized the kinds of guidelines that they either had received, knew of others having received or could imagine others receiving.

35 For example Latham, 'Nothing But the Truth' (2000), 653; Zhao, *Media, Market, and Democracy*; Donald *et al.*, *Media in China* (2002).

36 These kinds of narratives are too numerous and too widely distributed to be dealt with in detail here. For academic discussion on what some of the more prominent of these narratives were, particularly in the build-up to the Games; see Brownell, *Beijing's Games*; Price and Dayan, eds, *Owning the Olympics*; Cha, *Beyond the Final Score*; Polumbaum, 'Capturing the Flame'.

37 Beijing Radio broadcast an interview with opening ceremony organizer Chen Qigang who revealed how the voice of Lin Miaoke, who sang in the stadium, was dubbed over with the voice of Yang Peiyi, another girl who had been considered for the role, but rejected on the grounds of her facial appearance.

38 Many also simply read about the case in other media reports. It was widely covered across television, radio, newspapers and Internet news sources. After a few days, online videos of the interview were hard to find as they were blocked and removed by website operators. The interview was, however, still available in full on Beijing Radio's website a day or two after most other popular video-sharing sites had removed it before eventually being removed. The video was downloaded and saved by the author from the www.bjradio.com.cn website on August 12, 2008.

39 For further discussion see also Latham, 'Media and the Limits of Cynicism in Postsocialist China' (2009).

40 Latham, 'Media and the Limits of Cynicism in Postsocialist China' (2009).

References

Barthes, Roland. *Mythologies*. London: Paladan Books, 1973.

Brownell, Susan. *Beijing's Games: What the Olympic Games Mean to China*. Lanham, MD: Rowman and Littlefield, 2008.

Burgh, Hugo de. *The Chinese Journalist: Mediating Information in the World's Most Populous Country*. London: RoutledgeCurzon, 2003.

Cha, Victor D. *Beyond the Final Score: The Politics of Sport in Asia*. New York: Columbia University Press, 2009.

Chase, Michael, James Mulvenon, and Nina Hachigian. 'Comrade to Comrade Networks: The Social and Political Implications of Peer-to-peer Networks in China'. In *Chinese Cyberspaces: Technological Changes and Political Effects*, edited by Jens Damm and Simona Thomas, 64–101. London: Routledge, 2006.

Close, Paul, David Askew, and Xin Xu. *The Beijing Olympiad: The Political Economy of a Sporting Mega-event*. London: Routledge, 2007.

Donald, S. Hemelryk, M. Keane and H. Liu. *Media in China: consumption, content and crisis*. London: Routledge Curzon, 2002.

Fiske, John. *Television Culture*. London: Routledge, 1989.

Feng, F., X. Sun, X. Wang, P. Huang, Z. Zhao, S. Ji, G. Cheng, and Y. Ma. 'The Real China Brings the World Closer' ('zhenshi zhongguo ling shijie qinqie'). *Global Times* (huanqiu shibao), August 13, 2008, 1.

He, Zhou, and Jian-hua Zhu. 'The Ecology of Online Newspapers: The Case of China'. *Media Culture Society* 24 (2002): 121–37.

Hemelryk, Donald S., M. Keane, and H. Liu, eds. *Media in China: Consumption, Content and Crisis*. London: RoutledgeCurzon, 2002.

Humphreys, Lee, and Christopher J. Finlay. 'New Technologies, New Narratives'. In *Owning the Olympics: Narratives of the New China*, edited by Monroe E. Price and Daniel Dayan, 284–306. Ann Arbor, MI: University of Michigan Press, 2008.

Ji, S., Y. Li, X. Li, X. Sun, and C. Duan. 'The Olympics Enhance China's Communication with the World: According to Experts, if there are still People in the West who Criticise China without Reason, the Propaganda Effect will greatly be Diminished' ('aoyun shi zhongguo yu shijie goutong: zhuanjia cheng ruguo xifang zai yon ren huluan zhize zhongguo, xuan chuan xiaoguo jiang da zhektu'. *Global Times* (huanqiu shibao), August 27, 2008, 16.

Latham, Kevin. 'Nothing But the Truth: News Media, Power and Hegemony in South China'. *China Quarterly* 163 (2000): 633–54.

Latham, Kevin. 'SMS, Communication and Citizenship in China's Information Society'. *Journal of Critical Asian Studies* 39, no. 2 (2007): 295–314.

Latham, Kevin. *Pop Culture China! Media, Arts and Lifestyle*. California: ABC-Clio, 2008.

Latham, Kevin. ' Media and the Limits of Cynicism in Postsocialist China.' In *Enduring Socialism: Explorations of Revolution and Transformation, Restoration and Continuation*, edited by Harry G. West and Parvathi Raman. New York: Berghahn Books, 2009.

Lee, Chin-Chuan. *Power, money and media: Communication patterns and bureaucratic control in cultural China*. Evanston, IL: Northwestern University Press, 2000.

Lu, Xia. '人民日报人民时评: 突发敏感事件, 政府如何避免缺语、失语、妄语' (Renmin ribao renmin pingshi: tufa mingan shijian, zhengfu ruhe bimian que yu, shi yu, mang yu) [How should the government avoid lacking words, losing words or hiding words when sensitive events occur?]. Available at: http://opinion.people.com.cn/GB/70240/9529449.html. 24 June, 2009.

Lynch, Daniel. *After the propaganda state: media, politics and 'thought work' in reformed China*. Stanford, CA: Stanford University Press, 1999.

Ma Xiaofang, '奥运: 新媒体影响媒介生态环境' (Aoyun: xin meiti yingxiang meijie shengtai huanjing) [The Olympics: new media influences media situation and environment]. 第一财经日报 [First Financial Daily], 31 July, 2008.

Miao, M., F. Lu, D. Xie, M. Qing, and S. He. 'Dirty water sprinkled on Olympic security' ('Aoyun anbao bei po zangshui'). *Global Times* (huanqiu shibao), July 14, 2008.

People's Post and Telecoms Post. 'The Beijing 2008 Olympic Games Will Open Up an Era of New Media' ('Beijing 08 aoyunhui jiang Kaichuang xin meiti shidai'). August 1, 2008.

Polumbaum, Judith. 'Capturing the Flame: Aspirations and Representations of Beijing's 2008 Olympics'. In *Chinese Media, Global Contexts*, edited by Chin-Chuan Lee, 57–75. London: RoutledgeCurzon, 2003.

Price, Monroe E., and Daniel Dayan, eds. *Owning the Olympics: Narratives of the New China*. Ann Arbor, MI: University of Michigan Press, 2008.
Rafaele, V. 'The Cell Phone and the Crowd: Messianic Politics in the Contemporary Philippines'. In *Asia Unplugged: The Wireless and Mobilemedia Boom in the Asia-Pacific*, edited by M. Rao and L. Mendoza, 286–315. Thousand Oaks, CA: Response Books, 2004.
Smith, Briar. 'Journalism and the Beijing Olympics: Liminality with Chinese Characteristics'. In *Owning the Olympics: Narratives of the New China*, edited by Monroe E. Price and Daniel Dayan, 210–226. Ann Arbor, MI: University of Michigan Press, 2008.
Wang, W. 'New Media and the 2008 Olympic Games' ('xin meiti yu 2008 aoyun hui'). China News Research Centre, July 25, 2008. www.cddc.net.cn.
Xia Ming, '国外媒体如何报道08奥运' (Guowai meiti ruhe baodao 08 aoyun) [How did foreign media report the 2008 Olympics?]. Available at: http://www.cddc.net/cnnews/xwyw/200909/5383.html. 22 September, 2008.
Xu, Huiying. 'New Media should Rely on the Olympics to Reach the Heavens' ('xin meiti yu ping aoyunding tian'). July 1, 2008. www.1a3.cn/cnnews/cmjz/200909/3308.html.
Zhang, Lei. 'CCTV: The Realisation of the New Media Olympics' ('CCTV: xin meiti de aoyun shixian'). *Chinese Journalist* (zhongguo jizhe), July 31, 2008.
Zhao, Yuezhi. *Media, Market, and Democracy in China: Between the Party Line and the Bottom Line*. Urbana and Chicago, IL: University of Illinois Press, 1998.

The communication gesture of the Beijing Olympic Games

Weixing Chen

International Communication Studies Center, Communication University of China, No.1 Dingfuzhuang East Street, Chaoyang District, Beijing 100024, PR China

As a key example of the globalization of its communication, an Olympic host country's organizational capacity, level of sports ability and cultural charm become important items to be evaluated in international relations. That is, the symbolic performance of organizing global cultural activities serves as a communication platform to contend for soft power. To host the Olympic Games is the moment for a nation-state to shape its image via international public relations. China's communication gesture was to balance the value distribution of its public relations by transforming, as far as possible, the conflicts at an ideological level into the solemnity and enthusiasm necessary to fulfil her commitment to the international community. The Beijing Olympics were not only to show to the world the cultural impact of China's sports ability, but also to display her strength and sincerity by providing public goods through meeting the standards of organization and quality of services needed to host the event. Thereby the Chinese international concept of 'a harmonious world', to a large extent, was geared toward gaining the international community's understanding and praise. It should be mentioned that the globalization of communication not only reduces the marginal cost of information diffusion by enlarging the flow of knowledge, but also encourages sufficient interactivity to break each party's monopoly of information. China's peaceful rise on the world stage can not be divorced from the rise of its culture, which is necessarily accompanied by the profound changes in Chinese society itself.

Introduction

Seven years ago, on the night of 13 July 2001, when the International Olympic Committee made the decision that Beijing would host the 2008 Olympic Games, China's Xinhua News Agency said that this decision should be 'a milestone of China's rising international status'. The decision made by a non-political international organization resulted in a huge political significance, because this decision indicated that China would begin the countdown toward becoming the focus of international mass communication. The main question at the time was: as the country was to become the object of the international communications network, how best to shape her response?

A country's external communications, in a sense, is a kind of information guide to its foreign relations as they are shaped in order to achieve a specific effect. It is basically the symbolic reflection of real international relations and the current diplomatic status quo. The idea that the public opinion communication is a key element of international competition was formulated by British scholar E.H. Carr in 1939.[1] After the Cold War, US scholar Joseph S. Nye systematically put forward the theory of soft power which is fundamental to international communication studies.[2] In Nye's oft-repeated explanation, soft power is a type of attractive capacity that can manipulate others' desires; it is basically a symbolic mechanism, i.e. the attractiveness of a nation-state's culture, political ideas and policy. In an age of globalized communications, a test platform to display soft power might be a public event that could be 'mediated'. Given the possible scale of its transmission, the Olympics might well be the public event with the largest international audience. Through the application for, and hosting of, the Olympics, whether or not a country is able to culturally seduce all the world, to balance its value distributions in the flow of information and to provide credible high quality public goods is the criteria by which we evaluate the success of such an event.

The sincerity of international cooperation

In the international political processes that take place against the background of economic globalization, a country's economic power and political power are inextricably related and can even be converted into each other, thereby forming its own moral authority as well as competence, which in turn may allow it to gain a higher international status and more international resources. In the sense of communication, the position of a country in the economic global order decides its place in the international communication order. That is, national power can decide to some extent a country's right to speak and the quantity of content it may communicate. However, full consideration must be given in a climate of post-modernism that the world's political beliefs are often presented in a watered down form, i.e. the imposed political signification on the subject being communicated could become an obstacle to realizing the desired communication effect.

For example, almost two years after winning the right to host the Olympic Games, China put forward the 'peaceful rise' foreign policy at the BOAO Forum for Asia in 2003. However, the term 'rise' in the Occidental view carried a sense of 'conquest by force', and this goes against the Chinese government's intention. Shortly after this political slogan was officially proclaimed, it was revised to 'peaceful development' by some Chinese scholars in order to avoid a China threat theory that could add fuel to the fire. Since the second half of 2004, the phrase 'peaceful rise' in journalism, education and political propaganda gradually faded out and the more moderate 'peaceful development' concept was adopted. This conversion, which took place in order to ease Chinese foreign relations, can be regarded as the first instance in which China adjusted her policy in order to host the Olympic Games.

On 28 March 2002, the Beijing Municipal Government and the 29th Olympic Games organizing committee released the 'Beijing Olympic Action Plan' which pointed out that the primary strategic objective to hosting the Beijing Olympic Games was to organize the most outstanding Games in Olympic history.[3] Until 15 January 2004 when the Beijing Olympic Organizing Committee held its first plenary meeting, the leaders of the Chinese Government still proclaimed their intention to realize the objective of 'the most outstanding Olympic Games' by concentrating their efforts on this goal. The Beijing Olympic Organizing Committee held its second plenary meeting on 14 January 2005 which set the final objective of the organizing work as 'high-level Olympic Games with characteristics'.

This adjustment to the strategic objective represented a realistic political attitude. The term 'with characteristics' means 'a Chinese style, a humanist aura and mass participation'. And 'high level' is reflected in many aspects: high-level sports facilities and competition organizations, high-level opening ceremony and cultural activities, high-level media services, high-level security, high-level volunteer services and high-level traffic organization.

DOCUMENTING THE BEIJING OLYMPICS

China has become a spectacular power due to the rapid industrial and social development after her reforming and opening-up. But to build an image of a powerful country in the international arena necessitates that China must rationally face the international system dominated by Occidental values, respecting common values, common institutions and the common destiny of the international community while expressing her own attitudes, self interests and emphasizing the reciprocity and contribution to the world through various cooperative ventures. Thus, in recent years, China's aim has been to strengthen the institutional efforts and the substantial progress of her participation in the international arena, and to show to the world her sincerity and determination to promote peaceful development. In fact, because global communication does not eliminate differences in ideas, information errors and the asymmetry of knowledge, in other words, because China and the West still lack a relationship of institutional trust, problems in ethnic relations, economic, environmental, administrative and ideological aspects have been revealed and have frequently become hostages to, and the subject of, international discourses about China. Facing the pressure of public opinion, the Chinese government expressed its political attitude by making information known to public. On 24 May 2008, the Chinese Premier Wen Jiabao in the earthquake-stricken area of Sichuan spoke to the international press circles:

> Faced with such a big earthquake, we welcome reporters from all over the world to come to report. I believe you will use your conscience and humanitarian spirit to report justly, objectively and truly the situations of earthquake and suffering and what we have done. Dealing with the emergency and other issues, we will adhere to the people-oriented principle and to the opening-up policy that will never change.[4]

Two months later on 26 July, the General Secretary of CPC Central Committee Hu Jintao stressed that efforts should be made to make the Beijing Olympic Games and the Paralympic Games satisfying to the international community, to all the athletes, and to the people, so as to fulfil China's solemn commitment as promised to the international community.[5]

Obviously, the final fulfilment of these commitments also involves a technical process of cross-cultural communication that has significance for public relations. As early as 2005, the Beijing Olympic Organizing Committee invited tenders from all over the world in order to look for international public relations companies who could act as partners. The successful bidders were required to fulfil seven criteria: a clear publicity strategy; five languages in order to monitor international public opinion daily; to promote the image of the Beijing Olympic Organizing Committee; to make connections and invite the international media to come for observation; to maintain good relationships with and provide services for all involved; to help the 300 Beijing Organizing Committee for the Games of the XXIX Olympiad (BOCOG) officials in media training; and to demonstrate crisis management capabilities.[6] In the end, Hill & Knowlton, Inc. was the only company in charge of public relations during the Beijing Olympic Games. From 2007 to 2008, the Beijing Olympic Organizing Committee held more than 160 news conferences, one every two weeks in the first half of 2008.

Through the imposing opening ceremony of the Beijing Olympic Games, China displayed to the world a Chinese-style narrative, highlighting the theme of harmony. In the organization of the competitions the advanced technology to produce a spectacular scene, the ability to coordinate efficiently and smoothly, and the material resources of operation were fully demonstrated. In social participation, over 16 days, there were 100,000 Games volunteers, 400,000 city volunteers, one million community volunteers and 200,000 volunteer cheerleaders, who worked both inside and outside the stadium participating in different kinds of voluntary services in order to show to the world China's enthusiasm.[7]

The Games let the world see a comparatively authentic China where plainness and prosperity coexist; with an ability to succeed through diligence, and where, despite some embarrassing institutional flaws, there is hope and an emphasis on the future.

The breakthrough of the cultural ideas

It must not be forgotten that the Olympic Games are an international cultural event as well as a sporting event. From the perspective of cultural diplomacy, the host country in its role as a communicator should understand the objective of communication, i.e. to build a bridge between its values and those of the international mainstream where difference and parallels are more important than confrontation and conflict, thereby fully demonstrating the universal values incarnated by the Olympic Games. Observers of international public opinion noticed that hosting the Olympic Games put China's reality under the microscope: first of all, there was the emphasis on the role the Games play in enhancing national solidarity and promoting political unity. They were seen as positive in alleviating serious social divisions and slowing down the rising tendency of social conflicts which emerged several years ago in China. Additionally, we can find that China's politics are still coloured with conservatism while public opinion has called repeatedly for political system reform. But the tactics of nationwide mobilization are still frequently employed and this includes the means to launch a campaign as well as the ideological indoctrination used under the old authoritarian system.

The reality of China's actual politico-cultural inconsistencies leads to the fact that there exist differences between China and the Occident when social governance may take place through informal communication spheres: the Olympic Games in the Occident are mainly operated by non-governmental organizations with the involvement of a civil society that will not and cannot be supported or interfered with by the government. The Olympics in the Occident are mostly an activity with a city as its centre and with little relation to the central government. The budget is transparent, so a complex discussion will be carried out about any expenditure, especially when the public budget is touched. Westerners tend to be enthusiastic about the Olympics, with a fervour that is mostly spontaneous, voluntary and that rarely needs governmental mobilization; most feel a unity of propose, thus not caring about the protesting during the Olympic Games; and certainly, westerners tend not to politicize their uneasiness before and after the Games or bind it to the state's honour.

Of course, the Chinese Olympic Games were a mostly positive performance by China, who was able to act 'in line with international standards'; a principle adhered to since her reform and opening-up. At the same time, this process has provoked different reactions in the Chinese society, thereby becoming an open subject to talk about. It is worth noticing that during the last five years, all mediated public issues began to develop the civil consciousness of Chinese people. Indeed, with the popularization of new media technology in China, particularly the Internet, the field of public opinion, generally involving individuals voicing their concerns about public issues, gradually has come into being, as has an informal community. The sporadic opinion and criticism of common citizens is no longer limited to chats in such humble places as street corners and alleys. Internet technology is able to provide the public with the platform of blogs (private media), thereby pushing China into becoming a 'limited opinion society'. For example, during, and even after, the Olympic Games, discussion of and criticism by netizens, including officials and scholars, on China's current system of sports was a hot topic.

China's system of sports development, particularly the formal authoritarian mechanisms that produces national elite athletes, which was introduced in the 1950s from the former Soviet Union, means that the country concentrates its limited material resources on forging gold-medal-winning athletes with a political significance. This kind of sports system was exploited to the extreme during the Cold War by the former Soviet Union and East Germany. Here is a paradox. Such a system was often subject, in the past, to the nation-state's political aims in the sector of sports so that sports were a purely political symbol. Today, the gold medal athlete quickly can turn political labels into advertising resources,[8] thereby becoming a commercial darling; this means that the political significance embodied by the athlete encounters moral questions, for example, the exit of Liu Xiang, a hurdler, from the competition because of supposed over training, aroused very strong repercussions, including, criticism from Chinese netizens.

According to China's public opinion, there are three critiques to make of this system. First, this use of national resources lacks accountability and the material consumption of the elite athlete's training makes impossible the better development of public sports. Next, sports are games and it is human nature to play. Many sports often can't become a lifelong career. With the exception of a few sports (for example, basketball, football, track and field, tennis, etc.) that can be marketed, a large number of athletes will need to find jobs after their retirement. Finally, because of the lack of supervision by the public, this kind of system easily forms a huge interest group composed of athletic stars, coaches and sports bureaucrats. The rewards are great fame and fortune for the athletes and the coaches, while high achievement can bring promotion and power to the sports bureaucrats. Therefore, the authoritarian mechanism of sports becomes a catalyst for corruption in the sector of sports. At present, the discussion continues to be carried out on this issue.

In today's world of economic globalization, the rise of a new economic power will always raise political question marks and trigger off an examination of values. Queen Elizabeth II conveyed such a message at the banquet when Chinese President Hu Jintao paid a visit to Britain in 2005: 'China's development attracts much more global attention and admiration. But we would like to know, what kind of country do the Chinese people want to build? What role will China play in the international affairs in the twenty-first century? How will the international community regard this role?'[9] China is a big developing country. From the perspective of political marketing, it is necessary to build an international identity that is embodied by being either a collaborator or a stakeholder on the international stage. The school of constructivism represented by Alexander Wendt claims that international cooperation is completely probable, and that a country also can create an international culture which fundamentally tends to cooperation.[10] The construction of this sort of culture is embodied by the single country actor, that is, to update the existing national ideas so as to re-establish national identity while, furthermore, defining its national interest and levels. For China, on the basis of summing up the 30 year experience of reform and opening up, hosting the Olympics has meant that she can continue to exploit the local resources that promote political democracy and social progress.

The continuous promotion of China's reform-and-opening up and modernization needs to reconstruct a Chinese cultural subjectivity that will bring about the transformation from 'Made in China' into 'Created in China'. This doesn't mean that China will display her soft power on the international stage, but that she will use internationally identified concepts to normalize her international actions, while using Chinese cultural ideas to push forward the importance of cultural diversity and calmly playing a role of the creator of international public goods.

In fact, through the organization of the Olympic Games, we can see such logic; that is, behind the competition for political, institutional and ideological legitimacy lies a desire for cultural legitimacy. The historical transition of a political culture will become an important precondition for further development and, through this transition, the creative potential of the Chinese society will be further released. As a Chinese civil commentator pointed out, when the British Queen's guards recently gave up their bearskin helmets:

> It seems that no matter what a thing is, whether it represents a country's image or a local image, it should take as prerequisite not to encroach on and harm the animal's interests. Of course, it should even more take as prerequisite not to encroach on and harm the interests of human beings. In this world, no 'image' can be more important than the animal's interests, especially the interests of human beings.[11]

At this point, it is firmly believed that active and effective cross-cultural communication will help China and the Occident in the building of more and more common values, so as to promote world peace and development.

Notes

[1] Carr, *The Twenty Years Crisis*.
[2] Nye, *Soft Power*.
[3] Xinhua Net, March 28, 2008, released at 15:32:17. http://sports.sina.com.cn/o/2002-03-28/28253741.shtml.
[4] 'Wen Jiabao Accepted the Interview with Chinese and Foreign Reporters in Wenchuan, Epicenter of the Earthquake', *People's Daily*, May 25, 2008.
[5] People's Network 'The Central Collective Leadership's Commentaries on the Sports and the Beijing Olympic Games', *People's Daily*, July 27, 2008. http://su.people.com.cn/GB/channel 415/418/200807/29/16319.html.
[6] Liang, 'A Country's Public Relations'.
[7] '1.7 Million Olympic Volunteers are Ready in Position, Exceptional in the Games', *Xing Jing Bao*, August 2, 2008.
[8] On July 18, 2007, the Chinese Research Institute of Brands (*Yang Cheng Wan Bao*) released the report 'Value of the Chinese Gold Medal', calculating the value of ten gold medal winners: The leading figure is that of Liu Xiang, men's 110m hurdler champion, with a calculated commercial value (in terms of income) of 461 million yuan; the value of the other nine gold medal winners range from a minimum of 14 million.
[9] Chen and He, 'Strategic Reflections on the Interruption Encountered During the Torch Relay of the Olympic Games'.
[10] Wendt, *Social Theory*.
[11] http://news.sina.com.cn/pl/2008-09-03/075916222821.shtml.

References

Carr, E.H. *The Twenty Years Crisis, 1919–1939: An Introduction to the Study of International Relations*. Rev. edn. London: Macmillan, 1946.
Chen, G., and J. He. 'Strategic Reflections on the Interruption Encountered During the Torch Relay of the Olympic Games'. *Nan Fang Zhou Mo*, May 1, 2008.
Liang, S. 'A Country's Public Relations'. *Nan Fang Zhou Mo*, September 4, 2008.
Nye, Jr., Joseph S. *Soft Power: The Means to Success in World Politics*. New York: Public Affairs, 2005.
Wendt, Alexander. *Social Theory of International Politics*. Cambridge: Cambridge University Press, 1999.

Framing China and the world through the Olympic opening ceremonies, 1984–2008

Limin Liang

School of Communication, Northwestern University, 2240 Campus Dr., Evanston, IL, USA

This essay focuses on the coverage of the past seven Olympic Opening Ceremonies (1984–2008) through the lens of one national broadcaster: China Central Television (CCTV), which has been the sole Olympic TV rights holder within the Chinese mainland during this period. Through textual analysis of CCTV's live broadcast narrative, I hope to first shed light on how the concept of liminality may be used to analyze the coverage of a highly ritualized sports event. Second, I look for changes in the media's ritual practices and ritual language across these years and search for possible explanations.

Introduction

The Olympic Games is a classic ritual event that illustrates how liminality is dealt with in human society. Intended to be a time-out from ordinary life, the two-week long event every four years celebrates physical and moral excellence as it is embodied in athletes. During the Games, the usual political and economic structures that divide the world are supposed to be forgotten. The Games can be seen as a version of 'communitas', a stage of human existence that is 'between and betwixt.'[1] We recognize a generic human bond that ceases to be fragmentized. However, an over-emphasis on the liminal nature of the Games belies the behind-the-scene struggles to own the Games that takes place amongst various stakeholders, namely, heavy corporate sponsorship which is now the life-line of hosting the Olympic Games, co-optation by governments for chauvinistic purposes or by NGOs for their own causes, and even terrorists' attempts to hijack the events[2]. These 'out-of-frame'[3] activities raise doubts as to whether the Games truly represent a moment of 'human communitas'.[4]

The Olympic opening ceremony merits particular attention in this discussion because it captures well the tension between the national and the transnational aspects of the Games. During the opening ceremony, after athletes march into the stadium as representatives of their country, the national theme subsides with such rituals as the raising of the Olympic flag and the ignition of the Olympic flame. 'Symbols of the Olympic community are positioned hierarchically over and above the symbols of the nation-states, but without contravening them.'[5] However, the above mentioned 'out-of-frame' activities render this relationship a far more problematic one.

The media's role (in particular television) in capturing this tension cannot be overlooked. Ultimately, whether the audience finds the Games a liminal experience to a certain extent depends on the way the media present it. However, the media may easily deviate from such a theme. Once a national media organization becomes the Games' broadcast rights holder, it will more or less take a national approach as against the transnational approach favoured by the International Olympic Committee (IOC). In addition, it is also the media's judgment call whether they choose to report the various out-of-frame activities that detract from the Games' liminal image.

Specifically, this essay will focus on the coverage of the past seven Olympic opening ceremonies (1984–2008) through the lens of one national broadcaster: China Central Television (CCTV), which has been the sole Olympic TV rights holder within the Chinese mainland since the PRC returned to the Summer Olympic Games in 1984 after a long severance of relations with the IOC. Through the textual analysis of CCTV's live broadcast narrative, I hope to first shed light on how the concept of liminality may be used to analyse the coverage of a highly ritualized sports event. Second, I will look for changes in the media's ritual practices and ritual language across these years and search for possible explanations.

Competing approaches to understanding media events

In a pioneering work that brought anthropological theory to bear on media studies, Dayan and Katz proposed how the Olympic Games might fit into a typology of 'media events'.[6] Syntactically media events are characterized by 'elements of interruption, monopoly, being broadcast live, and being remote'. Their semantic dimension is 'typically proposed by its organizers and shared by the broadcasters ... The message is one of reconciliation'. In other words, during the Olympic Games media usually shed their critical stance and join 'the Greek chorus' with the IOC, promoting an internationalist theme.[7] Essentially this theory promotes a neo-Durkheimian notion of solidarity – the idea that the Olympic Games is a 'civil religion' whereby people overcome national, socioeconomic, racial and cultural barriers to celebrate a sense of human brotherhood.

However, critical scholars raise the question as to whether media events could always produce social solidarity or, if so, whose interests it serves.[8] Some Olympic Games obviously end up being hijacked by groups with countervailing agendas as were the Munich Olympics in 1976. Even if the successful hosting of the Games enhances social solidarity, there is the question of whether it is the national rather than the elusive international solidarity that is promoted. For one thing, national broadcasters are primarily a conduit for audiences to imagine a shared *national* community or a sense of *national identity*.[9] In covering the Olympic opening ceremonies, these broadcasters were found to selectively present the Olympic values, favouring values such as 'competition' and 'winning', which translate into a penchant for medal counting and references to potential medal contenders. Further, broadcasters repeatedly 'select, position and evaluate others relative to the home nation by dimensions of salience, hierarchy and similarity' so that other nations are cast in ways that are 'simplistic or even misleading'.[10]

All in all, while the structure of the opening ceremony is such that a harmony is struck between the international and the national aspects of the Games, with the former encompassing the latter, in actual media practice, such an accord is harder to strike. The time allotted to introducing each participating nation is not equal and the language used may be biased. Some nations may not be introduced at all.[11] The essence of internationalism could be rendered hollow.

Does the Chinese Opening Ceremony coverage present a sense of *communitus*?

How does the Chinese coverage fare against such criticism? In closely examining CCTV's coverage of the ceremony over 24 years, we find that first, the Chinese broadcaster managed to introduce every (or nearly every) participating nation in each opening ceremony, even though a majority of the nations before 1996 only received the briefest mention.[12] This is not a usual practice among commercial broadcasters. NBC, for instance, was once found to cover fewer than 80% of the national teams during the athletic parade of the opening ceremony.[13]

Second, CCTV hardly used any trivializing or marginalizing techniques (such as bantering) in introducing the nations. Sports status was the primary cue the commentator used to evaluate a participating nation while other criteria, such as degree of political stability and social and cultural references, were occasionally applied.

Third, CCTV managed to stage the entire live ceremony uninterrupted by commercials, on-spot interviews or other news programmes. This arrangement was faithful to the flow of the opening ceremony as intended by the Games' organizer. However, this is not to say that in the Chinese coverage there were no indications of any efforts to distinguish 'us' against 'them'; or that the deep-seated social and political tensions rife in the modern world simply were not papered over.

Presenting the national self and others in relation to the national self – it's a hierarchical world

As is quite natural, China was singled out from the rest of the world and given the most extensive coverage, often including favourable mentions of team manners and particular references to the team's medal potential in each sport. Among other nations, a small cluster of sports powers, a category which largely overlaps with political and economic power, also were considerably more mentioned than others. Earlier in the 1980s, or before the fall of the Soviet Union, USSR and Eastern European countries within the Soviet bloc also got more mentions.

In particular, as China's sports strength has continued to grow, there has been an attendant growth of awareness of China's potential 'rivals', who were more frequently identified. For instance, when Germany entered the stadium in the 2004 Olympic opening ceremony, the commentator made the following remarks,

> Since East and West Germany's reunification, they carried on their advantages and strengthened their power. Germany has won 67 gold medals in the three Summer Olympics since reunification. This year, Germany will be one of China's main rivals. In the last Olympiad, China replaced the position formerly retained by Germany.[14]

By the same token, during the 2004 coverage, the commentator remarked that 'Australia would strive to end up among the top five in the medal tally'. Speaking of the US team, the commentator made it clear that the USA is the world's unrivalled sports power. Even for the lesser known nations, a preoccupation with medal counts often led to repeated comments that many countries had not won a single medal in Olympic history.

While the Beijing Olympiad was widely suspected by western observers to be an opportunity for a state broadcaster to whip up nationalistic sentiments, CCTV's commentators were in fact told to diffuse a China-centred and Gold medal-oriented approach in covering the Games in the weeks and months leading up to the event.[15] But given the Games' widely acknowledged significance as a 'coming-out party' for China, commentators also took the opportunity to underscore China's sports strength and the point that hosting the Games embodied a century-long aspiration of the Chinese nation. They reminded the audience that until 1984, China had not won a single medal in the Olympic Games. In the 30 years since the PRC rejoined the Olympic family, however, China had won a total of 112 gold medals in the Summer Olympics and four gold medals in the Winter Olympics.

While competition may not contradict the values of the Olympics, highlighting this dimension conjures up an image of a battlefield where athletes do not convene to celebrate amateurism, but to compete on behalf of their sovereign states with the solitary goal being that they win. With China's growing awareness of its own sports strength, competition with other top players in the world inevitably starts to intensify, which returns to impact China's perception of itself. So it remains a hierarchical world, a world that is always seen through the prism of the national self.

Politics as usual in a sports media event – it is a divisive world after all

It is a well-accepted truism among sports media practitioners in China that politics should be separate from sports. Compared to the coverage by major western broadcasters, CCTV commentators continuously used euphemisms or chose to neglect the potentially divisive issues that could taint the friendly and apolitical theme of the Games. For example, mentions of the US-led boycott of the Moscow Olympics in 1980 (and vice versa in Los Angeles in 1984), terrorist activities (i.e. the Munich massacre), the ban on South Africa's participation due to Apartheid, and, most recently, the disruptions to the torch relay of the Beijing Olympics, were all avoided. Even when such a reference was made, as was with the case of boycotting, the mention was stripped of historical context. Furthermore, sensitive issues regarding the unity of a sovereign nation were also treated with great caution. But sometimes the scarcity of commentary, or even the decision not to comment, carries political meaning.

Throughout the four Olympiads under study, Taiwan participated in the Olympic Games under the name of 'Chinese Taipei', which was a compromise between the Chinese mainland, Taiwan and the IOC. Though Taiwan's participation in the Olympics has always carried political implications for the Chinese mainland, CCTV's introduction of the team was strictly confined to its sports strength. But in the 1996 opening ceremony, no mention was made at all regarding the team from Chinese Taipei. Given the extremely strained political relations between the two sides at the time,[16] the treatment was more likely a deliberate slight than an accident. What could be a more powerful expression of attitude than an outright negligence?

On the whole, however, it is very difficult to find even political insinuation in the CCTV's opening ceremony narrative. But because of their scarcity, when any political statements indeed find their way into the commentary, they become highly interesting. The following is the comment on the two Korean teams as they marched together for the first time in Sydney Olympics:

> The DPRK and South Korean delegations are entering the stadium. This time they form a unified team and each side sent 90 people to participate in the Opening ceremony parade … Now the IOC President Samaranch is rising to greet the Korean athletes. Once the Games start however, the Korean athletes will participate on behalf of their own nation, wearing their own national team's uniforms, raise their own national flag and sing their own national anthem.[17]

Reflecting the concept of 'Olympic truce' as proposed by the then IOC president Samaranch, the Korean teams marching side by side for the first time in 2000 was a highly symbolic event and merited media attention. What was interesting about the Chinese commentator in 2000 was that he broke with the tradition of deferring to the symbolic significance of such an event and revealed the fact that the Olympic truce only presented an image of rapprochement but had no substance. Recalling Turner's concept of structure versus anti-structure, we may say that for a moment, the structure that 'reigns' over ordinary life was loosened, and a certain version of communitas set in.[18] But the transformation was brief, and by the end of the 'media event' the old order would return. Ironically here the commentator went further by suggesting that the image of a truce would not even survive the opening ceremony as both teams would still compete on behalf of their own nation once the Games started. As Roche put it, the idea of an Olympic truce was after all, an 'arguably unachievable and unenforceable' one.[19]

The comment made in 2004 upon the entrance of the Russian team also offered an interesting window to the Chinese perception of global sports. The commentator suggested that during the Cold War an important dimension of the competition between the former USSR and the USA was manifest in the contention over the Olympic gold medals. This was another way of saying that, after all, politics could never be neatly separated from sports.

But these nuanced mentions of politics pale in comparison with the practice of major western broadcasters such as NBC. Take the latter's coverage of the 2008 Olympics opening ceremony as an example. The NBC commentator lost no opportunity in bringing politics into sports coverage. The Russian-Georgian conflict which had erupted on the eve of the Games, the Chinese mainland's relationship with Taiwan, issues with political hot spots such as Iran and North Korea, and many others, all found their way into the NBC narrative. The politicization of the Beijing Olympiad was also dissected. When the Thai team entered, Bob Costas rushed to add that it was the country where President Bush had made a strong speech against China's human rights problems shortly before he landed in China. In comparison, the Chinese broadcaster referred to none of the above mentioned issues, which it deemed as contradictory to the harmonious theme of the Games.

Different approaches to politics in sports were also revealed in the interpretation of the nuanced gestures that were embedded in the ceremony itself. Having a young earthquake survivor, Lin Hao, march alongside the national sports hero, Yao Ming, during the Chinese team's parade in 2008 speaks volumes about the interplay between sport and domestic politics. However, CCTV only gave this arrangement brief mention, noting that little Lin Hao had won the title of 'a young hero in fighting the earthquake'. Lin was not given proper close-ups either. In contrast, NBC went on at great length, telling the story of Lin Hao who risked his own life to save several of his classmates during the Sichuan earthquake in May. They also gave a careful analysis of the symbol's deeper meaning:

> So much that captures what we saw ... opposites being balanced with one another, hard and soft, light and dark. Here we have tall and short. Of course what's really being balanced is the incredible tragedy of the earthquake and the incredible joy of this moment and ... China, one of the reasons it's so hard to explain this place to people is it's not only a place of great success like Beijing and hundreds of millions of people lifted out of poverty, but also the country facing unbelievable challenges in the future.[20]

While this may reflect the broadcasters' different approaches to writing up scripts regarding particular personalities, it also shows a certain reluctance on the part of CCTV to comment on anything that came close to politics.

The extent to which media chose to cover topics that would diminish the liminal theme of the Games has an implication for the public's perception of the Games. Through the analysis of this section, one sees that national media unavoidably use various criteria to partition the world in relation to the national self. At the same time, there is an extent to which rituals and ritual language can paper over deep-seated social and political problems in reality. Even with the scarcity of such references in the Chinese coverage, it is still possible to spot signs of the cleavages that are simply too deep to ritualize. In spite of this problem, the Chinese media makers follow the principle that sports should be kept 'apart from politics'.

Table 1.   Content analysis of CCTV's coverage of the Olympic opening ceremonies' athletes parade, 1984–2008*

Number of comments by categories

Olympiad Year	Geographical Location	Olympic History	Medal History	Sports Strength	Team Attributes	Sports Stars or other Personalities	Team Manners/ Audience reception	Social, Economic or Cultural Comment	Political Comments	Total
1984	4	5	3	9	15	5	1	1	1	44
1988	9	2	7	22	108	11	1	0	1	161
1992	5	4	5	12	6	6	3	0	3	44
1996	44	17	18	61	36	42	3	1	1	223
2000	4	5	8	19	69	16	2	1	1	125
2004	31	117	104	54	35	23	0	27	12	411
2008	67	101	87	92	120	71	0	52	8	600

*Note: The video archives used here consist of self-recorded video material during two of the most recent Olympic opening ceremonies (2004; 2008) and the best available versions of the coverage of earlier Olympic opening ceremonies procured from the CCTV media library. Due to the passage of time, these latter may not represent fully the length of the ceremonies' live broadcasts. Of these archives, the 1984 video shows only 21 of the 140 participating national teams (NOCs); the 1988 video shows 126 of the 159 participating teams; the 1992 video shows 24 of the 169 participating teams, the 1996 video shows 176 of the 197 participating teams; the 2000 video shows 164 of the 199 participating teams. The 2004 and 2008 video show all of the participating teams, which were 201 and 204 respectively.

Changes and continuity in media rituals

A ritual approach to communication emphasizes the cohesiveness across time that communicative activities are able to produce, but ritual communication is also subject to change. Tracing such changes in a longitudinal study of a national broadcaster's coverage of the Olympic opening ceremonies – a highly ritualized occasion – can be illuminating.

To do this I coded CCTV's live broadcast comments on the athletes' parades in the previous seven Olympiads (see Table 1). Nations are the unit of analysis and nine coding categories have been used, including:

1. mentions of the country's geographic location;
2. Olympic history – references to the country's participation in the Olympic Games
3. medal history – references to the Olympic medals the country has won;
4. sports strength – general assessment of the country's sports power;
5. team attributes – references to the composition of the team and the prospects of winning;
6. team manners and audience reception – references to the demeanour of the athletes and the atmosphere in the stadium;
7. comments on sports stars or other prominent personalities associated with a country;
8. comments on social, economic or cultural aspects of the participating nations; and
9. political comments.

The number of comments is not calculated in terms of the sentences being articulated, but in terms of the ideas expressed.

The results have been combined with a more nuanced textual analysis. In general, two themes of continuity can be found through the coverage. First, even with a trend towards more diversified content, the majority of information being provided still concentrates on categories of sports related topics (categories no.2 to no.6 combined), which constitutes a low of 75% of all comments at the Barcelona opening ceremony to a high of 93.6% of all comments at the Sydney opening ceremony. As already demonstrated, in comparison with a number of western broadcasters that spent much time commenting on non-sports related factors for their domestic audience,[21] CCTV remained faithful to the nature of the Games being primarily a sporting event.

Meanwhile, political comment was, and to a large extent still remains, a very insignificant category. I use 'political comments' to designate any reference regarding the domestic politics of a nation (i.e. a team representing a newly independent nation), or the impact of important world events on the nations' sports power (such as references to the impact of the Cold War on sports competition), or any mention of the previous boycotts of the Olympic Games. Surprisingly, a 1995 study found that political commentary took up 24% of the Chinese coverage of the 1992 opening ceremony (23 comments).[22] Due to the incomplete data of the 1992 coverage gathered for this study, the accuracy of this finding could not be verified. One explanation may be that the 1992 Olympic Games were held in the aftermath of the disintegration of the former Soviet Union and the transition of power in a number of Eastern European countries. It is possible that the anchors made quite a few comments about such changes, which were counted as political comments.

Second, the Chinese commentary tended to be highly repetitive and more serious in nature compared to the humorous bantering among the western anchors.[23] Mostly the Chinese commentary focused on providing facts-based sports information. Also, the rehearsed nature could be strongly felt. Even with the adoption of the two-commentator format, there was virtually no communication between the two pundits. Instead, they merely recited prepared scripts. This in a way made the comments boring.

Amidst continuity, however, there are also various changes. First, there is a trend toward providing a greater diversity of information. In particular, the 2004 and 2008 CCTV commentary began to include certain categories of information that had not previously been found, such as comments about the social, economic and cultural attributes of the nations. Along the same lines, comments about the teams became more entertaining. Whereas previous references to a country's particular features included only occasional mention of its specific geographic location, more recent opening ceremony coverage has contained a greater variety of social and cultural references. Examples include: 'Cook Island is named after the British explorer Captain Cook in 1773'; 'Malawi is a country with beautiful scenery and is known for over 400 kinds of orchid'; 'Italy instantly reminds one of the great Roman Empire, the Colosseum, the Renaissance city of Florence, and Venice, the city of water'; 'Known for the Monaco Grand Prix, Monaco hosts the only race within Formula One that has tracks within a city. It is known as the jewel of the Formula One crown'; the French are an 'art-loving' people who 'care for sports with more artistic appeal such as fencing' while 'Iranians are usually of stout figures and are good at wrestling'.[24]

Moreover, human interest anecdotes began to show up more often. When the Spanish team entered in 2004, it was mentioned that King Juan Carlos had participated in the yacht race in 1972, won fifteenth place, and three years later became the King of Spain. In 2008, when the US team entered, the anchor included the fact that former President George Bush had served as the honorary president of the US team while the then-current President, George W. Bush, had led the cheerleaders. 'The flag-bearer of Switzerland is Roger Federer, the king of tennis, and it happens to be his 27th birthday today'; 'The choice of Salvatore's flag-bearer was the result of a national vote'.[25] The increase in this type of commentary follows a trend in news practice that puts more emphasis on human interest stories.

Some more nuanced changes are found in the way the Chinese team was introduced. Up until 2000, such introductions used highly hortatory language. For example:

> Now it's the team of the People's Republic of China in the stadium ... The Chinese team has 381 people, among them 251 athletes. They will participate in 28 sports and 105 events. The athletes will use their entire hearts and apply their thoughts, be confident, compete with style, compete to potential, strive to achieve good performances. They will express the aspirations of an advanced culture, express Chinese people's resolve, and win glory for the nation.[26]

> Now the team of the People's Republic of China, holding high the national flag in their hands, strides into the stadium with high spirits ... The Chinese team has 496 people, among them 392 athletes. They will participate in 22 sports out of 26. In the last Olympiad, China won 16 gold medals. The Chinese athletes are determined to give a brand new appearance and present themselves as 'the team of etiquette and manners'. They will embody the excellent cultural tradition of the Chinese nation, convey an image of China that enjoys social stability, economic development, and reform and opening up. They will compete with style, compete to potential, strive to achieve good performances and win glory for the nation. They will make their contribution to promoting the Olympic Movement and Olympic spirit as well as the friendship between different nations and regions.[27]

Given the role that sports played in the Chinese society up to the 1990s, such a tone was not uncommon. For a long time, mass sports aimed at preparing the Chinese for nation-building through body-building. They placed too much emphasis on winning rather than taking part in the sport and winning a gold medal was instantly linked to the idea of rejuvenating a nation. In the same token, a global sporting event calls for the use of solemn and grandiose language in order to galvanize the athletes as well as the audience back home. Brownell was correct when she noted that in the Chinese coverage of the Olympic

Games, a joyful mood always took a back seat to other more prized values such as 'progress' and 'civilization'.[28]

However, in the next two Olympiads, one could no longer detect such rhetoric:

> Now it's the team of the People's Republic of China in the stadium. The flag-bearer is Liu Yudong. He was also the flag-bearer in the last Olympics. Walking in the front row was the vice director of the Chinese delegation Yu Zaixin … followed by officials and leaders of the team. Walking behind them are the female athletes, followed by male athletes. This is Ping Pong player Wang Nan. The Chinese athletes will participate in 24 sports and 166 events. 203 people participate in the opening ceremony parade. Among the athletes the oldest is Wang Yifu, athlete in shooting and the youngest one is Shan Su, a swimmer who is only 15.[29]

> Now it's the team of the People's Republic of China in the stadium. Since 1984 China has participated in 5 Summer Olympic Games and has won a total of 80 gold medals. The flag-bearer is the world-famous athlete Yao Ming. In 2000, the Chinese team had their best ever performance, winning 28 golds, 16 silvers and 15 bronzes. For this Olympiad, China sent out its largest team ever, including 407 athletes, among them 269 male and 138 female. The Chinese athletes have gold medal potential in 7 sports, including diving, weightlifting, ping pong, badminton, shooting, gymnastics and judo. In 2000, 25 out of the 28 gold medals were from these 7 sports. In addition, they are expected to perform well in women's volleyball, fencing, yachts, cycling, etc.[30]

The change in the style of comment reflects the moving away from a more serious official media culture. A footnote to this change was exemplified through the bearing of the Chinese athletes. Whereas in earlier athletic parades the athletes displayed a military-like discipline, they walked with greater ease in the more recent parades. This shows that while in the 1980s and early 1990s, there were still ostensible efforts to use sports to 'bring about a spiritual shift towards greater unity … (and) to facilitate China's movement toward modern nationhood',[31] in the decade that followed, this strategy was applied with greater subtlety. MacAloon noted that because ritualistic moments in the West tend to be rare, ritualistic experiences in events such as the Olympic Games are highly desirable.[32] However, for a society like China which had been all too used to state occasions ornamented by political rhetoric designed to arouse people's nobler passions towards the state, a shift toward a plainer speech style is not unwelcome.

Backlash

The paramount ritual function of the Beijing Games' opening ceremony for China in a way dictates the use of a formal language that the ruling elites considered appropriate for China's 'coming-out party'. This is reflected in the way the Chinese team was introduced, which seemed more like a return to the rhetoric of a past era. For example, the commentator listed the four major objectives of the Chinese team as outlined by the state sports authorities:

> First, the athletes should promote the Olympic spirit and the Chinese spirit through hard work … since they serve to represent China's national image. Second, the athletes should compete to their potential and win glory for the nation. Third, the athletes should learn from other national teams and promote sports exchanges and friendship between China and the rest of the world. Fourth, the athletes' performance ought to add fuel to the public enthusiasm for sports … and promote the development of sports industry and other related sectors in China. In this way, they make their unique contribution to the construction of a harmonious socialist state.[33]

Also, towards the end of the opening ceremony, the commentators used a series of hortatory parallels to describe the exuberant national passion:

> Since 1908, the aspirations of Chinese for the Olympics have spanned a century. 100 years ago, we dreamed about the flame in Olympia. Today we ignited it in Beijing's night sky. Finally, the

western civilization originated in ancient Greece has met with the Chinese civilization with a history of 5,000 years. In the Los Angeles Games of 1932, there was only one athlete from China. Today, 1.3 billion Chinese join hands in hosting the Olympic Games. The love for the Olympics has been written into our national gene ... This is a moment belonging to Beijing. The world's eye is on Beijing ... We wish the athletes from around the world will compete to their best potential and will rewrite the beauty of the Olympics in a land of hope. We wish the Chinese Olympic heroes will emblazon their Olympic legend on the turf of motherland.[34]

The studied nature of these words seemed suited to the significance of how important this rite of passage was for China. The audience was being presented with a 'giant scripted show'.[35] Not only was every detail regarding the execution of the opening ceremony highly scripted, with meticulous rehearsals in the weeks and months before the event, but the commentary used to describe such an occasion was also highly scripted. In this case, interviews with CCTV anchors show that not even the commentators themselves were directly involved in the writing of the scripts. They were prepared by a team summoned by the highest communication arm of the government. Understandably, little spontaneity could be expected.

If the contrived manner of such a delivery style might still appear natural to an earlier generation, in an era when the audience is more used to straight talk and humorous bantering in media presentation rather than being 'talked-down to', such a style ended up sounding jarring to the average audience. Soon after the opening ceremony, criticism started to surface in major discussion boards on the Internet and in various blogs. Many wrote that the anchors' comments were an anachronism.

Organizational changes in CCTV's Olympic coverage and changes in the Chinese sports culture

The People's Republic of China rejoined the Olympic family in 1979 after severing relations with the IOC for 21 years and made a comeback at the Summer Olympics in Los Angeles in 1984. That Olympics also became the first Summer Olympics to be televised live in China by CCTV. Throughout the 1980s, CCTV's coverage of the Olympics was in collaboration with TVB of Hong Kong and very few people were sent to the Olympic city to do the coverage.

In 1992, the CCTV presence in Barcelona expanded and the team produced 250 hours of Olympic programming in total. But a cross-national study of the 1992 Olympic opening ceremony coverage found that CCTV provided the least amount of information among the 27 national broadcasters under study.[36] This was due to a heavy reliance on footage provided by other media organizations, inadequate translation and underdeveloped live TV coverage norms in China. Furthermore, the chief commentator recalled that he feared saying something that was politically or technically incorrect,[37] resulting in a minimum of comments.

The establishment of CCTV's sports channel, Channel 5, in January 1995 was a boost to the growth of sports TV and the Atlanta Olympic Games in 1996 became the first major live broadcasting exercise after the founding of the channel. It was also CCTV's first independent Olympic media coverage endeavour: 'It was the first time that the Olympic programming was produced, packaged and transmitted by CCTV on its own.'[38] CCTV set up its own studio at the International Broadcasting Center (IBC) and used unilateral live reporting from venues. About 60% of all news programmes and news commentary programmes were produced directly from IBC in Atlanta. The rest of the programmes were produced in Beijing. The coverage of the Atlanta Games also introduced the notion of 'human interest' when it comes to covering athletes.

In Sydney the TV team expanded to include 126 people and the total broadcasting hours were 584. Except for a morning programme that was produced in Beijing, all the other Olympic programmes were produced in Sydney. The story-telling nature of sports programming was further emphasized. The programmes became more dramatized and entertaining.

The next Summer Olympics in Athens saw still more intensive live broadcasting efforts. With a team of 208 reporters, anchors and technicians in Athens, CCTV produced 1,474 hours of live coverage throughout the Games. The coverage also became multi-channel. While CCTV Sports churned out 24/7 coverage, with a greater variety of programme formats including multiple newscasts, studio interviews and interactive programmes, two other channels were also devoted to extensive Olympic coverage.

The coverage of the 2008 Games, expectedly, topped all previous efforts. In a paper summarizing the legacy of the Olympic media operation, CCTV Sports' Supervisor Jiang Heping listed a number of 'Mosts' to characterize the coverage. It has the greatest output, with an unprecedented total of 2,796 hours of broadcasting time, spreading over seven terrestrial and HD channels. It involved the largest number of media makers, with more than 3,000 people within CCTV participating. It was noted that the programmes catered to the most diversified audience interests and showed competitions that were dominated by Chinese as well as foreign athletes alike. Also, the preparation for the Beijing Olympics coverage was the longest TV marathon ever, which spanned the entire Olympic cycle from 2004 all the way to 2008.[39]

The exponential growth of Olympic broadcast in China means that the importance of the opening ceremony coverage, which is the most ritualized aspect of the games, may be steadily decreasing in relation to the coverage of the entire Olympic event. In fact, if one looks at the news and news documentary programmes that constitute the bulk of Olympic programming today, they come much closer to similar programme genres in the West in terms of structure, content and commentator style.

Paralleling the organizational development in Olympic coverage is a change in media sports culture. Unlike the western tradition that often associates sports events with festival, in the past the Chinese coverage put more emphasis on 'solemnity' and 'the formulaic use of longzhong (grand, solemn)'.[40] Sports are also a means of social engineering in order to better prepare the populace for serving the socialist state.

Over the last two decades, however, China has slowly moved away from an emphasis on a homogenous socialist culture to embrace greater social and cultural pluralism. Sports have partly been dissociated from being a function of the state to becoming part of the market economy. Indeed professional and spectator sports are today an ever-expanding leisure industry in China. Practising sport is increasingly considered as an expression of life style and individual choice.

While the evolution in sports media's organizational setting and in sports culture may not fully account for the changes in the opening ceremony narrative, they do provide a background in which the opening ceremony narrative is embedded. In so far as media discourse has by now become an inseparable part of public rituals such as the Olympic Games opening ceremony, changes in the media discourse can be conceived as changes in the ritual practice.

Conclusion

The critical school of ritual studies believes that rituals serve to disguise deeper societal fault-lines, creating a false appearance of communitas. Given the Chinese tradition of insulating sports from politics in its media coverage, it would seem that the Chinese state broadcaster performs exactly such a role in covering the Olympic opening ceremony. It strives to provide a sanitized version of the Games. But even so, a tension between various conflicting forces is maintained and occasionally the veil is lifted to expose structural problems that simply cannot be papered over.

On the other hand, this essay shows that rituals, or more specifically ritual language, do change over time. Historically in China, covering an important international occasion such as the Olympic opening ceremony called for overblown rhetoric as a way of marking it apart from ordinary occasions. More recently, such grandiose language has given way to a plainer and more western-like style, although the use of casual bantering is still limited. This change can be mapped onto deeper changes in the media organizational practices and sports culture in China.

Rothenbuhler interprets ritual change as an outcome of competing ritual forms representing different social orders.[41] This essay instead looks into the changing ritual form presented by an evolving media organization. In China this change has been borne by successive generations of media-makers within the same state media organ.

While the TV producers and commentators do not create the rituals of the Olympics, they nevertheless add meaning to them. A particular type of language can serve as a marker of the importance of an occasion, i.e., once a certain threshold is crossed, such language becomes justified because the language suggests a proper social distance that the occasion demands of both the media producers and the audience. In this sense, media discourse can also be seen as demarcating the boundaries of acceptable values for a society, while changing discourses over time reveal changing values.

Occasionally there might be a discrepancy between the official criteria of introducing a public ritual and the proper standards in the eyes of the public. The highly choreographed narrative in the Beijing Olympic opening ceremony coverage is a case in point. While the state did succeed in imposing an orthodox reading of the event, the public response to such an interpretation was various. There is a growing challenge for official media organs to handle such important occasions in a manner that both honours the 'tradition' and satisfies an increasingly scrutinizing domestic audience.

In response to the different voices that emerged surrounding the opening ceremony coverage, there was a post-Olympics discussion within CCTV on the best form and style that the opening ceremony coverage should assume.

In an interview with Jiang Heping, Controller of CCTV Sports, after the Beijing Olympics, he said 'some believe that (contrary to the present model), the opening and closing ceremony commentary has to be interesting and attention-grabbing, which calls for an excellent command of language on the part of commentators. These people believe that the casual talk-show style of many foreign anchors is more effective and better matches the atmosphere of the ceremonies. There is no definite answer as to which one is more appropriate and we can leave this for future discussion'.[42]

In the interviews that I conducted with people involved in the Olympic media making, a majority of subjects actually expressed their preference for the NBC style of commenting. But many at the same time expressed reservations about whether or not the Chinese broadcasters would adopt a similar style in the near future, due to the 'different national characteristics' between China and the West and the official ritual function that is required of such an occasion in China. What can be said, however, is that a general trend towards the dilution of an older conception of public ritual emphasizing austerity has been begun, and is likely to continue in the future.

Acknowledgements

The author wishes to thank Professor James Ettema for his many valuable suggestions throughout the writing of the article. The author is also grateful to Mr. Zhang Zhaoxi of CCTV for his great help in gathering the video clips used for analysis in this article.

Notes

1 Turner, *The Ritual Process*, 96. Van Gennep, *The Rites of Passage*
2 MacAloon, 'Olympic Games', 262.
3 Goffman, *Frame Analysis*.
4 MacAloon, 'Olympic Games'.
5 Ibid., 253.
6 Dayan and Katz, *Media Events*.
7 Ibid., 10–14.
8 See Lukes, 'Political Ritual', 289–308; and Couldry, *Media Rituals*.
9 Anderson, *Imagined Communities*; Carey, 'Political Ritual'.
10 De Moragas Spà, Rivenburgh, and Larson, *Television in the Olympics*, 143.
11 Larson and Park, *Global Television*, 207–212.
12 The video material used here may not represent the full length of the actual CCTV coverage of each opening ceremony. But judging from the available material, CCTV did manage to introduce all or nearly all of the participating nations appearing in the video.
13 De Moragas Spà, Rivenburgh, and Larson, *Television in the Olympics*, 156.
14 From CCTV's coverage of the 2004 Olympic opening ceremony.
15 Interviews with various CCTV employees involved in the 2008 Olympic media production.
16 In response to Taiwan's pro-independence leader Lee Teng-hui's visit to the US, where he propagated his independence agenda, the Chinese government carried out military exercises over the Taiwan Straits in March, 1996. Alarmed, the US army sent two aircraft carriers to the region for intervention.
17 From CCTV's coverage of the 2000 Olympic opening ceremony.
18 Turner, *The Ritual Process*.
19 Roche, *Mega-Events and Modernity*, 197.
20 NBC's coverage of the 2008 Beijing Olympics opening ceremony.
21 De Moragas Spà, Rivenburgh, and Larson, *Television in the Olympics*.
22 Ibid.
23 Ibid. See Brownell, 'Cultural Variations', 26–41.
24 From CCTV's coverage of the 2004 and 2008 Olympic opening ceremonies.
25 From CCTV's coverage of the 2008 Olympic opening ceremony.
26 From CCTV's coverage of the 1992 Olympic opening ceremony.
27 From CCTV's coverage of the 1996 Olympic opening ceremony.
28 Brownell, *Training the Body for China*, 124.
29 From CCTV's coverage of the 2000 Olympic opening ceremony.
30 From CCTV's coverage of the 2004 Olympic opening ceremony.
31 Brownell, *Training the Body for China*, 145.
32 MacAloon, 'Olympic Games'.
33 From CCTV's coverage of the 2008 Olympic opening ceremony.
34 Ibid.
35 Interview with a US journalist involved in covering the Beijing Olympics.
36 De Moragas Spà, Rivenburgh, and Larson, *Television in the Olympics*.
37 Brownell, 'Cultural Variations', 26–41.
38 Interview with Zhang Wei, vice supervisor of CCTV Sports, October 28, 2008.
39 Jiang, 'The "Truly Exceptional"', 11–14.
40 Brownell, *Training the Body for China*, 124.
41 Rothenbuhler; *Ritual Communication*.
42 Jiang, Heping, Controller of CCTV Sports, 23 October, 2008.

References

Anderson, B. *Imagined Communities: Reflections on the Origin and Spread of Nationalism.* New York: Verso, 1991.

Brownell, S. 'Cultural Variations in Olympic Telecasts: China and the 1992 Olympic Games and Ceremonies'. *The Journal of International Communication* (June 1995): 26–41.

Brownell, S. *Training the Body for China: Sports in the Moral Order of the People's Republic*. Chicago, IL and London: The University of Chicago Press, 1995.

Carey, J. 'Political Ritual on Television'. In *Media, Ritual and Identity*, edited by T. Liebes and J. Curran, 47–70. London: Routledge, 1998.

Couldry, N. *Media Rituals: A Critical Approach*. London and New York: Routledge, 2003.

Dayan, D., and E. Katz. *Media Events: The Live Broadcasting of History*. Boston, MA: Harvard University Press, 1992.

Goffman, E. *Frame Analysis: an essay on the organization of experience*. Cambridge, MA: Harvard University Press, 1974.

Jiang, H. 'The "Truly Exceptional" and the Comparable: The TV Coverage of the Beijing Olympic Games'. *TV Research* 11 (2008): 11–14.

Larson, J., and H.-S. Park. *Global Television and the Politics of the Seoul Olympics*. Oxford: Westview Press, 1993.

Lukes, S. (1975) 'Political Ritual and social integration', *Sociology* 9(2): 289–308.

MacAloon, J. 'Olympic Games and the Theory of Spectacle in Modern Societies'. In *Rite, Drama, Festival, Spectacle*, edited by J. MacAloon, 241–280. Philadelphia, PA: The Institute of Human Issues, 1984.

de Moragas Spà, M., N.K. Rivenburgh, and J.F. Larson. *Television in the Olympics*. Eastleigh: John Libbey & Company Ltd, 1995.

Roche, M. *Mega-Events and Modernity: Olympics and Expos in the Growth of Global Culture*. London and New York: Routledge, 2000.

Rothenbuhler, E.W. *Ritual Communication*. Thousand Oaks, CA: Sage, 1993.

Turner, V. *The Ritual Process*. Ithaca, NY: Cornell University Press, 2007 (1969).

Van Gennep, A. *The Rites of Passage*. London: Routledge, 1977.

A study of Guangdong TV's Olympics coverage strategy

Yaohua Huang

Guangdong Television, Huanshi Dong Rd, Guangzhou, Guangdong, China

The 2008 Beijing Olympic Games were a magnificent and influential sports event which drew attention from all over the world. Television has long played a key role in broadcasting the Olympic Games and numerous broadcasters around the world had access to the event. As was authorized by the International Olympic Committee, Chinese Central Television (CCTV), the state-owned broadcaster, was the only station licensed to broadcast the Olympic Games. On the condition that the authorization would be exclusive of other TV stations, local media encountered a burning issue, that is, how could the local media share in broadcasting the games? A study of the strategies of local media during Beijing Olympic Games can reveal the environment of the national and local media, and the hidden cultures behind these signs of media ecology. A study of television from the perspective of a particular social environment can provide a better understanding of the role of culture in constructing TV as well as of the interaction between national culture and media organizations; consequently providing directions in theory that will aid the survival and development of television.

The Olympic Games: chance or challenge for local media

The Olympic Games were a sports event to which Chinese people had long been looking forward, and also was a significant event for the media. With the world's eyes on this sports event, all of the media in China had been well prepared to welcome its coming. On the one hand, the conflict between Olympic Games broadcasting and regular programmes would be decreased; on the other hand, more profit from advertisements would be made through broadcasting Olympic Games which would attract a larger audience. It was well known that Olympic Games broadcasting can bring great economic profit for a broadcaster.

Because Olympic Games Broadcasting should be authorized by the IOC, and CCTV was the only authorized broadcasting organization in China, most of the provincial television stations lost the rights to broadcast the Olympic Games. Moreover, the CCTV stations already had made a good profit through their monopoly on broadcasting, such as CCTV 5's monopoly of sporting events. It is said that the market share of CCTV has been stable through strengthening the monopoly of resources. The market share of CCTV 5 had risen to 35.8% due to the monopolization of the 2006 World Cup and it was ranked the second in China. After 2006 CCTV 5 evolved from a weak channel into a nationwide channel with an annual rising market share of 35.3%.[1]

In order to break the monopoly of CCTV on sports events, some provincial television stations (Liaoning, Jiangsu, Shandong, Hubei and Xinjiang, Jiangxi, Inner Mongolia stations, etc.) set up the Chinese and Sports Programming Network (CSPN) in 2007 in the hope that the shortage of sports resources would be solved by means of integrating the resources of the different members of CSPN. This strategy of integration was the original purpose of setting up CSPN with the further hope of making a breakthrough in broadcasting the Olympic Games. However, with the restriction of policies and funding, CSPN had no great advantage over the Olympic Games broadcasting which remained monopolized by CCTV.

The Beijing Olympic Games were a good chance for CCTV to consolidate and enlarge its market share. All provincial TV stations were permitted to broadcast the opening and closing ceremonies of the Olympic Games, but there was a strict restriction on broadcasting the Olympic Games live. Only a minority of local TV stations could broadcast some games live. CCTV hoped that there would be no direct competition for the live broadcasts of some games from provincial Satellite TV stations to divide the market share. Thus, for provincial TV stations, the Olympic Games brought more challenges than chances.

Through hard negotiation with CCTV, Guangdong TV station, a state-owned enterprise,[2] finally obtained the right to broadcast some games in Guangdong; that is to say, only the lesser terrestrial channels of Guangdong TV station – Guangdong Sports Channel and Pearl River Channel were able to broadcast certain games. Which games were they allowed to broadcast and why?

Local market or nationwide market?

When broadcasting sporting events, much depends on the specific situation of the media as to whether it is able to choose a local market or nationwide market. Much also depends on the ratio of the nationwide market to the local market, the contents of what is being broadcast and the watching preferences of local audiences. For example, there are six wireless terrestrial channels subordinate to Guangdong Television: Guangdong Satellite Channel, Pearl River Channel, Public Channel, Sports Channel, News Channel and Jiajia Cartoon Channel, as well as eight pay-per-view channels and mobile TV, mobile phone TV and subway TV, etc.

In terms of the coverage of wireless terrestrial channels, only Guangdong Satellite Channel has nationwide coverage and the other channels are local. Generally speaking, the economic profits for a nationwide channel are better than that of local channels. However, it is quite the opposite for Guangdong because the economic profits of Pearl River Channel are better than those of Guangdong Satellite Channel. Local culture plays a key role in attracting viewers and this is one of many factors that explains this phenomenon. Guangdong is situated in the south east part of China and is adjacent to Hong Kong, Macao. Cantonese is the dialect of Guangdong and a sphere of South China culture. Because of this, the Cantonese TV programmes are more popular than those in Mandarin. Hong Kong TV has drawn a large audience by means of its advanced production technology and programmes which are popular with the public. In the 1970s and 1980s, Hong Kong TV came into Guangdong and ever since then has gained high viewing figures.

In order to compete with Hong Kong TV, under the push to promote the use of Mandarin, the State Administration of Radio Film and Television permitted the creation of a Cantonese TV Channel in Guangdong: Pearl River Channel, which is the only provincial TV station broadcasting in Cantonese. And some Cantonese TV programmes are acceptable among the other terrestrial channels of Guangdong Television. It can be said that Cantonese culture has dominated the TV culture in Guangdong. Thus, the ratings for Guangdong Satellite Channel programmes broadcasted in Mandarin are lower than those of Pearl River Channel in Guangdong.

In terms of the market share, the Guangdong local market is still the main market for Guangdong Television. Since it was not permitted to broadcast the Olympic Games, Guangdong TV station put a great emphasis on ground channels such as the Pearl River Channel and the Sports Channel. As indicated above, there has been fierce competition amongst broadcasters in the Guangdong area from three aspects: first, from CCTV and all provincial satellite stations; second, from overseas media such as Hong Kong TV; and third, there also has been local competition among Guangdong Television, Southern Television and Guangzhou Television stations. If the local market share of broadcasting Olympic Games could not be ensured, Guangdong TV station would be a major loser. So when trying to ensure the market share in China, Guangdong TV station positively cooperated with CSPN to share the news on the Olympic Games. Guangdong TV station is not a member of CSPN, and the influence of its subordinate Sports Channel ranks the third in China, so this time the cooperation with CSPN revealed that Guangdong TV station had no other choice given the circumstances since the Olympic Games broadcasting was monopolized by CCTV.

As a matter of fact, other provincial satellite channels also encountered the same problem as Guangdong Satellite Television. During the Olympic Games, It was difficult for satellite channels to keep a regular market share because CCTV has a lot of channels of different types. So it often turned to its local media. However before the Beijing Olympic Games, provincial satellite channels were able to make some entertainment programmes that carved out a large market share by incorporating Olympic elements. For example, Hunan Satellite TV Station, which is famous for its entertainment programmes, created a major outside sports programme – *Olympic Games, Just do it*, which topped the ratings 11 times among the programmes broadcast nationwide with an audience share of 40 million viewers. This programme was changed to *Happiness, Just Do it* because the term 'the Olympic Games' wasn't allowed to be used on local TV stations' programmes by the State Administration of Radio, Film and Television. But during the Olympic Games, the ratings for this programme went from number one, from 4 August, to number five, to number seven during the period of 9–10 August.[3] So without the monopoly of sports resources, provincial satellite TV stations became weaker in the face of CCTV's competition.

The localization of strategies

The Beijing Olympic Games were a nationwide event. Before it occurred, all the media in China took full advantage of a national media agenda to introduce the Olympic Games from different aspects such as its history, culture and so on, showing the Olympic spirit to the audience. This strategy was aimed to ensure the success of Beijing Olympic Games by creating good public opinion, as well as a positive atmosphere and social environment.

Firstly, before Beijing Olympic Games began, some programmes relevant to the Olympic Games were broadcast on its subordinate wireless terrestrial channels, a strategy that was to set a goal for ratings and pave the way for the Olympic broadcasting; this included such programmes as *Olympic News, FUWA Olympic Journey* on Guangdong Satellite Channel, the *Special Program: Olympic Games are Coming* and *Olympics TV Collection* on Pearl River Channel. The live broadcast of the Guangdong Olympic Torch relay segment greatly stimulated audience viewing in Guangdong. The Olympic Torch relay became the focal point of worldwide attention and some live broadcasting events relevant to the Olympic Games also became their daily topic.

Second, Olympic broadcasting rooms were built in Beijing for all broadcasters. Guangdong TV station sent about 100 workers to broadcast the Olympic Games. These included the backbones of regular television programmes and famous anchormen, who are responsible for providing the news for different live programmes broadcasting news and special topics on Sports Channel, Pearl River Channel, Public Channel and News Channel. Moreover, a broadcasting room with advanced equipment was built on Pangu Plaza near to Bird's Nest Stadium, aiming to transmit the latest Olympic news for Guangdong Television.

Third, large Olympic programmes were created to broadcast Olympic Games from all aspects on ground main channels. Guangdong Sports Channel mainly broadcast live, together with the Beijing Broadcasting Room; both broadcasting, recording and playing games for entire days. Pearl River Channel, as the strong ground channel, aimed to be the best channel for Olympic broadcasting in Cantonese. So a prominent programme like *The Celebration of Pearl River* was made with the integration of special topics, consulting, the live broadcasting of games, etc. These programmes were broadcast for days during four prime times: from 7.00. to 8.00, from 12.00 to 13.00, from 17.50 to 18.30, and from 23.00 to 24.00. This programme transmitted Olympic information as soon as it was available, and focused on special topics including 'Gold Medal List', 'Olympic Starts', 'Professional Comments and Predictions' and so forth. At the same time, two exciting games were chosen to be broadcast live or recorded to broadcast according to the Games' agenda. The Olympic Games were broadcast and explained in Cantonese with famous anchormen, honoured guests, experts, sportsmen and stars of entertainment doing the commentating.

Last but not the least, the range of the Olympic Games was enlarged by new media. Since 2004 new media such as mobile television, mobile phone television and subway television have been created successively by Guangdong Television. These new media create a diverse broadcasting system along with the other wireless terrestrial channels of Guangdong Television, which had further enlarged the coverage of its programmes and fostered new points of economic growth for Guangdong Television. TV programmes could be received by viewers, even while they were travelling, on mobile television and mobile phone television by means of wireless digital radio broadcast technology. Since their foundation, these new forms of media broadcasting prepared intensely for the Olympic Games. During the Beijing Olympic Games, mobile phone television broadcast all Guangdong Satellite Television and Sports Channel programmes for the whole period, while mobile television and subway television mainly broadcast news programmes on other channels of Guangdong Television.

Ratings analysis

How was Guangdong television affected through its broadcasting of the Beijing Olympic Games? An investigation of the ratings and comparative analysis reveals a hidden pattern.

In terms of Beijing Olympic broadcasting, CCTV remained the strongest competitor for all provincial television stations including Guangdong Television. The advantage of CCTV consisted of its monopoly of Olympic resources, the support of the government polices and their nationwide coverage. In Guangdong, 15 channels of CCTV can be viewed. For the Beijing Olympic broadcasting, five wireless terrestrial channels and two pay-per-view channels were used to broadcast all the games and each channel had individual features geared to attracting particular audiences: CCTV-1 mainly showed the overview of the Olympic Games, CCTV-2 mainly broadcast the international Olympic Games which the Chinese audience were mostly likely to view; CCTV-5 mainly broadcast games which Chinese sportsmen took part in; and CCTV-7 was mainly for rural audiences and the channel for broadcasting the best/most highly competitive games. CCTV HDTV was the channel for all games, with a special focus on the best/most highly competitive games.

Such a great degree of saturation by CCTV and its subdivision of the market was beneficial to the density and level of Guangdong ratings coverage. According to the data of a market survey done by CVSC-SOFRES MEDIA from 3–9 August 2008, the market share for 15 of CCTV's channels was 26.60%, while the ratings for six of Guangdong TV stations was 30.056%. From 10–16 August, the market share of CCTV increased to 38.525%, while the market share of Guangdong TV station decreased to 27.002%. It seems clear that Olympic broadcasting did increase the ratings of CCTV. On the other hand, it could be said that Guangdong TV station was also a winner in relation to Olympic broadcasting because its ratings did not greatly decrease in the face of CCTV's strong broadcasting.

As an international top sports event, the host country generally pays a great deal of attention to the Olympic Games. It is also a good chance for the host country to show her understanding of the Olympic spirit, to show off her present capabilities and improve her image through the Olympic Games. Thus state television stations took the responsibility for representing these things. In the eyes of Chinese audiences, the CCTV stations represent the state's authority and trustworthiness as a representative of the country's and government's image. During the Beijing Olympic Games broadcasting, CCTV stations played the role of attracting all Chinese audiences in order to show Chinese ideology just as it does in programming like the *Spring Festival Entertainment Program*, which is highly popular with high annual ratings. The representation of ideology was fulfilled through the use of Mandarin, while the watching psychology and habits of the Guangdong audience have been shaped by Cantonese channels, which to some degree have weakened their loyalty to CCTV. This point can be proved by the ranking of ratings during the first week of the Olympic Games in Guangdong Province. According to CVSC-SOFRES MEDIA STUDY, four Pearl River Channel programmes were the top four from 10–16 August, while the broadcasting of the women's volleyball group games on CCTV-1 was ranked fifth. According to the ranking of ratings for this week in Guangdong, two live broadcast games on CCTV-5, and one each on CCTV-1, CCTV-5 and CCTV- 2 were the top five. Because the degree of Mandarin acceptance by city residents in Guangdong is higher than that of rural residents, they tended to accept the programmes broadcast in Mandarin on CCTV stations. So language usage also has an effect on programme acceptance.

Moreover, besides the Olympic Games, as far as international games broadcasting is concerned, Guangdong Television, compared with CCTV station, has its own advantage over the local ratings. Take 2006 World Cup Broadcasting as an example:

The ratings of Guangdong Sports Channel were higher by 0.7% than that of CCTV Sports Channel and the market share of Guangdong Sports Channel was higher by 7.5% than that of CCTV Sports Channel. For Chinese people, the influence of other international sports events cannot compare to that of Olympic Games, so the local culture of local television will play a greater role in ratings.

Conclusion

Due to the policy restriction and Olympic resources, provincial television stations are not dangerous competitors for CCTV. Within a specific local culture, Guangdong TV station aimed to create a local community of viewers on the basis of giving full advantage to Cantonese use, which allows it to reap social and economic profits from broadcasting

Table 1. Audience rating comparison between Guangdong Sports Channel and CCTV-5.

Date	Channel	Programme	Start	End	Second	Programme Type	Audience (Unit: thousand)	Audience Rating	Rating Share
01/07/2006	Guangdong Sports Channel	2006 World Cup Quarter-final (England v Portugal)	22:36:02	01:37:08	03:01:06	Sport	2079	2.3	23.4
01/07/2006	CCTV-5	2006 World Cup Quarter-final (England v Portugal)	00:52:42	01:30:16	00:37:34	Sport	1378	1.5	15.9

Source: From AGB Nielsen Media Research

sports events and other competitive activities not as popular as the Olympic Games such as the National Basketball Association (NBA), the Chinese Basketball Association (CBA), the English Premier League (EPL) and so on.

Notes

[1] See http://zhidao.baidu.com/question/62664609.html?si=5.

[2] Guangdong Television (GDTV), established in 1959, was the first provincial television broadcasting organization in China. It has been enjoying rapid development and has become the most influential of its kind in the country. Currently GDTV has six well-developed channels, namely: the Satellite Channel, Pearl River Channel, a Sports Channel, a Public Channel, a News Channel and Jiajia Cartoon Channel; eight digital pay-per-view channels: a Reality Show Channel, an European Football Channel, a Golf Channel, the Lingnan Opera Channel, a Pets Channel, an Exhibition Channel, a Property Channel, and an English Teaching Channel. Also some new media operations such as Mobile TV, Mobile Phone TV and Metro TV channels have come into existence.

[3] Data from CVSC-SOFRES MEDIA.

Personal, popular and information portals – Olympic news and the use of mobile phones among migrant workers in Fuzhou[1]

Jun Liu

Department of Media, Cognition and Communication, University of Copenhagen, Denmark School of Humanities and School of Humanities and Social Sciences, Fuzhou University, China

Based on theory regarding mobile communication in general, this essay relates the experiences of migrant workers from both rural and urban areas in Fuzhou, who used mobile phones to stay in contact with the Beijing 2008 Olympic Games, to how these contacts supported and encouraged migrant workers to persist in gathering Olympic Games information. In other words, does the relationship between demographics and knowledge about the Beijing 2008 Olympic Games differ according to the use of mobile phones among migrant workers? Results indicate that television became the primary source of Olympic Games news for migrant workers, but actually with few advantages as the respondents considered the mobile phone as their second source of information. Given the higher than average mobile media penetration rate among the sample of migrant workers and their information expectations, we cannot ignore the mobile phone's impact as a channel for information and public services. This essay's focus is also on how the government, the official press and service providers (China Mobile and China Unicom) appreciated the mobile phone as a means of spreading the Olympic Games' influence, making it possible for a large majority of people to enjoy the Olympic Games, and popularizing knowledge.

Introduction

Changes in technology have driven the development of new communication media. McLuhan's phrase 'The medium is the message'[2] encapsulates the fact that the form of a medium embeds itself in the message, creating a symbiotic relationship by which the medium influences how the message is perceived over time. Different media invite different degrees of participation on the part of a person who chooses to consume that medium. But the fast spread of new information technology often means that we fail to notice the structural changes in our affairs. Access to new technology also leads to a series of questions about what kind of information is available, whether information promotes an increase in real knowledge, and, perhaps most importantly, how are the relations of power in a society affected by the growth of information and communication technologies (ICTs)?[3]

In this age of mass media, it is certain that information will become more important in the future, as we move into an increasingly technology-dominant era. But it must be recognized that an information gap does exist and has been broadening since the advent of the Internet. This is mainly because the diffusion of the Internet across different areas is quite uneven, a process known as the 'Digital Divide'.[4] This divide exists between under-developed and developed countries as well as among people in the same country.

According to the 22nd Survey Report on the Internet Development in China,[5] the Internet penetration rate in China, 19.1%, is slightly lower than the average Internet penetration rate in the rest of the developed world, 21.1%. Currently most Chinese people still face technical difficulties when it comes to digital acquisition, processing, access, delivery and preservation as they adopt the virtual world, although the number of netizens in China had leaped to the first place in the world by the end of June, 2008.

The mobile phone in China

In contrast to the USA where Internet communication dominates,[6] another technology is being promoted particularly by Chinese consumers: cell or mobile phones which are labelled 'handy' in Chinese – a vivid expression for an increasingly personal approach to communication. Digital technology has expanded the mobile phone's potential from a talking device to a more dynamic tool, shaping individual and organizational life, doing new things one had previous not even thought of doing.[7] After 20 years' development in China, the total number of mobile phone users had surpassed 592 million by the end of July 2008, an average of one in less than three people (see Figure 1).[8] The figure illustrates at least the quantitative relevance of this new communication media in China.

On the other hand, mobile phone use is largely unregulated, unpredictable and unknowable. It is impossible to know when they will be used, what will be said, by whom, to whom, or for what purpose. The mobile phone can't be easily switched off, controlled, or made safe by centralized supervisory authorities.[9] It breaches information blockage and challenges the traditional communication order, helping people to receive information about the outside world, to maintain contact with each other and even make political waves. As low-cost, higher credibility phones gain popularity, there are now new competing models of citizen journalism, with more outlets delivering news.

Furthermore, the mobile phone is depicted not only as an opportunity to send and receive personal-interest messages, but also as a new medium for information retrieval.[10] To sate the Chinese thirst for cheap prices, fast connections and global information, China has become the biggest mobile communication carrier in the world, both in terms of customer base and network scale since 2007. The mobile phone as a medium affords

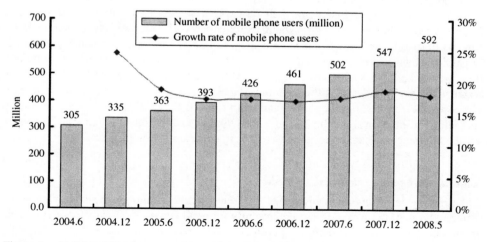

Figure 1. Valid mobile phone users' growth in China: 2004–08.
Source: CNNIC.

a useful model to understand how the media and ordinary people in China interact. Based on a theoretical outline of mobile communication in general, this essay discusses the specific role of mobile communication during the Beijing 2008 Olympic Games using the example of Chinese migrant workers. The intent of this essay is to analyse some of the effects of mobile media on Olympic Games knowledge among migrant workers in both rural and urban areas in Fuzhou, the capital city of southeast China's Fujian Province. It also discusses some implications for using mobile telephony in order to provide both possible connections within society and necessary information for migrant workers, in addition to taking part in and contributing to any aspect of knowledge spreading and citizenship development in China.

The Beijing 2008 Olympic Games and mobile phones

The Beijing 2008 Games is the first time that digital media coverage of the event – including live broadband Internet coverage and mobile phone clips – was widely available throughout the world from official rights holders' websites. Mobile phones were the high-speed wireless connection service that allowed for a personal approach to get Olympic information; also they became the most important new carrier to spread news in the 2008 Beijing Olympic Games.[11] Both the third-generation (3G) mobile phone, based on the Chinese 3G standard, known as TD-SCDMA (Time Division Synchronous Code Division Multiple Access), and cell phones with common functions such as messaging, Multimedia Messaging Service (MMS) and Internet access also were able to act as media to receive the Olympic news. With these applications, work staff, volunteers and ordinary people could enjoy high-speed data transmissions, which allowed them to watch televised games, receive mobile newspapers, and surf the Internet on their cell phones. China Mobile, the sole cooperative partner for the Beijing Olympics of mobile communications services, provided promotional events for the Beijing 2008 Olympic Games information service. It cost only RMB 0.4 Yuan each hour to watch the Olympic Games via cell phone, while the official mobile phone broadcaster of the Beijing 2008 Olympic Games had the ability to support 10,000 subscribers for real-time video transmission and 10,000 users for video-on-demand at the same time.[12]

In addition to the cheap cost of receiving the Olympic news, we should not omit to note that over 46% of the audience got their Olympic news from the Internet and Wireless Internet via cell phones, while more young white-collar workers, according to a survey from Iimedia Research, preferred to use mobile phones to catch up with the latest news about the Olympic Games, especially when they were on their way to work or the restroom, or before they went to bed.[13] In China, over the 17 days of the Olympic Games, 153 million people watched the live broadcasts of the Olympic Games online, with an average 20 million page views per day on the mobile phone platform provided by CCTV.com.[14] As a result, in spreading information about the Beijing 2008 Olympic Games, the use of mobile phones to get the Olympic news emerges as a very striking communication technique.

Migrant workers and their use of media

Although the term *migrant worker* has different official meanings and connotations in different parts of the world, it is used currently for residents from China's less-developed areas who go to work in more prosperous coastal areas and big cities.[15] According to statistics from *Study Times* (學習時報), an official newspaper of the Party School of the Central Committee of the Communist Party of China, the current number of migrant workers in China is estimated at 200 million, or nearly 15.4% of the population.[16] One of important characteristics Chinese migrant workers have, according to state statistics,[17] is that they are fleeting transients in cities easily attracted by a high-income, better work opportunities and living conditions in urban areas. Recent estimates put the number of migrant workers migrating to urban areas (urban working population) to over 140 million, with the growth rate of 6 to 8 million each year.[18] And the total number of working population in urban areas has already surpassed that in rural areas. When placed in a new social context such as the urban environment, however, migrant workers are always faced with concomitant physical, emotional and intellectual demands.[19] Moreover, city governments cannot offer enough housing, education and other environmental infrastructures to temporary residents. Most migrant workers do not enjoy the same basic rights as ordinary urban citizens, nor are their family members allowed to live in cities, unless they are able to find urban jobs as well. As a result, ways of information seeking have become an important tool used by migrant workers to search for jobs, find better work opportunities or seek health information. As the country tries to bridge the widening income and literate gap, according to Professor Ge Jianxiong,[20] fair competition and information seeking for migrant workers is on the top of the government agenda. Media literacy, or the ability to access, analyse, evaluate and create messages in a wide variety of media for finding useful information, is an important component of individual information seeking ability.

It is interesting to note that the mobile phone penetration rate among migrant workers, according to the survey from China Youth and Children Research Center, is 72.9%, much higher than the average mobile phone penetration rate in China, 45.5%.[21] A study by Renmin University of China also reveals that the mobile phone penetration rate among left-behind children, 7.8%, has lagged *far behind* the average mobile phone penetration rate amongst migrant children, 38.2%.[22]

Research question

Based on the above brief overview, this study will now consider the questions relevant to knowledge of the Beijing 2008 Olympic Games and the mobile phone use of migrant workers between rural and urban areas in Fuzhou, the capital city of southeast China's Fujian Province, as of June 2008 to September 2008. With over 40% of farmers seeking jobs outside their local areas, Fujian Province also has attracted migrant workers from all over China after the strategy of building-up the Economic Zone on the West Side of the Straits was announced, calling for more workforces from rural areas. Taking No.1 Centre Elementary School of Gulou District, Fuzhou as an example, the population of children of migrant workers, 1,080, soared to 72% of total students there.[23]

The study reported here focuses on the key research question: How does the relationship between demographics and knowledge about the Beijing 2008 Olympic Games issues differ according to the use of mobile phones among migrant workers?

The study focuses on the following characteristics of migrant workers, among others: 1) demographics; 2) orientation toward the mobile phone as an information source; 3) community involvement and attachment; 4) social contact; and 5) communication with news sources. Also I will focus on the role of the mobile phone in producing transformations in values and personality. Changes in values and attitudes, it can be argued, are far more important to modernity than mere changes in behaviour. The focus is also on how the government and the official press appreciate mobile media as a means of broadcasting official information, such as calling for participation in the Olympic torch relay; the popularizing of knowledge in the future; and for experiencing an increase in the awareness of participation in public affairs. Focusing on data collection, fieldwork and survey, and population selection based on their relevant surrounding mobile communications, I shall also provide further recommendations on how to harvest the potential of mobile communication among migrant workers.

Perspectives and relevance

Acting as a complex sparkplug for human life, the mobile phone enables people to create their own micro-cultures, change cultural norms and values, and demonstrates consumers' ability to modify and repurpose technology for their own use.[24] Critical studies argue that mobility does not inevitably oppose centralized power; mobility can reinforce central hierarchical imperial power, or have the ability to disrupt the structure of social interaction at several levels, and even can frustrate users' attempts to communicate.[25]

Some studies have focused exclusively on the mobile phone's development in China. Looking into the hierarchy of relative influences on the intention to adopt a mobile phone, Louis Leung and Ran Wei sampled Hong Kong and suggest that the effects of age and social differences far outweigh those of the technological differences.[26] Tao Jianjie once investigated media access,[27] both traditional ones and mobile phones, for migrant workers in Shanghai's Xuhui District. Field observation and interviews on the spread and use of mobile phones among migrant workers were conducted by Yang Shanhua and Zhu Weizhi in South China's Pearl River Delta,[28] although it only captured an early stage of such a spread mostly from the motivation of mobile communication use. The *China Youth Daily* published the above mentioned study on *Media Literacy between the Left-behind Children and the Migrant Children in Cities* which made public the fact that the mobile phone penetration rate among the left-behind children at 7.8%[29] has lagged *far behind* the average mobile phone penetration rate in the migrant children, 38.2%.

Literature evaluation

Most Chinese studies have emphasized the influence of mobile phones during the SARS epidemic.[30] The mobile phone has been used to mobilize supporters of political causes while the government has made concerted attempts to not only to register SIM cards and identity cards, but also to block these messages at source. There are specificities to mobile adoption as well as the urban and information ecologies of China that make it something of an outlier case, at least in comparison to Asian countries such as Japan and Korea. Discussions only recently have begun to revolve around exterior features, such as SMS, although they have lacked in-depth arguments or comprehensive investigation of the sociological impacts. Little attention was paid to a less unequally distributed technology, such as the ubiquitous mobile phone and its media reliance and media preference within migrant workers. The spread of the Olympic Games influence on migrant workers had not attracted any attention in previous studies.

Method

Survey research

A two-step approach was adopted for the empirical research. Firstly, the study aimed to find out the existence of differences in adoption, acquisition and usage of mobile phones among migrant workers. I differentiate between those people in the rural and urban areas because they represent one of the largest mobile phone user groups and are easily influenced by mobile phones in China, trying to find out how and why their patterns of mobile phone usage vary.[31] Random interviewees were chosen among the sample population of migrant workers in urban and rural areas in Fuzhou, in representative factories and shopping malls, spanning both the metropolitan areas and the surrounding, less industrialized, belt. Local official statistics departments, the CNNIC's annual report, data from Fujian Branch of China Mobile and China Unicom companies provide demographic information.

The second step was to design a questionnaire for face-to-face interview, after preliminarily drafting the demographic data about the relationship between the mobile media use and attitudes toward communication preferences and knowledge on the 2008 Beijing Olympic Games.

The graphs included:

- Basic data: age, gender, education, career, socio-economic status, usage time, browse content and preference;
- Attitude data: attitude and knowledge towards the Olympic Games and usage time with mobile phone;
- Behaviour data: improved understanding of media using performance. More importantly, it can be used to segment customers based on behaviour, thus to define criteria for different categories of mobile media owners.

Ethnographic research

We obtained detailed information about migrant workers using mobile phones in natural settings like factories, companies, as well as on the street from personal observation with in-depth exploration and interviews over extended periods of time. My research group also joined factories and communities as participant observers to examine and assemble a picture of how the migrant workers used mobile media to explore their own identities and to create new ones. In particular, I summarized the raw data to understand the information demands of mobile phone users from low-income and migrant workers. An open-ended questionnaire was introduced. Interviewees were able to talk freely within these questions, encouraging a full, meaningful answer using the subject's own knowledge and/or feelings.

Progress plan

Sample procedure

At first we selected companies which had over 50% migrant workers amongst their total worker population from both rural and urban areas in Fuzhou, then sent out our requests and sample questionnaires at the beginning of May 2008. After receiving permission,[32] we went to the companies to popularize the questionnaire knowledge and dispel any misgivings among migrant workers. The survey data collection procedure used a random sampling protocol, and followed voluntary principles, to produce a statistically representative sample of the migrant workers' population in companies we interviewed. We started to obtain detailed information about migrant workers using mobile phones in natural settings like factories, companies, as well as on the rural streets from personal observation with in-depth explorations and interviews over extended periods of time at the end of May. The research group joined communities once a week as participant observers to examine and assemble a picture of how these sample migrant workers used mobile phones. Two days after the Beijing Olympic Games started (10 August), we began an open-ended questionnaire on the information about the Olympic Games and mobile phone use, then left the questionnaires with interviewees during the Olympics. The questionnaires were sent back by the sampled migrant workers from 25 August. We finished the data collection on 5 September 2008.

Demographic data

The number of sampled migrant workers in this study is 111. The proportion of females among the sample is 29%, while males take up 63% of the total sample. The remaining 8% did not provide their gender information in the questionnaires. The majority of the sample are young people of 26 to 30, which accounts for 25% of migrant workers interviewed, reaching one quarter of the total amount of people; the next groups include people aged 31–35 and 21–25, which account for 17% and 16% respectively, then, people aged 36–40 and 41–45, both of which account for 12%. The young age structure of migrant workers has exerted great influence on the in-depth application of the mobile phones in the sample, for example, in the use of the online function.

The proportion of migrant workers regarding the mobile phone and television as their most frequently used media is the largest, both accounting for 27% (see Table 1). But most of migrant workers in urban areas did not have televisions in their dormitories.

The proportion of migrant workers with mobile phones in both urban and rural areas is very large, both accounting for over 90% (see Table 2), which reflects the popularization of mobile phones.

Findings and discussion

The data below is summarized from the questionnaire survey conducted from June to August 2008, designed and administered by the author. The survey data collection procedure followed random sampling protocol to produce a statistically representative sample of the migrant workers population in companies we interviewed.

Comparison of results between the rural and urban surveys

Table 1 lays out the relationship between the use of mobile phone and workplaces in rural and urban areas. Both the rural interviews and the urban survey show that migrant workers in both samples consider the mobile phone as one of the most important ways to get up-to-date information and frequently used the medium. But the chi-square test shows that the

Table 1. Most frequently used media among sample migrant workers.

Media	Percentage
Mobile phone	27
Television	27
Internet	22
Newspaper	12
Friends, colleagues, family members	8
Radio	3
Magazine	1

Table 2.   Mobile phone ownership among sample migrant workers

Urban (65 respondents)	Rural (45 respondents)	Missing (1 respondent)
91.7%	95.6%	100%

differences (the relationship of mobile phone use in the past workplace to the present workplace) are not significant (see Table 3, no.1).

The chi-square test shows that the differences between the present use of mobile phone and the workplace are significant (P = 0.002 < 0.05, see Table 1, no.2). The present workplace has a certain influence on use of the mobile phones.

Comparison of results between the workplace and the Olympic news

Two of our hypothesis propose the existence of differences in the present workplace and when and which channel was used to get the latest Olympic news. The chi-square test shows that the differences are not significant (see Table 1, no.3 and 1, no.4)

Regarding the existence of differences in the present workplace and the favorite media sources to get Olympic Games news in the future, the differences are statistically

Table 3.   Comparison of results between rural and urban survey (**t significant at p < .01)

		Pearson Chi-Square Asypm. Sig.(2-sided)	Lambda
1.	Self-assessed level of mobile phone use before	0.361	
2.	Self-assessed level of present use of mobile phone and workplace	0.002**	0.235
3.	The existence of differences of time for getting the latest Olympic news in present workplaces	0.457	
4.	The existence of differences amongst channels for getting the latest Olympic news in present workplaces	0.145	
5.	The existence of present workplaces for the favourite media sources to get Olympic news in the future	0.000**	0.067
4.	The existence of differences in present workplace and suggestions for media channel for migrant workers groups to get Olympic Games news in the future	0.006**	0.226
6.	The most frequently used media and when did you get the latest news about Beijing Olympic Games	0.498	
7.	The most frequently used media and the favourite media sources to get Olympic Games news in the future	0.580	
8.	The most frequent used media and which channel did informants use to get the latest Olympic news	0.000**	0.122
9.	The most frequently used media and suggestions about media channels for migrant workers groups to get Olympic news in the future	0.000**	0.126
10.	The frequency of mobile phone use and when informants got the latest Olympic news	0.146	
11.	The frequency of mobile phone use and which channel informants got the latest Olympic news from	0.098	
12.	The frequency of mobile phone use and the favourite media sources to get the Olympic news in the future	0.058	
13.	The frequency of mobile phone use and suggestions about media channel for migrant workers groups to get Olympic news in the future	0.000**	0.052

significant at the 95% level (P = 0.000 < 0.05, see Table 6.1–5). It indicates that both the rural and urban workplaces have had an impact on the sampled migrant workers' decision on which are their favourite media sources they would prefer to use to obtain Olympic news in the future. However, the influence is little due to the extremely low correlation (Lambda = 0.067, see Table 1, no.5).

Also regarding the existence of differences in the present workplace and the suggestion on media channels for migrant workers groups to get the Olympic news in the future, the differences are statistically significant at the 95% level (P = 0.006 < 0.05, Lambda = 0.226, see Table 1, no.6). It indicates that both the rural and urban workplaces have an impact on the sample migrant workers to decide by themselves which media approach will be best for them to receive the Olympic news in the future.

Comparison of results between the most frequently used media and the Beijing Olympic Games

Two of our hypotheses were about the most frequently used media and when did informants get the latest Beijing Olympic Games news and their favourite media sources to get Olympic news in the future. The chi-square test shows that the differences are not significant (see Table 1, no.7 and no.8)

Regarding the most frequently used media and which channel was employed by informants to get the latest news about the Beijing Olympic Games and their suggestions on media channels for migrant workers groups to use to get the Olympic news in the future, the differences are statistically significant at the 95% level(P = 0.000 < 0.05, Lambda = 0.122, see Table 1, no.9; P = 0.000 < 0.05, Lambda = 0.126, see Table 1, no.10). It indicated that the most frequently used media has an impact on the sample migrant workers to decide by themselves which media approach would be best for migrant workers to receive the news about Olympic Games in the future, as well as where they got the latest Olympic Games news.

Comparison of results between the use of mobile phones and the news on Beijing Olympic Games

Regarding the frequency of mobile phone use and when and which channel informants used to get the latest news about the Beijing Olympic Games and the favourite media sources to get Olympic news in the future, the chi-square test shows that the differences are not significant (see Table 1, no.11, no.12 and no.13)

Regarding the frequency of mobile phone use and suggestions about media channel for migrant workers groups to get the Olympic Games news in the future, the differences are statistically significant at the 95% level (P = 0.006 < 0.05, see Table 1, no.14). It indicates that the frequency of mobile phone use now has an impact on the sampled migrant workers to decide by themselves which media approach will be best for migrant workers to receive the new of Olympic Games in the future. However, the influence is small due to the extremely low correlation (Lambda = 0.052, see Table 1, no.14).

Comparison of results on the workplaces, the use of media and the frequency of mobile phone use

The present workplace has an influence on the use of the mobile phone. The existence of differences in present workplaces (rural or urban areas) had the biggest impact on the sample migrant workers' decisions about which media approach will be best for migrant workers to use in order to get the Olympic news in the future. The most frequently used media also indicates its impact on both the media channels about the latest new and future information on the Olympic Games.

The frequency of mobile media use, as well as the existence of differences in the present workplace (rural or urban areas) influences the sample migrant workers to decide which media approach would be best for migrant workers to receive Olympic news in the future. But both influences are statistically insignificant.

Comparison of the results on media use, media preference and audience expectations on Olympic Games news in urban areas

As shown in Table 4, TV is the primary source of Olympic Games news for all three groups (the media use, media preference and audience expectations), but actually not significantly more as the respondents considered mobile phones and the Internet as their second and third sources, due to the lack of television sets in the dormitories of migrant workers according to our interviews.

Examples from the field

Migrant workers seemed to experience a bit of anxiety at the time of their first interview. It seemed to be particularly challenging because this interview also contained a presentation component with personal information. Over the period of two months of pre-field research, April and May, the author used text messaging to encourage and support the migrant workers who had completed their first interviews. Often all that was required was a short text message to the migrant workers, telling them that what they had provided would improve the understanding of media use among migrant workers. The information also gives advice to organizations, such as those working on the protection of migrant workers' rights, to collect migrant workers' complaint data via new media.

Zhang Qixun (張其訓)

The father of an 8-year-old girl, phoned his left-behind daughter in his hometown Longyan, a prefecture-level city in south-eastern Fujian province, twice a week on average. By being able to stay in touch via SMS, Zhang and his daughter were able to have a talk usually to provide the support and encouragement that his daughter needed to complete course assignments and to keep track of the course requirements, while performing an important family connection. Zhang had learned about multimedia messaging and mobile on-line

Table 4. Comparison of results on media use, media preference and audience expectations on the Olympic news in urban areas.

Media	Media Use	Media preference	Audience Expectations
Mobile phone	23.1%	16.9%	4.6%
Television	30.8%	44.6	83.4%
Internet	21.5%	21.5%	0%
Radio	1.5%	3.1%	3.1%
Newspaper	13.8 %	7.7%	3.1%
Others	9.3%	6.2%	5.8%

functions from his employers but never used that. He thought it was 'useless and a waste of money' for him and the migrant workers.

He took out his mobile phone and showed me a text message when I asked him which Olympic event holds most interest for you? This message came from his daughter telling him that He Wenna, who also came from Longyan, just had won the first Olympic trampoline gold on 18 August 2008. Zhang remembered that he shared the news immediately with his colleagues while he also forwarded the message to his fellow-villagers as he was an opinion leader.

Wen He (文和)

A 22-year-old graduate from the senior middle school who was working as a home delivery staff member. He was one of the migrant workers who was familiar with accessing the Internet via mobile phones. Wen's mobile online duration was over five hours every week, the longest one in our survey. Funds, the stock market and news became the main topics when he surfed the Internet with his mobile phone. Wen He received the news that Michael Phelps and the US team squeaked in to win the 4x100m freestyle relay on 11 August 2008 from the mobile phone three days before our interview.

Wen had already changed his mobile phone number three times. But he never changed his mobile phone, saying it was 'unnecessary'. He once sent a text message expressing his concern at the latest pricing package from China Mobile, since he appreciated the service provider's promotion programmes, saying: 'I always pay attention to the promotion programs by China Mobile. I prefer to switch to a new number to top up my mobile as soon as I know there are some promotion programs.'

Such a trend, according to Luo Guoquan, director of the news centre, Fujian Branch China Unicom Corporation Limited,[33] was supported by the implementation of the zero-monthly-fee cards that allowed mobile phone use without a basic monthly rate. Moreover, calls can still be received when the card runs out of credit.

Huang Xiaoyan (黄小燕)

A 25-year-old, worked as an assistant in a building material company in Luoyuan Bay and often used the computer during her work time. The Internet jumps to the most frequent used medium with Huang, who spent between half an hour and one hour everyday surfing the Internet. Online chatting was currently the top internet application and an important entertainment source for her. Most of the Olympic news, as a result, was obtained from the Internet by Ms Huang; however, she could not remember and specify any details. Ms Huang chose the newspaper as her favourite media source for the Olympic Games news since she earned her junior college diploma and 'it's convenient to read a newspaper as an assistant'.

A migrant worker L (anonymous)

Works as a carpenter in Fuzhou Higher Education Mega Center. He did not have and never had used a mobile phone since he did not think it was necessary to have one. However he intended to buy a second-hand mobile phone, mainly to use to contact his family members. Information about the Olympic Games came from his friends, but he could not remember any details or when he received it, because 'it already took me all day time to finish my work and I don't have time to concern myself with the Olympics'.

The majority of migrant workers in our fieldwork seemed to use mobile phones for maintaining family and social relationships. Messages received from migrant workers over the three months of June to August ranged from anxious requests for leave to apologies for missing or being late for work, and messages of seeking work opportunities, to appointments to even dirty jokes.

Conclusion

During this study, using mobile phones to communicate with others and obtain Olympic Games news was a way of providing connection and up-to-date knowledge on the Olympic Games, where migrant workers were likely to spend fewer hours at home and were also more likely to lead a busy, complex life in which the work, family and social interactions made demands on their time. Migrant workers were managing the rest of their time with the aid of mobile phones and text messaging, being able to manage their lives in the same fashion seems to make sense. Results also show that the mobile phone is essentially an urban medium for communication, because the sharing and requisition of information is relatively small in the villages.

The existence of differences in workplace (rural or urban) areas had the biggest impact on the sampled migrant workers to decide by themselves which media approach would be best to receive the Olympic news in the future. The most frequently used media channel also indicated an impact on both the media approaches about the latest news and future information on Olympic Games. It is interesting that television became the primary source of media used to obtain Olympic Games news, and was also the main media preference and fulfilled audience expectations from migrant workers, but actually this was only slightly significant as the respondents considered mobile phones and the Internet as their second and third sources. *Renmin Daily* cited a migrant worker's feedback as an example, saying that he could receive the latest Olympic news and cheer for the athletes' success through the *People's Mobile Newspaper on Olympic Games*, overcoming difficulties such as the shortage of TV sets in his workplace.[34] We should not omit that interviewees remembered well the exact information they got from mobile phones while they invariably failed to recall the news from the Internet or their friends. Due to the limitation of 160 characters, including letters, spaces and numbers in a text message, as well as the limited screen and size of mobile phones, information left a deeper impression on users. In relation to the average mobile media penetration rate as discussed in previous studies,[35] the sampled migrant workers and their information expectations, we should not ignore the mobile phone's effect on the spread of the Olympic Games influence.

Many modern problems will be resolved through information use and a highly informed public. One of the great promises of mass communication is that it will help alleviate these problems by providing people with the information they need. Mass communication has the potential of reaching people who have not been reached by other means. These people include low-income rural dwelling families as well as the ethnic minority groups in China. Mass communication will also provide vital information to the needy in under-developed countries in the world, many of whom have even less access to the media than those in China. Communication is regarded as a mean of influencing learning motivation.[36] Song and Cornford suggest the government increasingly regards the mobile phone as a channel for information and public services.[37] Technology influences human actions and social structures, and human action and the social context of these actions also shapes technology. Mobile phones will be a relevant approach toward that aim.

Notes

[1] An earlier version of this essay was presented at 'Documenting the Beijing Olympics' conference, organized by the School of Oriental and African Studies (SOAS) at the University of London, September 12–13, 2008. I wish to thank Dr Kevin Latham and Ms Ding Yimin for their invaluable suggestions on earlier drafts of this essay. I also acknowledge Dr Lola Martinez and Dr Kevin Latham for their editorial assistance in the preparation of this essay. The essay is a product of a research project funded by the Innovation and Technology Fund, Fuzhou University (project no. 2007-XY(S)-06). It's also a product of a research project by the Central Committee of the Communist Youth League of China (project no. 2008GH158).

[2] McLuhan, *Understanding Media*.

[3] Lax, *Access Denied*, 3.

[4] Cooper and Kimmelman, *The Digital Divide*; Hoffman and Novak, 'Information Access'; Katz and Aspden, 'Motives, Hurdles, and Dropouts'; McConnaughey and Lader, *Falling through the Net II*.

[5] CNNIC (China Internet Network Information Center), *Statistical Reports*, 10.

[6] Calum MacLeod, 'China Vaults Past USA in Internet Users'. *USA TODAY*, April 20 2008, 1.

[7] Levison, *The Story*; Sieber and Valor Sabatier, 'Uses and Attitudes'.

[8] CNNIC, *Statistical Reports*.

[9] Latham, 'SMS, Communication', 303.

[10] Rice and Katz, 'Comparing Internet'; ITU, 'Asia-Pacific Telecommunication/ICT Indicators 2008 Broadband in Asia-Pacific: Too Much, Too Little?' 2008, 7th ed. http://www.itu.int/ITU-D/ict/publications/asia/2008/index.html.

[11] XINHUANET, 'Mobile Phones Become the New Carrier to Spread News in the Beijing 2008 Olympic Games'. August 15, 2008. http://news.xinhuanet.com/olympics/2008-08/15/content_9346917.htm.

[12] Zhao, 'Only RMB 0.4 Yuan Each Hour to Watch the Olympic Games via Cell Phone', 7.

[13] Zhang, 'Survey: The Beijing 2008 Olympic Games will Make a Thorough Face-lift of China's Structure of Wireless Internet Users'. 2008. http://jeszhang.blog.163.com/blog/static/32112258200871711825865/.

[14] EBU (European Broadcasting Union), 'Beijing 2008: The Digital Games'. 2008. http://www.ebu.ch/en/union/news/2008/tcm_6-62839.php.

[15] Li, *Urban Migrant Workers*.

[16] Liu, 'Survey on the Migrant Workers in China', 4.

[17] Research Office of the State Council, *Report of the Survey*; Wei, *Survey on the Migrant Workers*.

[18] Xu, 'Report on State Council's "Opinion on How to Resolve Problems Related to Migrant Workers" in 2006', 2.

[19] Ge, 'Immigration and China's Modernization', 12.

[20] Ibid.

[21] Wang, 'Migrant Workers in New Generation: The Most Noteworthy Social Group', 5; CNNIC, *Statistical Reports*.

[22] Deng, 'It's Beyond our Expectation that the Average Mobile Phone Penetration Rate in the Migrant Children is Very High', 2.

[23] Liu, 'Survey on the Migrant Workers in China'; Lai, 'Three Expectations for Migrant Workers in the New Year, Expert Advise to Speed Up the Reform of the Household Registration'. February 18, 2007. http://news.cnwest.com/content/2007-02/18/content_432073.htm.

[24] Levinson, *The Story*; Katz and Suygiyama, 'Mobile Phones'.

[25] Agar, *Constant Touch*; Ling, *The Mobile Connection*; Katz and Aakhus, *Mobile Communication*.

[26] Leung and Wei, 'Who are the Mobile Phone Have-nots?'.

[27] Tao Jianjie, 'Media Access', 44–95.

[28] Yang and Zhu, 'Mobile Phone'.

[29] Deng Jing, 'It's Beyond our Expectation', 2.

[30] Liu, 'On Communication'; Xia Qianhua and Ye Xiaohua, 'National Media Coverage'; Xu and Yan, 'An Investigation'.

[31] CNNIC, *Statistical Reports*; Wang Qinghuan, 'Migrant Workers in New Generation', 5.

[32] One company in urban and four from rural areas were chosen. They are Fuzhou NANXI Garment Co., LTD (福州市南夕服装有限公司) in an urban area with 75% migrant workers population; Fuzhou Minlian Wood Industry Limited Company (福州闽聯木業有限公司) with over 70% migrant workers population; Flexible Packaging Science & Technology Garden at Economic Zone on the West Side of the Straits (海峡西岸軟包裝科技園) with 50% migrant workers

population; and Luoyuan Shanlin Food Products Co. Ltd (羅源山林食品) with 51% migrant workers population from rural areas. We also selected migrant workers in Fuzhou Higher Education Mega Center to finish our interviews. The companies in rural areas were all located in the Luoyuan Bay Economic Technical Developing Zone, one of Fujian Province's six over-50,000-ton deep-water port terminal berths. A resource for a further development of the waterfront building, Luoyuan Bay's transportation and air transportation is convenient. It had been identified as Fuzhou's output bay, and the second largest category of commercial bay in Fujian province, opened the air line to Hong Kong, Japan, Singapore and other routes directly.

[33] Interviews with Mr Luo Guoquan (羅國權), director of news centre, Mr Wang Yukun (王宇坤) and Mr He Guidong (何桂東), both operation managers, at the office of Fujian Branch, China Unicom Corporation Limited, July 17, 2008.

[34] *People's Daily* Online, 'People's Mobile Newspaper on Olympic Games had been Well Received by the Readers'. 26 August, 2008. http://wireless.people.com.cn/GB/113340/113370/7731655.html.

[35] Wang Qinghuan, 'Migrant Workers in New Generation', 5; Deng Jing, 'It's Beyond our Expectation'.

[36] Horstmanshof, 'Using SMS', 426.

[37] Song and Cornford, 'Mobile Government'.

References

Agar, Jon. *Constant Touch: A Global History of the Mobile Phone*. Cambridge, UK: Icon Books, 2003.

CNNIC. *Statistical Reports on the Internet Development in China: The 22th Survey Report*. 19 July, 2008. http://research.cnnic.cn/img/h000/h10/attach200906151611110.doc.

Cooper, Mark, and Gene Kimmelman. *The Digital Divide Confronts the Telecommunications Act of 1996: Economic Reality Versus Public Policy*. Washington, DC: Consumer Union, 1999.

Deng, J. 'It's Beyond our Expectation that the Average Mobile Phone Penetration Rate in the Migrant Children is Very High'. *China Youth Daily*, April 14, 2008.

Ge, J. 'Immigration and China's Modernization'. *China Press and Publishing Journal*, June 6, 2008.

Hoffman, D., and T. Novak. 'Information Access: Bridging the Racial Divide on the Internet'. *Science* 280, no. 5362 (1998): 390–1.

Horstmanshof, Louise. 'Using SMS as a Way of Providing Connection and Community for First Year Students'. In *Beyond the Comfort Zone*, R. Atkinson, C. McBeath, D. Jonas-Dwyer and R. Phillips, 423–427. Perth: Proceedings of the 21st ASCILITE Conference, 2004. http://www.ascilite.org.au/conferences/perth04/procs/horstmanshof.html.

Katz, James E., and Mark Aakhus. *Mobile Communication, Private Talk and Public Performance*. Cambridge, UK; New York: Cambridge University Press, 2002.

Katz, J.E., and P. Aspden. 'Motives, Hurdles, and Dropouts: Who is On and Off the Internet, and Why'. *Communications of the ACM* 40, no. 4 (1997): 97–102.

Katz, J.E., and S. Suygiyama. 'Mobile Phones as Fashion Statements: The Co-creation of Mobile Communication's Public Meaning'. In *Front Stage–Backstage: Mobile Communication and the Renegotiation of the Social Sphere*, edited by R. Ling and P. Pedersen, 63–81. London: Springer-Verlag, 2006.

Latham, Kevin. 'SMS, Communication, and Citizenship in China's Information Society'. *Critical Asian Studies* 39, no. 2 (2007): 295–314.

Lax, Stephen, ed. *Access Denied in the Information Age*. New York: Palgrave, 2000.

Leung, Louis, and Ran Wei. 'Who are the Mobile Phone Have-nots? Influences and Consequences'. *New Media & Society* 1, no. 2 (1999): 209–26.

Levinson, Paul. *The Story of the World's Most Mobile Medium and How It Has Transformed Everything!* New York: Palgrave Macmillan, 2004.

Ling, Rich. *The Mobile Connection: The Cell Phone's Impact on Society*. Amsterdam: Elsevier, 2004.

Li Qiang. *Urban Migrant Workers and Social Stratification in China* (農民工與中國社會分層). Beijing: Social Sciences Academic Press, 2004.

Liu Hailong. 'On Communication and Control of Rumors from the "Atypical Pneumonia" Case in Guangzhou'. *Journal of International Communication* 2 (2003): 40–46.

Liu, W. 'Survey on the Migrant Workers in China'. *Study Times*, January 9, 2006.

McConnaughey, J., and W. Lader. *Falling through the Net II: New Data on the Digital Divide.* Washington, DC: US Department of Commerce, 1998.

McLuhan, Marshall. *Understanding Media: The Extensions of Man.* New York: A Signet Book, McGraw-Hill Book Company, 1964.

Research Office of the State Council. *Report of the Survey on the Migrant Workers in China.* Beijing: China Yanshi Publishing House, 2006.

Rice, Ronald E., and James E. Katz. 'Comparing Internet and Mobile Phone Usage: Digital Divides of Usage, Adoption, and Dropouts'. *Telecommunications Policy* 27 (2003): 597–623.

Sieber, Sandra, and Josep Valor Sabatier. 'Uses and Attitudes of Young People toward Technology, and Mobile Telephony'. eTransformation, 16th Bled eCommerce Conference, Bled, Slovenia, 9–11 June, 2003.

Song, G., and T. Cornford. 'Mobile Government: Towards a Service Paradigm'. *2nd International Conference on e-Government*, University of Pittsburgh, Pittsburgh, 12–13 October, 2006.

Tao Jianjie. 'Media Access for Mobile Labors in Shanghai Xuhui District'. *Journalistic University* 44–7 (Winter 2003): 95.

Wang, Q. 'Migrant Workers in New Generation: The Most Noteworthy Social Group'. *Guangming Daily*, June 22, 2007.

Wei Cheng, ed. *Survey on the Migrant Workers in China.* Beijing: Law Press China, 2008.

Xia Qianhua, and Ye Xiaohua. 'National Media Coverage of SARS Crisis (February to May 2003)'. *Journalism & Communication* 2 (2003): 56–65.

Xu Huiming, and Yan Sanjiu. 'An Investigation on Rumor Spreads in Guangzhou SARS Incident'. *Journalistic University* 4 (2003): 36–43.

Xu, J. 'Report on State Council's "Opinion on How to Resolve Problems Related to Migrant Workers" in 2006 (國務院關於解決農民工問題的若干意見起草紀實)'. *People's Daily*, March 30, 2006.

Yang Shanhua, and Zhu Weizhi. 'Mobile Phone: Selecting on Their Own Initiative under the Background of Globalization'. *Social Sciences in Guangdong* 2 (2006): 168–173.

Zhao, W. 'Only RMB 04 Yuan Each Hour to Watch the Olympic Games via Cell Phone'. *Beijing Daily*, July 29, 2008.

Olympiad, a place of linguistic struggle – the discursive constitution of 'human rights' in the 2008 Beijing Olympics

Yihjye Hwang

Modern East Asia Research Centre, Leiden University, PO Box 9515, 2300 RA Leiden, The Netherlands

This article investigates the Beijing Olympics as an event that incited people in the contemporary international community to talk about 'human rights', and to engage in the discursive proliferation of human rights. China experienced three waves of this discursive proliferation of human rights in 2008: firstly, through anger at foreigners over Tibet and the torch relay; secondly, in grief after the Sichuan earthquake, and thirdly, in pride at the successful games. Certain conceptions of human rights were brought to the fore during these three periods of time. This article aims to study the competing discourses over human rights among different political forces, such as international human rights groups, pro-Tibetan Independence groups, and the Chinese government. All of them speak, or appear to be speaking, of one and the same thing: the 'human rights'. Things being said in turn underpin the production of particular conceptions of 'human rights'.

Introduction

Zhang Danhong, a Chinese woman working as an editor at the Deutsche Welle radio station in Germany, was suspended from her job in mid-August of 2008 following remarks she had made in the media four days before the opening of the Beijing Olympics. She said that 'The Communist Party of China has more than any political force in the world implemented Article 3 of the Declaration of Human Rights'; referring to the fact that the Chinese authorities were pulling more than 400 million people out of poverty. This remark, however, was met by a strong reaction from German society as well as various overseas Chinese communities, i.e. political dissidents and Falun Gong practitioners. They attacked Zhang as someone who was 'courting' China's Communist Party regime, a regime with one of the worst records on human rights in the world. A couple of days later, Zhang was temporarily relieved of her duties. The suspension brought about an equally strong backlash however. A group of German Sinologists signed a petition, asking the radio station to restore Zhang's position. Many people in China have also voiced sympathy and concern for Zhang, accusing those in the West who chant the slogans of human rights and freedom of speech of hypocrisy. Zhang's case demonstrates the clash of different conceptions of human rights that occurred as Beijing hosted the 2008 Olympic Games.

Hosting a modern Olympics in China is said to be a century-old dream of many Chinese. Committed to the concepts of 'Green Olympics', 'Hi-Tech Olympics' and 'People's Olympics' under the theme of 'One World, One Dream', China aimed to create an unforgettable sporting event, which indeed proved to be highly successful. The games were also intended to present to the world an image of China as a nation whose human rights record has improved significantly, in the sense that the quality of people's lives has made considerable progress.[1] The choice of the concept 'People's Olympics' was intended mostly to present China as a nation that cares about its people. Nevertheless, in the run-up to and throughout the Games, China also faced international scrutiny over its human rights' record. Many parties in the international community used the Games to draw attention to various political/human rights issues that were associated with China. They argued that while the Chinese government was facing the dilemma of sacrificing either Olympic glory or its standpoint on various political issues, there was an opportunity to pressure Beijing into making concessions. In this sense, the Beijing Olympics suddenly became not simply a physical site of competition among athletes, but a discursive space in which different political forces, with different positions, forms and organizations, mutually competed and contested, interacted and intersected in a field structured by relations of power. The whole event was a confrontation between discourses, conducted discursively. This essay aims to speak of those political battles, of those confrontations, and to discover the interaction of discourses as weapons of attack and defence over the issue of people's 'human rights'.

The concept of 'human rights' often refers to the basic rights and freedoms to which all humans are entitled. Those rights are normally taken as given. Indeed, it is now widely held that all human beings possess certain political, civil, economic, social and cultural rights simply by virtue of their humanity.[2] Some, at least, further extend this position by arguing that the international community ought to act to ensure that all human beings are able to claim these rights when they are violated. The given-ness of such rights might be questioned, however, if we follow Friedrich Nietzsche's suggestion that everything that we hold as solid, taken-for-granted, and certain about the world is, upon closer examination, accidental and contingent.

In his *On the Genealogy of Morality*, Nietzsche presents a critique of taken-for-granted moral concepts. He asks: 'under what conditions did man invent the value judgements good and evil? And what value do they themselves have?'[3] What is required in studies of morality, according to Nietzsche, is 'a revaluation of all values'. For Nietzsche, the principle of these values (good and evil) themselves must be called into question. What Nietzsche tells us here is that the idea of 'truth' is itself a kind of construction made under specific conditions. Inspired by Nietzsche, Michel Foucault paid attention to the discursive nature of those taken-for-granted 'truths'.[4]

The social entity, for Foucault, is itself a form of discursive constitution. Foucault argues that discourse 'systematically forms the object of which they speak'.[5] When we 'speak' of an object/subject, the object/subject is formed as a result of our 'speaking'.[6] The term 'discourse' in common usage means 'a *coherent* or *rational* body of speech or writing'.[7] Foucault however uses this term with a much broader and involved meaning. 'Discourse' is understood as highly diverse, fragmented and heterogeneous in nature. It is a realm that includes both linguistic and non-linguistic acts, a synthesis that encompasses discursive practices and social practices, and a domain in which discursive practice and social practice are exercised.[8] In view of this understanding, when it is stated that an object/subject is constituted in discourse, the term 'discourse' refers to a domain of dispersion, in which various discursive and social practices intersect, intertwine and interact. The social entity, accordingly, resides only in discourse, in its exteriority – that is, discursive and social practices – and this is all there is.

Moreover, it is noted that the discourse involves a complex set of practices that keeps certain statements, utterances and conducts in circulation, while silencing other statements, utterances and conducts.[9] One cannot just 'say' and 'do' what one wishes to 'say' and 'do'. The use of words and actions has limits. The complex sets of practices involve the play of power, thereby implying the production of exclusion and inclusion. Indeed, only certain discourses are disseminated in society, accordingly only certain forms of object/subject are formed. 'Truths', which are generally regarded as complete and absolute, are in fact limited and contingent. They are not naturally given, but contingent socio-historical constructs of discursive practices. Accordingly, Foucault suggested to 'reverse' what we believe to be 'truths', and to study 'truths' from their exteriorities.[10]

Following Nietzsche and Foucault's line of thought, this essay problematizes the concept of 'human rights'; it aims to analyse the concept in its exteriority rather than its hidden core of meaning. The essay argues that: There was no such thing as 'human rights' in the first place; nor is 'human rights' a single thing; it is subject to different practices – people's speech and actions. The idea that there is such a thing as 'human rights' grew gradually. What this thing amounts to is subject to different kinds of practices. Each practice has an input, making it possible to talk about 'human rights' and attach a specific substance to it. And this process of construction is not simply one way, either. Particular discourses of human rights in turn make certain actions possible, sustaining or undermining what people say and do. The concept of 'human rights' is therefore conditional, lodged in contingency. 'Human rights' in this aspect should be seen as a dynamic and fluid, rather than as a static, value. The connotation of 'human rights' is always deterred and deferred. It never has final or fixed meaning, and each 'stop' is arbitrary and contingent. The value of human rights is not naturally given, but exists in the way people talk and act. In other words, there is no such thing as 'human rights' outside of this process of constitution; 'human rights' exist only in discourse.

Moreover, this essay investigates the Beijing Olympics as an event that has incited people in the contemporary international community to talk about 'human rights', and to engage in the discursive proliferation of human rights. China experienced three waves of this discursive proliferation of human rights in 2008: firstly, through anger at foreigners over Tibet and the torch relay; secondly, in grief after the Sichuan earthquake, and thirdly, in pride at the successful games. Certain conceptions of human rights were brought to the fore during these three periods of time. This essay aims to study the competing discourses over human rights among different political forces, i.e. international human rights groups, pro-Tibetan Independence groups, the Chinese government, and the Chinese netizens. All of them speak, or appear to be speaking, of one and the same thing: 'human rights', and all try to define the term 'human rights' or conceptualize 'human rights'. This essay will scrutinize their discourses, analysing the statements, utterances and conducts that were made by those who have various positions, in an attempt to comprehend how the discourses of human rights reciprocally conflict and compete with each other in ways that produce different conceptions of human rights.

In sum, this essay is about how we ought to understand the issue of human rights in general. By taking the Beijing Olympics as an illustration, it argues that we need to treat the issue of human rights as a realm of discursive conflict. The question of human rights is no longer one of whether Asian nations accept human rights or reject it as a 'Western notion', as the debate over so-called 'Asia values' has touched upon,[11] but a question of what we mean by human rights – who gets to define them and how. In what follows, the essay in succession shows how different discourses competed with each other in the torch relay, the earthquake and the Games. The conclusion argues that although 'human rights' are non-fundamental, the essay does not claim that human rights are fictitious entities. Rather, it is a notion that needs to be sustained, substantialized, and promoted on the discursive ground – what people say and do.

Right to self-government: a conception of human rights in the torch relay

On 31 March 2008 China launched the Olympic torch relay with a televised ceremony in Tiananmen Square. Chinese officials hailed it as the 'journey of harmony'. Nevertheless, the torch relay had been marked by protests and disturbances since it started in Athens, representing a wide range of political issues related to China's human rights record. The most prominent issue, among many others, was the issue of Tibet,[12] as the torch relay was held right after the unrest that took place in Tibet in March 2008.

The 2008 Tibetan unrest began with a series of demonstrations in Lhasa and elsewhere in Tibet on 10 March 2008, the forty-ninth anniversary of the failed 1959 uprising against China's rule. In the beginning, the demonstrations were peaceful, but they quickly turned violent. On 14 March the demonstration in Lhasa grew into a riot, in which mobs attacked civilians – mainly ethnic Chinese – along with burning and looting. Beijing, in response, sent troops in to crackdown on the protest. The riot caused the deaths of many people. The Government of Tibet in exile claimed that over 200 Tibetans were reported to have died, and thousands had disappeared. Beijing disputed these figures, placing them at less than a tenth of this total.[13]

The Tibet riot cast a harsh light on China just as it prepared for the Olympic Games. The torch relay, in particular, became a magnet for critics of China's policies in Tibet and human rights activists. Protesters disrupted stops in many cities along the route of the international leg, especially in London, Paris and San Francisco. The leaders of many countries in the West, such as France, also voiced their indignation at Beijing, threatening to boycott the opening ceremony. Those protests in turn provoked a fierce reaction from many Chinese who felt their country was being humiliated. Counter-demonstrations were held in a number of cities around the world. During this period of time, several conceptions of human rights were being articulated. The collective right to self-government in particular, advocated by many overseas Tibetans and their sympathizers, was brought to the fore. This line of argument – the Tibetan rhetoric, as this essay terms it – contended that the collective right to self-government is the most fundamental basic right.

First of all, in the Tibetan rhetoric, the indigenous right of the Tibetan people, a nation that possess its own tradition, language, culture, religion, etc., has been violated under the 'colonial' rule of the Chinese. Tibetans are being outnumbered in their own land due to the huge wave of Han-Chinese settlement. Its distinctive culture and identity have been gradually fading away as many Tibetans have been obliged to adopt the community standard of the majority in Tibet, the Han-Chinese people. This is said to constitute a form of 'cultural genocide', resulting cultural, social, economic, and political marginalisation of the indigenous population. Tibetans are therefore entitled to resist the Han-Chinese culture in the name of preserving their own culture and their distinctive identity. This conception of 'human rights' was clearly revealed in the statement of Tibetan's spiritual leader, the 14th Dalai Lama, on the 49th Anniversary of the Tibetan National Uprising Day. In the statement, the Dalai Lama noted that

> In Tibet today ... as a result of their [the Chinese government's] policy of population transfer the non-Tibetan population has increased many times, reducing native Tibetans to an insignificant minority in their own country. Moreover, the language, customs and traditions of Tibet, which reflect the true nature and identity of the Tibetan people are gradually fading away. As a consequence, Tibetans are increasingly being assimilated into the larger Chinese population.[14]

Other 'rights' that are affiliated to the indigenous right in the Tibetan rhetoric include linguistic, cultural and religious rights. In terms of linguistic rights, the freedom to use and develop the Tibetan language needs to be guarded. It is said that the Tibetan language is the primary means of daily communication among Tibetans. Tibetan's historical, literary, spiritual as well as scientific works are all written in the Tibetan language. In terms of cultural rights, Tibet's distinct cultural heritage and tradition need protection, as they are facing threats at various levels. In terms of religious rights, Buddhism is regarded to be fundamental to Tibetans, intimately connected to their identity. Religious rights ought to cover the freedom of the manner of belief or worship. Thus Beijing should not interfere in religious practices and traditions, such as 'the relationship between a teacher and his disciple, management of monastic institutions, and the recognition of reincarnations'.[15]

Moreover, economic rights are also stressed in the Tibetan rhetoric. The Tibet plateau, the world's highest plateau, is regarded as rich in natural resources untouched by human exploitation, including minerals, forests, water and so forth. Although various development projects that Beijing implements such as the Western Development Economic Plan or the Qinghai-Tibet Railway have benefited the indigenous population, many Tibetans believe that the Chinese people have reaped more benefits from the development and utilization of Tibetan's natural resources. As a British newspaper noted, 'life might have got better for some indigenous Tibetans after years of economic growth, but they see Han-Chinese migrants doing a whole lot better and at their expense'.[16] 'Development' in this vein, for Tibetans, turns out to be a brutal exploitation and the dispossession of their inherited lands. In the view of Tibetans, the right to possession of land is the foundation on which economic activities are based. It is therefore essential that only the indigenous population is entitled to have the legal authority to formulate and implement developmental plans, and have rights to profit from the development.[17]

Because a collective wrong has been perpetrated, a collective cure is represented as the appropriate solution. One of the remedies supported and advocated by the Dalai Lama for the disappearance of Tibetan culture/identity and economic inequality is a 'genuine autonomy' for Tibet. Over time, the Dalai Lama has been promoting what he calls 'Middle Way Approach', in which Tibetans accept Chinese sovereignty in exchange for genuine autonomy. The Dalai Lama and his proponents argue that the Tibetans' culture and identity can only be preserved and promoted by the Tibetans themselves, but not by others. Affairs that are associated with Tibet/Tibetans ought to be decided by Tibetans. Hence, it is imperative that the right of Tibetans to govern themselves is implemented throughout the region where the Tibetans reside. This approach is audibly elaborated in a memorandum proposed by the Government of Tibet in exile in the eighth round of Tibetan-Sino talks held between 31 October and 5 November 2008. The Dalai Lama's position on 'genuine autonomy' can be summarized as follows.

Firstly, the integrity of the Tibetan nationality must be recognized. The memorandum notes: 'There is no dispute about the fact that Tibetans ... belong to the same ethnic group and that they have a strong sense of common identity.' Secondly, the memorandum notes that it is indispensable that 'the entire [Tibetan] community, comprising all the areas currently designated by the PRC as Tibetan autonomous areas, should be under one single administrative entity'. Before 1949, Tibet was comprised of three provinces known as U-Tsang, Amdo and Kham, which, nowadays, are divided and administered under different Chinese provinces. The so-called 'Tibetan Autonomous Region' (TAR), established in 1965, is less than half the landmass of Tibet with only one-third of the total Tibetan population. Hence, the boundaries of Tibetan national autonomous areas ought to be modified, incorporating TAR and all other historically Tibetan-inhabited areas. Thirdly, there ought to be a restriction on the movement of other peoples – mainly, the Han-Chinese people – migrating to Tibet. The memorandum states:

the very principle and purpose of national regional autonomy is disregarded if large-scale migration and settlement of the majority Han nationality and other nationalities is encouraged and allowed. Major demographic changes that result from such migration will have the effect of assimilating rather than integrating the Tibetan nationality into the Han nationality and gradually extinguishing the distinct culture and identity of the Tibetan nationality.[18]

Finally, the practice of 'genuine autonomy' ought to include the right for Tibetans to create their own government that possesses powers to legislate on all matters within the competencies of the region, and to execute and administer decisions independently. Beijing, without the consent of the Tibetan regional government, cannot change the basic features of this autonomy.

In contrast to the Dalai Lama's position, another solution, advocated by many exiled Tibetan groups – most prominently, the Tibetan Youth Congress (TYC)[19] – works toward more radical goals, calling for political independence of Tibet. Their political standpoint was in evidence in a series of protests in the run-up to, and throughout, the Beijing Olympics. One example among many is a hunger strike lunched by the TYC in New Delhi between 28 July and 24 August 2008, entitled 'Indefinite Fast for Tibet – without Food and Water'.[20]

The protest began on 28 July with an inaugural ceremony, followed by three groups of six hunger strikers, each sitting and fasting for nine days. The selection of six hunger strikers in each group – 18 strikers in total, aged from 19 to 63 including monks as well as laypeople – was to symbolically represent the plight of the six million Tibetans. The organizers aimed to demonstrate that their movement transcended age as well as class, having a pan appeal in the Tibetan community, in opposition to the idea presented by Beijing that only the monks supported their appeals. A speaker at the inaugural ceremony told the hunger strikers that they were 'fighting for a just cause, for human rights, for Tibet's sovereignty, for your own culture and to protect your own education system'.[21] A press release issued on 21 August 2008 spelt out the reason for the strike. It stated:

> Human life is truly precious, but also what's the use of life if there is the absence of the basic dignity, associated with life, the absence of honour and of a satisfaction which can only be described as 'identity'. It is for this basic Tibetan identity, encompassing numerous elements that the six have set on this path of martyrdom.[22]

In this context, the term 'human rights' is conceptualized as upholding distinctive Tibetan culture and identity. China's rule over Tibet, a colonial occupation, is regarded as a violation of Tibetans' rights, in a sense that Tibetans have been deprived of their culture and identity. The demonstrations that took place in March therefore not only reflected the Tibetan people's dissatisfaction with the status quo, but also demonstrated their determination to continue their struggle for the inherent right to be a Tibetan. Moreover, Beijing's crackdown on the demonstrations further violated various civil and political rights of Tibetans, such as freedom of expression, assembly and association, and freedom from torture, arbitrary arrest and detention. During China's occupation the cultural, civil and political rights of the Tibetan people have been seriously violated.

It is interesting to note that although various human rights violations are touched upon in the aforementioned discourse, the origin of those violations is crucially said to be Tibet's lack of sovereignty. The appropriate cure is therefore to regain its sovereignty. Only on the day when Tibet becomes again an independent country, as the TYC noted in the hunger strike, will Tibetans be able to enjoy 'freedom of speech, of religion, of association, of equal opportunity, of electing their own government, of feeling safe in their own homes'.[23] Hence, to end the Chinese occupation is the single largest, if not the only, challenge to the principles enshrined in the contemporary human rights regime for

Tibetans. And Tibetans wanted to seize the Olympic opportunity to shine a spotlight on the Tibet issue and their quest for complete, sovereign and political independence.

In short, it is Tibetan identity that is at stake in the Tibetan rhetoric, and its culture that is under duress. Only by full implementation of the rights to self-government – either genuine autonomy or complete independence – can the Tibetan identity be safeguarded, thereby ensuring respect for the Tibetan people's cultural, economic, civil and political rights. Collective human rights in this rhetoric are the prerequisite and guarantee for the full realization of individual human rights. Individual human rights cannot be truly realized until self-government is made in a nation – the Tibetan nation – as a whole.

Counter-discourses in the torch relay: right to security and other conceptions of human rights

Responding to this sort of criticism, Beijing tried to present its own version to the international community. Beijing rejected the claim that the 'human rights' of Tibetans have deteriorated. In Beijing's version, the Chinese government has improved the lives of indigenous Tibetans considerably, compared to the Dalai Lama's rule prior to the 1940s. A press conference held by the Chinese government on 9 April 2008 in response to the March unrest in Tibet clearly conveyed this line of argument.[24]

Qiangba Puncog, an ethnic Tibetan and the chairman of the Chinese Government of the TAR, said that 'human rights' in every aspect have made huge progress in Tibet since 1959. In terms of economic rights, Puncog noted that Tibet has registered an annual GDP growth rate of over 12% for seven consecutive years, and the region's infrastructure has improved greatly. Indeed, Beijing has frequently emphasized economic developments, livelihood improvements and the construction of infrastructure in Tibet. In China's White Paper on Tibet published in 2004, the document indicated that GDP in Tibet today is 30 times greater than it was before integration into the PRC. The result of this economic growth is an increase of life expectancy (from 35.5 in 1950s to 67 in 2004) and a growth in the Tibetan population (from 1.20 million in 1964 to 2.50 million in 2003).[25] The Chinese government proceeded to say that they would stick to those measures to accelerate economic development in the future. In contrast to the Tibetan view, Beijing understands its development plans as a benevolent project to help Tibet to improve its prosperity and living standards. Alongside economic development are the improvements of social and cultural rights. According to Qiangba Puncog, Tibet had witnessed a rapid social development, by which he referred to education, medical services and other social welfare. Moreover, he noted that Beijing has also invested a fortune to repair Tibet's temples, cultural relics and religious sites.[26] The claimed cultural accomplishments were further reiterated in China's White Paper on Tibetan Culture published in September 2008, in a defence against accusations made by Tibetan exiles.

Nevertheless, if people in Tibet have achieved huge progress in the region's economic development, along with the social and cultural rights, why was there unrest in Tibet in March? The unrest, according to Beijing, was not about the human rights, but about the ethnic conflict instigated by the Dalai Lama and his proponents. Beijing openly accused the Dalai Lama of using his moral and religious authority to foment the unrest, in an attempt to use the Olympics to publicize the cause of Tibetan independence, with the ultimate aim of trying to restore the old feudal order of serfdom.

According to Beijing, Tibetan exiles intended to take the Games hostage and force the Chinese government to yield on the Tibetan independence issue. In Beijing's rhetoric, the Dalai Lama and his proponents staged various coordinated activities in order to create sensational effects and attract the world's attention, calling for international pressure on Beijing. For instance, some pro-independence Tibetan exiles in early March 2008 launched the 'Marching into Tibet' campaign in Dharamsala, with a plan to penetrate the China-India border and arrive at Lhasa on the eve of the Games. Meanwhile, the 'Tibet Independence Torch Relay' was also staged to revive the spirit of the Tibetan National Uprising of 1959 and to counter China's Olympics torch relay. The Dalai Lama himself, before the conclusion of the 2008 Beijing Olympics, had an extensive speaking schedule in the UK, India, Germany, Britain, Australia and the USA. All those activities, in the opinion of Beijing, were by no means a coincidence but coordinated, planned and linked. In this vein, the riot in Tibet in March was interpreted as part of a Tibetan independence movement, 'premeditated, organised and instigated by the Dalai clique', in Chinese officials' words.[27]

To publicize its version of the March unrest in Tibet, Beijing highlighted innocent civilians being assaulted by rioters. The Chinese state-controlled Xinhua News Agency reported that many ethnic Han-Chinese shop owners or employees were left dead or critically wounded. State television showed in its footage dozens of monks and crowds of rioters throwing rocks and bombs. Videos that depicted protesters attacking stores in Lhasa were disseminated throughout China. In addition, Beijing allowed websites in China – which are usually heavily censored – to show graphic, violent images of Tibetans looting and attacking civilians in Lhasa. The nature of Tibetan protests was defined as 'criminal' and 'violent', portrayed as a 'serious criminal act of violence involving beating, destruction of property, looting and arson' – a situation which prompted the Chinese officials to question 'if any democratic government under the rule of law would tolerate such violence' as they had in Lhasa?[28]

The specific conception of human rights being raised here is the right to security. In Beijing's rhetoric, security, defined as a 'state of existence free from fear', is a fundamental human right. 'Everyone has the right to live peacefully and safely. Threats to peace and security come not only from international wars and conflicts but from domestic violence, organised crimes, terrorism and weapons of mass destruction.'[29] If the right to security is not respected, one can enjoy neither political and civil, nor cultural and social rights. Society is capable of offering individuals more freedoms only under the conditions of peace and security. The March riot was regarded as a threat to the security of the people in Tibet.

Moreover, given this conceptualization of the term security, poverty also endangers people's security. In Beijing's narrative, Tibet before 1959 was a society languishing under theocratic rule and a system of feudal serfdom. Ordinary people did not have any rights to speak of. In that period of time, the Dalai Lama, as a leader of Tibetan Buddhism and also head of the Tibetan government, monopolized power in every aspect. The serf owners, making up less than 5% of the total population of old Tibet, possessed all the resources in Tibet and absorbed the whole wealth of the region. The rest of the population – the serfs and slaves – suffered destitution and famine. The majority of Tibetans could hardly be assured of their basic right to survival. Tremendous changes have taken place in the region since 1959, particularly after the China's adoption of a reform and opening-up policy. In Beijing's rhetoric, the Chinese government has made great efforts to eliminate poverty in Tibet. It is in this respect that Beijing claims that the human rights situation 'has never been so good in Tibet as it is today'.[30]

This conception of 'human rights' in fact overlaps with another notion: that of 'basic rights'. According to Henry Shue, basic rights are 'everyone's minimum reasonable demand upon the rest of humanity', which is composed of two rights: The first is the right to security, which refers to 'physical security' – a right to be free from 'murder, torture, mayhem, rape, or assault'. And the second is that of subsistence rights, or the 'minimal economic security', which alludes to 'unpolluted air, unpolluted water, adequate food, adequate clothing, adequate shelter and minimum preventive public health care'. Shue argues that without physical security and minimal economic security, no one is in a position to exercise any other kind of right, i.e. political and civil rights. These two rights are basic because 'enjoyment of them is essential to the enjoyment of all other rights'.[31] In other words, they are the rights upon which other rights rest.

In Beijing's rhetoric, the majority of the Tibetans under feudal serfdom were subjected to ruthless oppression, exploitation and barely possessed any personal freedom. Tibet's integration into the PRC which led to the abolition of theocratic feudal serfdom in 1959, is accordingly interpreted as the 'liberation' of the broad masses of serfs and slaves from the monopoly of a minority of nobles and senior monks. The failed uprising against the Chinese rule in 1959 is read as a movement initiated by a group of people in the upper ruling strata of Tibet, trying to preserve feudal serfdom, opposing 'democratic reform'.[32] In promoting this version of Tibetan history, Beijing in 2009 declared a new annual holiday in Tibet, called 'Serfs' Emancipation Day', falling on 28 March, the date on which Beijing announced the dissolution of the Dalai Lama-led government in 1959.[33] On that account, Beijing argued that those Tibetans in exile who claim to be speaking on behalf of Tibetan people – i.e. the Government of Tibet in exile – do not represent all of their constituents. Their political entreaty to be independent, it is argued, involves overriding the rights of individuals in the name of collective rights. Here, ironically, Beijing privileges the rights of individuals over communities, while its critics speak for collective rights against individual rights.

In short, in Beijing's rhetoric, the features of political practice in Tibet under the Dalai Lama were patriarchy, hierarchy and indeed anti-democracy. The Chinese Communist Party organ *People's Daily* therefore commented that it was paradoxical that those who present themselves as the defenders of human rights asked the Dalai Lama to dwell on human rights in Tibet.[34] In addition, they also sharply criticized foreign/Western reporters over their coverage of the riots in Tibet. What happened in Lhasa, in their view, was 'far more complicated than "the Chinese government's ruthless crackdown on Tibetan protest"', in the words of a Chinese writer.[35] Noting that the West 'always brags about human rights and freedom', they asked 'so why does it turn a deaf ear to the serious human rights abuse of attacks on and killings of innocent people in Tibet?'[36] Not only the official, but also the ordinary Chinese contended that the Western media are biased and irresponsible, spouting anti-Chinese opinions.

The Olympics are hugely popular among the Chinese. As Susan Brownell contends, it is a projection of national sentiment wishing to wash off the historical humiliation of being invaded by the Western powers in the nineteenth century. China is no longer 'The Sick Man of East Asia', and wishes to demonstrate its return to global power in the twenty-first century.[37] The disruptions in the torch relay entrenched the feeling held by many Chinese that their country was being insulted again. This sentiment was particularly strong among young, educated Chinese, including those who were studying aboard. This bottom-up nationalist indignation found a place to grow in cyberspace. Chinese netizens set up the website Anti-CNN.com to strike back at CNN for 'fabricating news', and many MSN users put a 'Red Heart China' in their screen name. Several Internet campaigns were organized to boycott foreign businesses in China, such as French supermarket chain Carrefour. As a result, much of the Western criticism of China's human rights record became discredited in the eyes of ordinary Chinese. Western conceptions of human rights were eclipsed to some degree in Chinese communities.

In addition to Beijing's rhetoric, many other conceptions of human rights also emerged. Following on the heels of the unrest in Tibet, several political issues associated with China, such as Falun Gong, China's treatment of North Korean refugees, the imprisonment of Chinese political dissidents, Taiwan independence and the Xinjiang problem were also brought forward, becoming big news in the world media. Various dimensions of human rights were emphasized, such as religious freedom, the right to pursue freedom and a better life, freedom of expression and legal rights. Although these issues cannot be elaborated upon within the scope of this essay, it is worth noting that they collaborated with each other in achieving their respective goals. Many political/rights activists during this period of time were urged to form a united front in the protest against Beijing. For instance, some Chinese dissidents held a press conference in Taipei a few days before Taiwan's 2008 presidential election to boost the bid of the pro-independence candidate of Democratic Progressive Party. While condemning Beijing's crackdown on Tibet, they spoke of other human rights abuses associated with China, and urged that anyone threatened by the Beijing regime – whether they are 'Tibetan, Taiwanese, a Falun Gong member, underground churches, or a democracy activist' – should all stand together to protest against the Chinese government.[38]

It should also be noted, however, that as those engaged with various political issues collaborated under the banner of human rights in the aftermath of the Tibet riot, they were at the same time excluded or marginalized from the human rights agenda due to the unrest in Tibet. For instance, some Taiwanese independence advocates during this period of time seemed very anxious about the Taiwan issue being ignored. They published several articles in Taiwan appealing to put more efforts into advocating Taiwanese independence. One of these articles argued that international pressure over the Tibet issue had been well earned, but in terms of sheer scale, the Taiwan issue did not receive equal attention.[39] Another example is the Darfur issue. Before the unrest in Tibet, much international pressure over human rights had focused on the Darfur problem. But after the unrest, the world community seemed much less concerned over the genocide in Darfur. Hence, the whole event cannot simply be described as a single battle, fighting between Beijing and exiled Tibetans. In effect, several separate yet intersecting battles were being fought out at the same time.

In short, many human rights activists were being driven by the belief that the Beijing Olympics Games were their opportunity to challenge the Chinese government's position. During the torch relay it seems that they had succeeded in making 'Tibet' and 'human rights' the dominant issues. The torch relay, being a component of a Chinese public diplomacy or soft power strategy, was intended to improve China's image. Yet, as many political commentators noted, it turned into a public relations disaster. As those activists vowed to step up their protests in the run-up to the Games, the Sichuan Earthquake, nevertheless, shifted the ways in which people talked about 'human rights'. It was indeed a 'tectonic shift'.[40]

'People coming first' in Sichuan earthquake: the discourse of the right to live

An earthquake measuring 7.9 on the Richter scale occurred on 12 May 2008 in Sichuan province of China. The disaster killed at least 87,000 and left millions of people homeless less than three months prior to the Beijing Olympics. The disaster, however, provided 'a good opportunity' for China to repair the damage to its international image that had resulted from the unrest in Tibet, turning it overnight from the status of victimizer to victim. New faces of 'China' – humane, benevolent and efficient – emerged.

Beijing was quick to respond to this natural catastrophe, a response quite unlike its dire management of the Tangshan earthquake in 1976. Rescue teams were quickly dispatched to disaster-hit areas within hours. Just 90 minutes after the earthquake occurred, Chinese Premier Wen Jiabao flew to the affected area to oversee relief efforts in person. On the same day, the People's Liberation Army (PLA) also dispatched tens of thousands of troops to help with disaster relief work. The government also accepted all foreign offers of aid, including foreign rescue teams from Japan and other countries. Moreover, Beijing decided to allow media to show the full scale of the disaster. China's national TV services such as CCTV gave rapid response, providing timely and round-the-clock coverage of the earthquake. The Western media's praise of the government's rapid, efficient and open disaster relief efforts was worded as strongly as its earlier condemnations of China's appalling human rights records and its brutal suppression of the Tibetan people.[41]

The Chinese government tried to link its responses to the earthquake with its human rights' record. The spokesman of Chinese Foreign Ministry made the following remarks at a regular press briefing: 'In this earthquake you can see that the Chinese government has carried out a "people-centred" relief effort ... this clearly shows that the Chinese government respects and protects human rights.'[42] The political message in this remark is that the Chinese government puts people first and is dedicated to maintaining and promoting its people's right to life. This message can be summarized into a single political motto of the Chinese Communist Party (CCP), 'People Coming First'.

The notion is not new to the CCP's propaganda rhetoric. In fact, it could be said to have been the principal ideology of the CCP for a long time. The term has been briefly defined as putting the people's interests above everything and serving the people wholeheartedly. Mao Zedong, in his report to the 7th National Congress of CCP in 1945, noted:

> Our point of departure is to serve the people whole-heartedly and never for a moment divorce ourselves from the masses, to proceed in all cases from the interests of the people and not from the interests of individuals or groups, and to understand the identity of our responsibility to the people and our responsibility to the leading organs of the Party.[43]

In this statement, Mao reiterated that the CCP should always exercise its power solely for the sake of people, safeguard the public interest, and let people see the prospects for the prosperity and rejuvenation of the nation as well as for the happiness of its people. In the CCP's rhetoric, the term has been regarded as China's/CCP's implementations of promoting human rights. Beijing had earlier dismissed the expression of 'human rights', as it had been identified as 'bourgeois idea'. It was not until 2004 that China incorporated 'respect for and protect human rights' into its Constitution.[44] Nevertheless, according to Beijing, this by no means implies that the Chinese government did not value human life or ignore 'human rights'; China instead exercised its human rights practice by adhering to the spirit of 'putting people first'.

In 2008, 'People Coming First' was vividly spoken about in Chinese official rhetoric in the wake of Sichuan earthquake. It was the main theme of Chinese discourse on 'human rights' amid the earthquake rescue and relief. 'People's lives' were particularly stressed in the elaborations of the notion. As an editorial of *People's Daily* noted, the essence of the term is 'the people's lives being above anything else'. The article wrote:

> life, either an individual life or the life of every Chinese citizen, is placed at the place of paramount importance. It is essential to show the respect and solicitude for and the understanding of people, to protect them and be at their service, and to explain the connotation of the concept of 'making people first'.[45]

In this rhetoric, the right to life is enunciated as the highest value in a country like China, which has to encounter frequent natural calamities and an acute shortage of per-capita resources.[46] The rescue and relief efforts were to put 'People Coming First' into practice. Political mottos such as 'Ensuring the safety of the people's lives', 'Saving lives is the priority' and 'A gleam of hope, a hundred percent of effort' were frequently used and quoted by Chinese officials during that period of time. And, as the Chinese People's Liberation Army (PLA) was the backbone of the rescue and relief efforts in the earthquake, it is said that the army represented a strong guarantee for the existence of human rights.

Furthermore, the rhetoric of 'People Coming First' discredited values that emphasize individual liberties and rights. It argued that individual liberties and rights are not without limitation. This way of thought was reinforced in a debate right away after the earthquake, stirred by a schoolteacher who left all his students behind, dashing to the playground by himself while the quake was taking place. When asked by his students why did he not wait to take them out, the schoolteacher replied that he was only concerned about his own life. He further noted that he was a person who was in pursuit of liberty and justice, but not one who would sacrifice his own interest for the good of others. The schoolteacher later reiterated this viewpoint in his blog, and added that he felt no moral guilt at all.[47]

The aforementioned remarks caused strong resentment among the Chinese population. Many netizens in China lambasted the schoolteacher and argued that, as many people like the PLA soldiers went to the stricken areas to save lives, some even dying during the rescue operation, the schoolteacher's remarks that built upon 'Western individualism' were inappropriate and deplorable. An article in *Human Rights Magazine* writes:

> The 'universal values' that emphasise individual freedom and rights also made some show during the disaster. However, amidst thousands of people who fought the disaster and saved others in spite of their personal safety, the sporadic shows of 'universal values' appeared alien like noise.[48]

To those critics, the rule of 'universal values' could not be equivalent to the sacrifice of those who fought the disaster and saved others in spite of the risk to their personal safety.

On the basis of the above conception of human rights that give priority to people's lives, Beijing further condemned Western countries, which often see themselves as defenders of universal human rights, as hypocritical. For instance, an article in *People's Daily* strongly criticized the British House of Commons for holding a hearing on the issue of China's human rights and for inviting the Dalai Lama to speak at the hearing amid the earthquake rescue and relief. It wrote that at the time 'when the Chinese government and people ... are plunging themselves into the earthquake relief work and making every possible effort to save lives', such a move only 'poses a bitter sarcasm about some Western forces on the so-called human rights issue', treating 'the vital human rights issue merely as a trifle matter'. The article then continues saying that it is the governing concept of putting the people first and the national will of safeguarding human lives above anything else that have turned a tragic quake into a nationwide rescue of human lives. Therefore, according to the article, the evidence of China's human rights record lies in the actual relief efforts of the Chinese government.[49]

In short, amid the earthquake Beijing aimed to show that even an authoritarian government is capable, perhaps even more capable than 'the West', of responding to the needs and suffering of its people, and therefore, in a way, better at respecting 'human rights'.[50] This line of rhetoric appeared to be somehow convincing during this period of time. Even international human rights groups acknowledged Beijing's earthquake response as morally correct. A director of a human rights group in China said that '[t]he Chinese authorities have made efforts to demonstrate their respect and concern for human life'.[51] Indeed, amid the earthquake many in the outside world felt deep sympathy for China, and the bad feelings stirred by the Tibetan unrest seem to be fading, though the situation in Tibet did not fundamentally make much progress. The Sichuan earthquake not only offered Beijing an opportunity to improve China's national image; more importantly, it redefined the discursive agenda on human rights. The conception of the human right to life emerged as the dominant discourse.

The opening ceremony and the Games: the discourse of right to development

China finally got its Olympic moment on the night of 8 August 2008, when billions of television viewers watched the spectacular opening ceremony, with more than a hundred heads of state or government in attendance. The four-hour opening ceremony, directed by the Chinese filmmaker Zhang Yimou, could be read as the showcasing of China's 5,000 years of cultural splendour and its comprehensive national strength. However, equally importantly, through the opening ceremony, together with the Games itself, China also tried to convince the world that it had made considerable progress in its human rights record throughout 30 years of reform and opening up since 1978.

Beijing frequently noted that the adoption of China's reform-and-opening-up policy has not only scored remarkable achievements in terms of economic development, but also made great progress in terms of human rights in China and the world as a whole. The foremost achievement has been to lift millions of people out of poverty. The Chinese government claimed that poverty alleviation has turned out to be a brilliant success in China. The reform-and-opening-up policy has reduced the number in poverty significantly, which counts two thirds of the people worldwide being lifted out of poverty in the most recent 25 years. *People's Daily* wrote:

> In the past 30-year period ... China has reduced its poverty-stricken population to 20 million from the 250 million. Relevant data released by the World Bank last year [2007] showed that over the past 25 years, China accounted for 67 percent of the achievements in global poverty reduction.[52]

In addition to eliminating poverty, it is said that the policy has also rapidly improved the quality of life for the majority of ordinary people, building a society of relative prosperity in all aspects. In the opinion of Chinese officials, two historic leaps have been realized: firstly, from poverty to adequate food and clothing, and secondly, from adequate food and clothing to a reasonable standard of living.[53] The Beijing Olympics was particularly intended to present the latter facet, which was manifested in the following aspects.

The first is the improvement of infrastructure facilities. Infrastructure developments are regarded as an effective support for the promotion of human rights in the Chinese officials' view. In preparing to host the Games, the Chinese government devoted huge resources to building infrastructural facilities. Railways, roads, energy and other infrastructure were all upgraded. These developments have been said to come as a benefit to ordinary citizens.

Secondly, the Chinese government aims to show that its country has met Western standards of living. Environmental issues were in the spotlight. In preparation for the Olympics, many polluting factories were shut down and removed. There had been a large-scale project involving the reclamation of emissions at gas stations across Beijing areas since China won the bid in 2001. Other measures were also implemented to reduce pollution and improve air quality and environment in Beijing, such as the transformation of residential heating from coal to electricity, stricter vehicle exhaust standards, and the operation of an alternate-day driving system for odd-and-even-numbered license plates. Moreover, the newly constructed sports venues incorporated advanced building technologies and energy-saving systems. The National Stadium (or 'Bird's Nest') and its neighbouring Water Cube, for instance, are praised for their energy efficiency and sustainable design. They have been claimed to have a deeper influence in China's future development pattern in terms of its environment. The impression China means to convey is that 30 years of reform and opening up does not merely bring exterior transformations, but internal refinements in the country.[54]

Thirdly, the Beijing Olympics were intended to demonstrate the 'quality' of the Chinese population itself has been improved. The government embarked on a crusade in the run-up to the Games to 'civilize' its population by improving its manners. A number of campaigns were launched to fight against the so-called 'bad habits' and 'improper etiquette', such as spitting, littering, bad language or queue jumping. Banners urging good behaviour were raised across Beijing. Moreover, a large number of Olympics volunteers played the role of 'educators' helping the ordinary citizens to behave properly. The volunteers were trained to work hard to serve others, and to enforce small details like stopping at red lights and giving up seats for the elderly on public transportation. They were the crème de la crème of what 'a good Chinese citizen' is expected to be. The vice-chairman of the Chinese Olympic Committee told the local media that the Games 'is not simply a matter of competitive sports; it is also a question of raising the quality of the people'.[55]

In addition, Beijing tried to weave the story that the Chinese people today have a more mature attitude, featuring them as open, magnanimous, rational, tolerant and pluralist. The local media in China during the Games particularly highlighted this aspect. *People's Daily*, for instance, noted that the Chinese people during the Games showed none of the excessive nationalism feared by some foreign media prior to the Games.[56] The newspaper wrote:

> When sprinter Liu Xiang, gold medallist of 110m hurdle in Athens 2004 ... quit the games ... most Chinese expressed their understanding. Just 20 years ago, Chinese gymnast Li Ning, who won three gold medals in 1984 Los Angeles Games, found a bullet in an anonymous envelope after his poor performance in Seoul Games in 1988. Thanks to 30 years of development, China is more open-minded and confident, and hopes to merge more with the world in the spirit of the Olympic slogan 'One World, One Dream'.[57]

Likewise, an article in *Guangzhou Daily* described the Games as having served as a 'growing-up ceremony' for the Chinese population. It praised Chinese spectators at the Games for cheering for every wonderful performance and not booing at poor showings. The article commented that this phenomenon reflects the fact that the Chinese nation has built up its confidence, thereby becoming more tolerant.[58]

The changing quality of the Chinese population is said to be a result of incessant improvement in the economic, social and cultural rights of the citizens in China. In Beijing's rhetoric, the government since 1978, alongside economic development, has adopted various measures to strengthen support for education, culture, public health and other social undertakings. According to Chinese officials, China has almost eliminated illiteracy among the young and middle-aged population. The country now has a fairly high level of education. Beijing aimed to show this feature to the international community. *People's Daily*, when speaking about the opening ceremony, wrote:

In today's world, there are probably not many people who still perceive the Chinese people as a nation of 'men with pigtails and women with bound feet' as depicted in the Hong Kong Kung-fu movies, but the anecdotes about uncivilised and orderless Chinese are widespread around the world ... In reality, the Chinese people has become better educated with the development of the economy in recent years. As Chinese and Beijingers, are we ready? What should we show to the world?[59]

With those aforementioned achievements, Beijing's narrative about the past three decades claims that it has improved China's human rights record. In 1978, the story goes, the country had just emerged from the catastrophe caused by the Cultural Revolution – by that time the people were more focused on trying to feed themselves, and hosting the Olympic Games was inconceivable. Since then China has not only lifted millions of people out of poverty, but has helped them to become more a prosperous, open and better people. The Beijing Olympiad was a demonstration of this material and spiritual progress in terms of human rights achieved over the past 30 years. In this narrative, the notion of 'development' seems to be an all-inclusive key to the solution to all sorts of social problems in China.

Many scholars have argued that 'modernization' is the foremost, if not the only, theme of modern and contemporary Chinese history, and that 'development' is the indispensable way to achieve this goal whichever ideologies or approaches are adopted.[60] Deng Xiaoping's most famous quotation uttered in 1961 – 'I don't care if it's a white cat or a black cat. It's a good cat so long as it catches mice' – explicitly demonstrates this pragmatic mode of thought. In this vein, Beijing's leaders also believe that by choosing 'development' as its priority it has managed to improve the human rights of its people.

In Beijing's rhetoric, 'development' brings a very positive result in terms of 'human rights' in China's society. As represented through the Beijing Olympics, people in China now live a much better and far more secure, prosperous and well-off life; many of them have received a good education, and look outwards to the world with an open mindset. Moreover, development has given the Chinese people unprecedented personal freedom. The state has retreated from many parts of people's lives. People in China can now move around the country and travel aboard more freely; they can buy their own house, choose their own job, or even criticize government corruption in their daily conversations. In the meantime, society as a whole has opened up much more compared to a generation ago when it was still isolated from the rest of the world. Beijing contends that those who attack China over its human rights record overlook these points.

In this rhetoric, the 'right to development' is particularly highlighted. For the Chinese government, the right to development is a fundamental human right and of primary importance. A forum on human rights held by the Chinese government in Beijing in April 2008 fully elaborated this conception of human rights. Luo Haocai, the president of the China Society for Human Rights Studies, remarked in his speech at the opening ceremony:

> The right to development is an inalienable human right. Every person and every country have the right to pursue development and enjoy its fruits ... Development is the central agenda for the overwhelming majority of developing countries and the biggest human rights problem facing the world today. That's because development lays the groundwork for the full realisation of human rights. To advance other human rights, we should first of all realise the right to development, eliminate starvation and poverty and provide basic health care services.[61]

At the forum another speaker further contended that the Chinese government since 1987 has always put the realization of the people's right to life and development at the top of its agenda. He noted that by taking development as its central task, human rights in China have been considerably advanced. Chinese officials claimed in this way that 'China has made historic progress in human rights and that China's human rights conditions are in the best historical period'.[62]

In short, during the Beijing Olympics, China was at the centre of world attention. The Beijing's Games, to a certain extent, successfully represented the achievements made during 30 years of reform and opening up. Indeed, while there were still many negative stories about China in the Western media,[63] it should be admitted that at this point the scale and density of the criticism were much lower and more moderate. Even though the Games have not seduced everyone, a certain number of people in the West were dazzled by them. The fading of criticism over China's human rights record is a reflection of the precedence that China's conception of 'human rights' took over other alternatives, for example the rights of Tibetans to self-determination or civil and political rights in general.

Conclusion

The Olympic Games are never free from politics; the Beijing Olympic Games were no exception. They cannot be free from politics because they provide a space, an occasion, to bring different people with different political views together, interacting, intersecting and competing with each other. The Games incited people in the contemporary international community to 'speak' about the idea of 'human rights'.

In 2001 when Beijing won the bid for the 2008 Games, it promised the world that hosting the Olympics would improve its human rights record. The Beijing Olympics were indeed intended to demonstrate the achievements made in China in the last three decades, including the lifting of hundreds of millions out of poverty, prioritizing people's lives, and making them more prosperous, open and 'better'. Such achievements are interpreted as an improvement of China's human rights record. For the critics, the Beijing Olympics was conversely a chance to bring various human rights abuses, such as the authoritarian rule over, and unfair treatment of, minorities into the international spotlight. Many international human rights groups argued that China has broken promises made to Olympic organizers to improve human rights in the country. The riot in Tibet, particularly, demonstrates various cases of human rights abuses associated with China. Both sides speak of the human rights situation in China, but they speak about different 'human rights'. The Beijing Olympics, as this essay has shown, brought different conceptions of 'human rights' to the forefront. The whole event took place within the discursive realm of political battles and power relations, in which the different discourses constructing 'human rights' mutually interact, intersect and compete with each other.

Acknowledging the discursive nature of 'human rights' is crucial when the international community is trying to promote human rights globally, or to establish a moral foundation of universal human rights. As argued in this essay, the notion of 'human rights' rests upon a discursive ontology. It needs to be sustained, substantialized and promoted on the discursive ground – what people say and do. The Beijing Olympics in this particular aspect could be interpreted as promoting 'human rights' in general, as it incites people to talk about it in what might be described as the discursive proliferation of 'human rights'. However, we should keep in mind that many other potential conceptions of 'human rights' are excluded in this process of discursive proliferation. Moreover, the discursive proliferation does not necessarily lead to a coherent, or single conceptualization of 'human rights'. Instead, those conceptualizations are highly diverse and fragmented, not only in the way they are uttered but also in the content of what is uttered. Indeed, however much some may seek to monopolize the conceptualization of 'human rights', it is unlikely that reaching a consensus is possible. Counter-discourses are always there.

This essay finally suggests that the international human rights regime ought to be flexible enough to fully accommodate alternative conceptualizations of human rights in order to realize its essential purpose: to promote and protect vital human interests. Promoting 'human rights' in a way that does not seriously engage with alternative conceptions risks widening misunderstanding and setting the stage for hostility, resulting in the deterioration of the legitimacy of the notion. This was demonstrated in the event of the Beijing Olympics, where many Chinese resented the Western monopolization of the notion of 'human rights' and where there was anger among China's human rights critics about the repressive policies of the Chinese government. It should be noted that this essay by no means speaks for, or prioritizes, any particular conception of 'human rights', e.g. the rights to security or development, while undermining alternatives, e.g. political, civil or cultural rights. But it insists that the alternative voices have 'rights' to be heard. It is truly absurd that someone should seek to silence others while claiming that one is protecting the right to freedom of expression, as demonstrated in the case of Zhang Danhong mentioned at the beginning of this essay.

In this vein, this essay is not a deconstruction of the notion of human rights. Acknowledging the discursive nature of 'human rights' does not inevitably lead to the abandonment of the concept. Richard Rorty, for example, argues that human rights have no foundation, but defends and promotes human rights on pragmatic grounds.[64] This essay, in sum, is intended to be an exposition of the limits of the current international human rights regime, driven by a concern for the fuller inclusion of alternative voices of human rights into the current regime.

Notes

[1] See especially Brownell, *Beijing's Games*; Guoqi Xu, Olympic Dreams (2008). Many studies on the 2008 Olympics pay attention to its relationship with Chinese nationalism, economic developments and modernity. For nationalism, see Jinxia Dong, 'Women, Nationalism'; Xiaobo Liu, 'Authoritarianism'. For economic development, see Tomlinson, 'Olympic Values'. On modernity, see Collins, 'The Fragility'; Humphreys and Finlay, 'New Technology'.

[2] Brown, *Sovereignty, Rights and Justice*, 115–16. It is common to distinguish between three generations of human rights. The first generation of rights – civil and political rights – are laid down in Article 2-21 of the Universal Declaration of Human Rights (UDHA), including freedom from torture, arbitrary arrest, right to participate in government, freedom of thought, expression, association religion, etc. The second generation of rights – economic, social and cultural rights – are listed in Articles 22–27 of the UDHA, and elaborated upon in the International Covenant on Economic, Social and Cultural Rights. Examples of such rights include the rights to food, clothing and housing, rights to social security, etc. The third generation of rights – solidarity rights – are reflected in global protection of the rights of indigenous people, and some regionally specific declarations of human rights, such as Banjul Charter and Vienna Declaration of 1993. Those rights are more concerned with collective rights of 'peoples', which include the rights to political, economic social and cultural self-determination, and the rights to economic and social development of 'people'.

[3] Nietzsche, *On Genealogy of Morality*, 5.

[4] In his interview with Alessandro Fontana and Pasquale Pasquino, Foucault noted that 'Truth is a thing of this world: it is produced only by virtue of multiple forms of constraint. And it induces regular effects of power. Each society has its regime of truth ... that is, the types of discourse which it accepts and makes function as true; the mechanisms and instances which enable one to distinguish true and false statements, the means by which each is sanctioned; the techniques and procedures accorded value in the acquisition of truth; the status of those who are charged with saying what counts as true.' (Foucault, 'Truth and Power', 131) Foucault's series of historical analysis in works such as *Madness and Civilization* (1965), *The Order of Things* (1970),

Discipline and Punish (1977), and *History of Sexuality* (1978) can be read as studies of various modes of the construction of 'truths' in discourse.

[5] Foucault, *The Archaeology of Knowledge*, 49.

[6] For Foucault, the distinction between subject and object is interchangeable. This essay therefore punctuates these two terms with a slash.

[7] Turner *et al.*, *Penguin Dictionary of Sociology*, 'Discourse'. Emphasis added.

[8] The distinction between discursive practices and social practices for Foucault is highly ambiguous and, indeed, interchangeable. Laclau and Mouffe further elaborate this point, as they argue that any social practice has its discursive dimension; any discursive practice has its material foundations and is, in effect, a social practice (*Hegemony and Socialist Strategy*, 107–8).

[9] Foucault, *The Archaeology of Knowledge*, 31–9, 215–29; see also McNay, *Foucault*, 74–6.

[10] Foucault, *The Archaeology of Knowledge*, 229.

[11] The so-called Asia values discourse has been growing since the Bangkok Declaration on human rights of 1993, made by Asian ministers in the run-up to the Vienna Conference of that year. Some advocates of the Asia values denied the human rights promoted by the international society are genuinely universal. They argued that the contemporary human rights thinking is actually established upon, and indeed privileges, a Western view of what it is to be human and its conception of politics. For the debate about Asia values, see: Tang, ed., *Human Rights*; Bauer and Bell, eds, *The East Asian Challenge*; Jacobsen and Bruun, eds, *Human Rights*.

[12] Other issues include the war in Darfur, China's support to regimes in Myanmar and Zimbabwe, North Korean defectors, Falun Gong, Taiwan Independence, etc.

[13] 'Fire on the Roof of the World', *The Economist*, March 14, 2008. http://www.economist.com/daily/news/displaystory.cfm?story_id=10870258&top_story=1; 'China Keeping Tight Grip on Tibet', *BBC News Online*, June 3, 2008. http://news.bbc.co.uk/1/hi/world/asia-pacific/7433659.stm.

[14] The Office of His Holiness the Dalai Lama, 'The Statement of His Holiness the Dalai Lama on the Forty-Ninth Anniversary of the Tibetan National Uprising Day'. March 10, 2008. http://dalailama.com/march10/49thMarch10.html.

[15] The Official Website of Central Tibetan Administration, 'Memorandum of Genuine Autonomy for the Tibetan People'. 2008. http://www.tibet.net/en/index.php?id=78&articletype=press.

[16] 'Whatever China Does, Tibet will still Demand its Freedom', *The Observer*, March 16, 2008. http://www.guardian.co.uk/commentisfree/2008/mar/16/tibet.china.

[17] The Official Website of Central Tibetan Administration, 'Memorandum of Genuine Autonomy'.

[18] Ibid.

[19] TYC was founded by some Tibetans in exile in 1970 with the aim to struggle for the restoration of independence for Tibet.

[20] Tibetan Youth Congress Press Release, 'TYC Launched Indefinite Fast for Tibet – Without Food and Water'. July 28, 2008. http://www.tibetanyouthcongress.org/day1.html.

[21] Ibid.

[22] Tibetan Youth Congress Press Release, 'Hunger Strikes Battle Out Day 6 As Their Health Gets Critical'. August 21, 2008. http://www.tibetanyouthcongress.org/3-day06.html.

[23] Tibetan Youth Congress Press Release, 'Tibetan People's Mass Movement: No Olympics in China until Tibet is Independent'. July 28, 2008. http://www.tibetanyouthcongress.org/day1.html.

[24] Press Conference on the Recent Situation in Tibet. April 9, 2008. http://www.scio.gov.cn/zt2008/zdssyzx/gxbfbh/200804/t159773.htm.

[25] Ibid., May 23, 2004.

[26] Information Office of the State Council of the People's Republic of China, 'Opening Statement at the Press Conference'.

[27] Ibid., May 23, 2004.

[28] Ibid.

[29] Luo, 'China Embarks on a Road'.

[30] Information Office of the State Council of the People's Republic of China, 'Opening Statement at the Press Conference'.

[31] Shue, *Basic Rights*, 19, 20, 23, 19.

32 Xinhua, 'Backgrounder: Historical facts of Tibet'. March 25, 2008. http://news.xinhuanet.com/
    english/2008-03/25/content_10080334.htm.
33 China Tibet Information Centre, 'Tibet Endorses Serfs Emancipation Day'. January 19, 2009.
    http://eng.tibet.cn/index/news/200901/t20090119_448458.htm.
34 'Which Issue "the Tibet Issue" is?' (西藏问题是什么问题?), People's Daily, April 16, 2008.
    http://opinion.people.com.cn/GB/40604/7125203.html.
35 'Time to Stop Criticising China – We've already Come So Far'. The Observer, August 3, 2008.
    http://www.guardian.co.uk/commentisfree/2008/aug/03/china.olympigames20081.
36 'Beijing Claims Weapons Discovered in Monastery', Taipei Times, April 15, 2008, 1.
37 Brownell, Beijing's Games, 19–47.
38 'Activists Condemn Crackdown', Taipei Times, March 21, 2008, 2.
39 'Taiwan is Missing its Chance in Tibet Issues', Taipei Times, April 16, 2008, 8.
40 Cull, 'The Public Diplomacy', 117–44; Elisabeth Rosenthal, 'China Earthquake Pushes Tibet to
    Sidelines', New York Times, May 22, 2008. http://www.nytimes.com/2008/05/22/world/asia/
    22tibet.html.
41 'China's Earthquake: Days of Disaster' The Economist, May 15, 2008, for example, wrote that
    China reacted to the disaster 'rapidly and with uncharacteristic openness', particularly in contrast
    to Burma's secretive response to Cyclone Nargis.
42 'Quake Reveals Softer Side to China'. BBC News Online, May 28, 2008. http://news.bbc.co.uk/2/
    hi/asia-pacific/7424262.stm (emphasis added).
43 Mao, On Coalition Government, 123–4.
44 Information Office of the State Council of the People's Republic of China, 'White Paper: China's
    Progress in Human Rights in 2004'. January 4, 2005. http://www.lawinfochina.com/WBK/
    display.asp?db=1&id=46&keyword=.
45 'Learning to Experience "People Coming First" Concept Amid Quake'. People's Daily, June 11,
    2008. http://english.peopledaily.com.cn/90001/90780/91342/6428348.html.
46 'A Special Lecture on China's National Conditions'. People's Daily, May 26, 2008. http://
    english.peopledaily.com.cn/90001/90780/91342/6418410.html.
47 'At the Moment When the Earth Rocked – A diary of 512 Wenchusan Earthquake'. Tianya.cn,
    May 22, 2008. http://cache.tianay.cn/publicforum/content/books/1/106727.shtml.
48 Xia, 'From Tangshan to Wenchuan', 'Wang Chen' (2008).
49 'Tendentious Loss of Sight for "Human Rights Defenders"'. People Daily, June 4, 2008. http://
    english.peopledaily.com.cn/90001/90780/91342/6424369.html.
50 Hurricane Katrina of 2005, in the opinion of the Chinese media, was the contrast to Sichuan
    Earthquake. Hurricane Katrina was one of the deadliest hurricanes in the history of the United
    States, causing thousands of deaths in the actual hurricane and in the subsequent floods. The
    criticisms of the American government's response to the hurricane primarily focused on delays in
    government response to the flooding of New Orleans, lack of planning and coordination in the
    relief effort, and the subsequent state of chaos of the flood-hit areas. For those criticisms, see
    '"Katrinagate" Fury Spreads to US Media'. Television New Zealand, September 7, 2005. http://
    tvnz.co.nz/view/page/425822/609550.
51 'Quake Reveals Softer Side to China'. BBC News Online.
52 'Orientation and Path of Reform and Opening Up Entirely Correct'. People's Daily, December 3,
    2008. http://english.peopledaily.com.cn/90001/90780/91342/6545553.html.
53 Chen, 'China Registers Historical Progress in Human Rights', 'Wang Chen' (2009).
54 'The Glory of the Olympics'. People's Daily, December 12, 2008. http://english.people.com.cn/
    90001/90780/91345/6473401.html.
55 Beijing City Government launched 'queuing day' on the 11th of each month to encourage people
    to queue. One local football club hired university students to teach fans how to chant politely.
    Beijing City Government even issued etiquette guidelines for citizens on their contact with
    foreigners. For instance, a district of Beijing City handed out a list of 'Eight Don't Asks' to its
    citizens, which asked them not to question foreigners about their age, wage, marital status, etc.
    According to Beijing, there were about 100,000 Olympic event volunteers, 400,000 city
    volunteers, one million social volunteers and two million cheering squad volunteers. Reported in
    'Olympic Crackdown on China's Bad Habits'. BBC News Online, August 6, 2007. http://news.
    bbc.co.uk/1/hi/world/asia-pacific/6927361.stm.
56 In the 2004 Asian Football Confederation Championships, the loss of the Chinese team to Japan
    caused thousands of Chinese fans to riot afterwards.

57 'Beijing Olympics Showcases a Mature China'. Xinhua, September 29, 2008. http://news. xinhuanet.com/english/2008-09/29/content_10132319.htm.
58 'Nine Treasures Contributed by Beijing Olympics' (北京奧運獻給世界九大寶藏), *Guangzhou Daily*, August 25, 2008, A7.
59 'What Do We Display to the World in the Olympics'. *People's Daily*, August 10, 2008. http:// english.peopledaily.com.cn/90001/90780/91345/6470797.html.
60 See: He Ping, *China's Search for Modernity*; Yongnian Zheng, *Discovering Chinese Nationalism*; Weiming Tu, *China in Transformation*; Dittmer and Kim, eds, *China's Quest*.
61 Luo, 'China Embarks on a Road'.
62 Ibid.
63 For instance, some human rights groups and Western media outlets have focused on the political, social and economic impacts of Beijing Olympics on the rights of China's minority people, i.e. migrant workers.
64 Rorty, 'Human Rights', 111–34.

References

Bauer, Joanne, and Daniel A. Bell, eds. *The East Asian Challenge for Human Rights*. Cambridge: Polity, 1999.

Brown, Chris. *Sovereignty, Rights and Justice: International Political Theory Today*. Cambridge: Polity, 2002.

Brownell, Susan. *Beijing's Games: What the Olympics Mean to China*. Lanham, MD: Rowman & Littlefield, 2008.

Collins, Sandra. 'The Fragility of Asian National Identity in the Olympic Games'. In *Owning the Olympics*, edited by Monroe E. Price and Daniel Dayan, 185–209. Michigan: University of Michigan Press, 2008.

Cull, Nicholas J. 'The Public Diplomacy of the Modern Olympics Games and China's Soft Power Strategy'. In *Owning the Olympics*, edited by Monroe E. Price and Daniel Dayan, 117–44. Michigan: University of Michigan Press, 2008.

Dittmer, Lowell, and Samuel S. Kim, eds. *China's Quest for National Identity*. New York: Cornell University Press, 1993.

Dong, Jinxia. 'Women, Nationalism and the Beijing Olympics: Preparing for Glory'. *International Journal of the History of Sport* 22, no. 4 (2005): 530–44.

Foucault, Michel. *Madness and Civilization: a History of Insanity in the Age of Reason*. New York: Vintage, 1965.

Foucault, Michel. *The Order of Things: An Archaeology of the Human Sciences*. New York: Vintage, 1970.

Foucault, Michel. *The Archaeology of Knowledge*. New York: Pantheon, 1972.

Foucault, Michel. *Discipline and Punish*. London: Penguin, 1977.

Foucault, Michel. *History of Sexuality, Volume I: An Introduction*. New York: Vintage, 1978.

Foucault, Michel. 'Truth and Power'. In *Power/Knowledge: Selected Interviews and Other Writing 1972–1977*, edited by Colin Gordon, 109–33. Sussex: Harvester, 1980.

He, Ping. *China's Search for Modernity*. New York: Palgrave Macmillan, 2002.

Humphreys, Lee, and Christopher J. Finlay. 'New Technology, New Narratives'. In *Owning the Olympics*, edited by Monroe E. Price and Daniel Dayan, 284–306. Michigan: University of Michigan Press, 2008.

Information Office of the State Council of the People's Republic of China. 'White Paper: Regional Ethnic Autonomy in Tibet'. May 23, 2004. http://www.scio.gov.cn/zfbps/ndhf/2004/200905/ t307903.htm.

Information Office of the State Council of the People's Republic of China, 'Opening Statement of the Press Conference on the Incident of Beating, Destruction of Property, Looting and Arson in Lhasa'. March 17, 2008. http://www.scio.gov.cn/zt2008/zdssyzx/gxbfbh/200804/ t159493.htm.

Jacobsen, Michael, and Ole Bruun, eds. *Human Rights and Asian Values: Contesting National Identities and Cultural Representations in Asia*. London: Curzon, 2000.

Laclau, Ernesto, and Chantal Mouffe. *Hegemony and Socialist Strategy: Toward a Radical Democratic Politics*. London: Verso, 1985.

Liu, Xiaobo. 'Authoritarianism in the Light of the Olympic Flame'. In *China's Great Leap: The Beijing Games and Olympian Human Rights Challenges*, edited by Minky Worden, 263–272. New York: Seven Stories, 2008.

Luo, Haocai. 'China Embarks on a Road towards Human Rights Progress with Chinese Characteristics' (中国特色的人权发展道路). *Human Rights Magazine* 7, no. 3 (2008): 2–4.

McNay, Lois. *Foucault: A Critical Introduction*. Cambridge: Polity Press, 2005.

Mao, Zedong. *On Coalition Government*. Beijing: China News Agency, 1945.

Nietzsche, Friedrich. *On Genealogy of Morality: A Polemic*, edited by Keith Ansell-Pearson. Cambridge: Cambridge University Press, 2000.

Rorty, Richard. 'Human Rights, Rationality, and Sentimentality'. In *On Human Rights: The Oxford Amnesty Lectures 1993*, edited by Stephen Shute and Susan Hurley, 111–34. New York: Basic Books, 1993.

Shue, Henry. *Basic Rights*. New Jersey: Princeton University Press, 1996.

Tang, Tuck-Hong, ed. *Human Rights and International Relations in the Asia Pacific Region*. London: Pinter Press, 1994.

Tomlinson, Alan. 'Olympic Values, Beijing's Olympics Games, and the Universal Market'. In *Owning the Olympics: Narratives of New China*, edited by Monroe E. Price and Daniel Dayan, 65–85. Michigan: Michigan University Press, 2008.

Tu, Weiming. *China in Transformation*. Boston, MA: Harvard University Press, 1994.

Turner, Bryan, Nicholos Abercrombie and Stephen Hill. *The Penguin Dictionary of Sociology*. New York: Penguin, 2006.

Wang, Chen. 'China Promotes International Human Rights with the International Community'. *Human Rights Magazine* 7, no. 3 (2008): 3–10.

Wang, Chen. 'China Registers Historic Progress in Human Rights'. *Human Rights Magazine* 8, no. 1 (2009): 3–10.

Xia, Li. 'From Tangshan to Wenchuan: Human Rights Practice of Chinese Characteristics' (从唐山到汶川:中国特色的人权实践). *Human Rights Magazine* 7, no. 4 (2008): 5–6.

Xu, Guoqi. *Olympic Dreams: China and Sports, 1895–2008*. Cambridge, MA: Harvard University Press, 2008.

Yongnian, Zheng. *Discovering Chinese Nationalism in China: Modernization, Identity, and International Relations*. Cambridge: Cambridge University Press, 1999.

Public diplomacy games: a comparative study of American and Japanese responses to the interplay of nationalism, ideology and Chinese soft power strategies around the 2008 Beijing Olympics

Christopher J. Finlay[a] and Xin Xin[b]

[a]The Annenberg School for Communication, The University of Pennsylvania, 3620 Walnut Street, Philadelphia, PA 19104, USA; [b]Communication and Media Research Institute, The University of Westminster, 309 Regent Street, London W1B 2UW, UK

The Olympic Games are global communication events that offer host-nations the unique opportunity to promote a soft power agenda by allowing them to construct global messages about their cultural identities and work towards public diplomacy goals that may be more difficult to achieve under normal circumstances. At the same time, however, the Olympics accentuate nationalist and patriotic sentiment, especially in host-nations. Nationalist conviction must be conceptually differentiated from support for the national government. Indeed, we suggest that one of the tasks of governments of Olympic host cities is to manage strong nationalist emotions in order that they support the public diplomacy efforts associated with the Olympic Games. In this paper, American and Japanese media responses to the interplay of China's 2008 Olympics public diplomacy efforts and Chinese nationalism are comparatively analyzed for each of three periods: 1) the international torch relay; 2) the 2008 Sichuan earthquake; 3) the Olympic Games. Our findings suggest that in the West, the Chinese nationalism that was prompted by a controversial torch relay overpowered other aspects of the Games and that thus the Olympic Games ultimately gave new power to familiar discourses emphasizing a fear of China. In Japan, on the other hand, the Olympics presented modest, albeit important, new opportunities to test and promote positive portrayals of Sino-Japanese relations

Introduction

In August 2008, an estimated 4.7 billion people, or 70% of the global population, watched part of the 17-day Beijing Olympic Games on television. In the United States, NBC's television coverage made the Beijing Olympics the most watched event in American television history, with over 215 million tuning in.[1] As a television spectacle, the Beijing Olympics was an unqualified success. And yet, the Chinese government, the International Olympic Committee (IOC) and Games organizers had hoped it would be much more. As Nicholas J. Cull argues, the Beijing Olympics were meant to be 'the latest phase in a sustained Chinese government campaign to woo the world and engage foreign publics'.[2] And yet, in February 2009, less than six months after the Games ended, a BBC World Service survey of public opinion in 21 countries found that across the countries surveyed, China's positive ratings fell six points over the year to 39% and its negative ratings rose from 33% to 40%.[3] Europeans had become more negative toward China and a majority of Americans remained negative, with 'views essentially unchanged at 52 per cent'.

Doug Miller, the poll's representative in the BBC press release, stated that the 'results suggest that China has much to learn about winning hearts and minds in the world. It seems that a successful Olympic Games has not been enough to offset other concerns that people have.' As a central component of what Joshua Kurlantzick calls China's 'Charm Offensive',[4] the Beijing Olympic Games appear to have failed.

In this essay, we explore responses to the 2008 Beijing Olympics in the United States and Japan, two nation-states who have particularly complicated historical relationships with China and with whom China continues to have tense relations. Working with the assumption that Olympics audiences in different societies responded differently to China's soft power overtures, we examine how key events in the final months leading to the Games were framed by the media in the two countries. These final months can be understood as a preparatory period in which international attention focused on China and in which media frames for understanding what would transpire in August 2008 emerged and, arguably, crystallized. Given that the Olympic Games have historically been a vehicle for public diplomacy and a powerful trigger for nationalist sentiment, this essay focuses on the interplay between nationalism and soft power around the 2008 Games. Our essay analyses the relative influence of nationalism on China's potential soft power dividends with the two nation-states. Through the exploration of similarities and differences in the responses of the United States and Japan to China's Olympic diplomacy efforts, we critically interrogate whether the messages distributed via global mega-events such as the Olympic Games enable effective diplomatic interventions or if a nation-state's soft power strategies may in fact require more nuanced applications that are specific to the unique norms and paradigms of different global audiences.

The interplay of soft power and nationalism in the Olympic Games

The reach of Olympics mega events, unparalleled in the contemporary world, has enticed a series of nation-states to use the Games to promote their public diplomacy *or* soft power agendas. Joseph Nye identifies soft power as a key dimension of a nation-state's power, along with military power and economic power. Nye argues that a nation-state has three soft power resources: 'its culture (in places where it is attractive to others), its political values (when it lives up to them at home and abroad), and its foreign policies (when they are seen as legitimate and having moral authority)'. Nye argues that a nation-state obtains a greater amount of soft power if these three resources attract and persuade groups outside the nation-state to adopt similar goals. Soft power can be differentiated from traditional forms of public diplomacy, such as academic exchange programmes and government-sponsored global broadcasting, in that the currency of soft power resides not just in government programmes, but in the private production and distribution of goods and texts that represent the cultures and values of a nation-state. Nye notes, however, that 'soft power is more difficult to wield [than military or economic power because] many of its crucial resources are outside the control of governments, and their effects depend heavily on acceptance by the receiving audience'.[5]

In an argument that has resonances with Dayan and Katz's *Media Events*,[6] Nye suggests that participation in global institutions can enhance a nation-state's legitimacy and soft power by indicating that they are following international rules and standards. While this holds for participation in the Olympic Movement, the Games are a particularly complex and imperfect vehicle for those states who wish to use their host status to add to their soft power reserves. First, the soft power dividends that nation-states may gain via hosting the Games must be understood as the product of what could be called cooperative soft power. This is to say that Olympics diplomacy is the discursively negotiated product of multiple actors involved in the production of the Games. These different actors each have their own soft power or public relations goals. The IOC, for instance, uses the Games to promote the internationalist ideology of Olympism, while corporate sponsors and official Olympics broadcasters have their own agendas and audiences. The soft power goals of a nation-state may not exactly match those of the IOC or of other actors involved in the modern Olympic Movement. Thus, a nation-state's Olympics soft power project must be read as a necessarily curtailed enterprise that emerges out of negotiations between key members of the Olympics Family.

Further, despite the Movement's commitment to internationalism, the Games, both as spectacles[7] and as international sports competitions, intensify nationalist sentiment. As deLisle observes: 'nationalism is a familiar element in the Olympic experience'.[8] Anderson argues that the spectacle is an important vehicle for official nationalism because it affords the political powers of the nation-state the opportunity to promote specific representations of the past that empower current conceptions of the nation-state and define visions of its future. Numerous researchers have examined how the Olympics, as a sports spectacle, accomplishes the task Anderson describes.[9]

As an international competition, the Olympics have also historically accentuated existing tensions between nation-states and regions with competing ideologies. This was perhaps best demonstrated during the Cold War, when the Games acted as spaces where athletes, as products of Eastern and Western ideologies, essentially fought proxy wars. When both the Soviet Union and the United States participated in the same Olympics, medal counts became a method by which to judge who was winning the Cold War. In the post-Cold War era, global audiences witnessed a resurgence of this type of behaviour in Beijing as the American and Chinese media obsessed over their respective medal counts. At the end of the 2008 Games, China won the highest number of gold medals, while the United States won the highest number of medals. A controversy ensued over whether or not the number of gold medals won or all medals won was the ultimate measurement of which country was the top performer in the Olympic Games. As Kevin Eason, writing in the *Times Online*, wryly observed: 'China celebrated achieving its ultimate aim of heading the Olympic medals table for the first time. Unless you are in America, where you will discover that Team USA remain the force in world sport.'[10]

In Beijing, as in other Olympics, soft power agendas exist in uneasy company with the potential for nationalist foment that the Games can excite. Anderson and Hobsbawm contend that elites use nationalism as a form of social engineering to construct the nation-state.[11] However, both scholars stress the volatile nature of nationalism. Further, as Ien Ang writes: 'the cultural constitution of national identity, as articulated in both official policies and informal popular practices, is a precarious project that can never be isolated from the global, transnational relations in which it takes shape'.[12] As we saw in the lead-up to the Beijing Games, evolving controversies in transnational relations between China and other states had a profound impact on the power of nationalist sentiment in all of the states involved. While some level of nationalism can be quite productive, such as nurturing the national pride associated with hosting an Olympic Games, extreme displays of hostile nationalism can negatively affect a nation-state's strategic international relationships and goals. Thus, the management of nationalism ought to be understood as one of the essential tasks of the nation-state. This task is especially important during the Games, when the Olympic spotlight focuses international attention on host-nations and when events associated with the Games risk the potential of souring national pride into negative nationalist zeal.

Case study 1: The United States, NGOs and Western conceptions of global civil society

Western cultural imperialism: global civil society responds to Beijing 2008

In the West, the Beijing Olympics provided non-governmental organizations (NGOs) and global civil society activists the opportunity to focus global attention on China's continued refusal to adopt human rights practices that are informed by Western norms. High profile groups, including Human Rights Watch, Reporters Sans Frontières, Dream for Darfur and Amnesty International, began concerted media campaigns years in advance of the 2008 Games.[13] Through the sophisticated use of online activist networking sites and offline media interventions, from well-placed op-eds by high profile commentators, such as the article by Mia Farrow in the *New York Times* linking China to the genocide in Darfur, to publicity stunts such as the unveiling of a 450-foot banner on the Great Wall of China proclaiming 'One World, One Dream, Free Tibet 2008'[14] on the one year anniversary countdown to the Games in August 2007, the official media narrative of the Beijing Olympics had been challenged in Western media long before the Games had become a common part of American public discourse.[15] Thus, the introduction of the Games for many in the United States was via reports about the controversies surrounding them.

One of the most effective aspects of these campaigns was the production of compelling imagery that re-imagined the symbols, mottos and mascots of the Games as representations of coercion, abuse and murder. As Smith contends, creating a coherent and compelling set of Olympics symbols that appeal to both domestic and international audiences are central to the staging of a successful Games. As each successive symbolic component in the lead-up to the Games was introduced, from the *Dancing Beijing* Games emblem[16] to the *Friendlies* or *Fuwah*, the Games mascots, activists reworked them, challenging their potential to contribute to a coherent Games narrative.

It is particularly important to note that Olympic sponsors and the IOC were also targets of this campaign. Reporters Sans Frontières, for instance, reworked the Olympic rings into five interlocked handcuffs. Olympic sponsors and the IOC itself were painted as Western enablers of China's abysmal human rights record and were thus vilified along with the Beijing Organizing Committee for the Olympic Games (BOCOG) and the Chinese government. Critics of the IOC's decision to award Beijing the 2008 Games made frequent allusions to the 1936 Berlin Olympics, suggesting that the organization had given a dangerous regime a global platform to promote a regressive agenda.[17] This comparison was particularly powerful because it suggested the IOC had turned its back on some of the key functions that it has been associated with in the post-Second World War period. As Henry and Al-Tauqi argue: 'what has been portrayed as a global phenomenon, and which according to the Olympic Charter aspires to principles of universality, has been undeniably a species of political and cultural particularism',[18] This is especially evident when the Games are hosted in periphery states. Black and Van Der Westhuizen found that the West has tended to frame periphery host-nations as either the nation-states that have graduated into the community of civilized nation-states (Mexico City 1968; Seoul 1988) or as nation-states that had done penance for breaking from the norms shared by core states and who were on the road to rehabilitation (Tokyo, 1964; Munich, 1972).[19]

During the final bid presentation for the 2008 Olympics, Beijing framed its bid via an appeal to the theme of rehabilitation: 'Eight years have already gone by since our first bid for the 2000 Games. During this period of time, my country has made tremendous strides on the road to modernization and social progress.'[20] Despite this appeal, China did not follow through on the implicit task it had set for itself during the 2008 bid period as an Olympic host that would engage in major human rights reforms. Instead, China began to pursue a goal whereby the 2008 Games would 'challenge the West to abandon the occidental interpretation of Olympism and to embrace the Oriental view' through cultural displays and attempts to introduce Asian sports, with their associated values, into the Olympic Games.[21] We contend that China's dogged commitment to autonomy despite agreeing to host the Olympics, a role that traditionally demands assimilation, was ambitious but naive.

Creating a new global Olympics media frame that moved beyond the normative rehabilitation and graduation narratives would have required a sophisticated campaign that engaged Western audiences and that had some level of support from external actors who had credibility in the West. The chance that China's nascent voice in the global media sphere would be able to convey such a dramatic message was particularly challenging because Beijing had to contend with a powerful 'hegemony of discourse, since most of the world's news is expressed within the framework of Western concepts and ideology and dominated by the English-language media'.[22] In the West, links between the Olympics and a range of issues had been discursively constructed by a range of global civil society actors and NGOs. As Economy and Segal point out: 'Chinese leaders simply saw no relationship between the pageantry of the Olympics and Tibet, Sudan, or broader human rights concerns, and they never figured out how to engage and disarm those who did.'[23] A key element of creating a media strategy that would have engaged Western audiences and opened up the possibility for introducing a new periphery state narrative would have been to enlist the support of credible Western actors. The IOC, for instance, would have been a powerful and obvious choice. Yet, while the IOC did little to force China to address the concerns of global civil society actors – in December 2008 Rogge noted that although the IOC had delivered 'a few very clear messages to the Chinese', China's decision to act 'upon some and not upon others' was their sovereign right[24] – the IOC did virtually nothing to aid China in promoting their alternative narrative.

Expanding on Close, Askew and Xu, who suggest that NGOs and civil society actors play a role in facilitating Olympics-related Western cultural imperialism, we argue that in the case of the 2008 Olympics, these groups created media interventions that only promoted a cultural assimilationist solution to human rights questions. In effect, the failure of China to 'balance between Chinese and Americanized/Westernized trends', to 'express itself in its own way but at the same time in the way that the world can understand and likes to hear'[25] was compounded by the failure of NGOs and global civil society actors in the West to explore how to express their own goals in a way that would balance Chinese and American trends and appeal across existing socio-political and cultural divides. Further, existing divides were accentuated in the West through linking, perhaps inadvertently, anti-Beijing Olympics media to existing Western anti-China narratives. This became especially evident in the four-month preparatory period leading to the Games.

Preparatory period one: the torch relays (April–May 2008)

The Beijing Olympics torch relay began in Greece on 24 March 2008. When BOCOG had announced the torch route in 2007, they claimed that it would be the longest torch relay in the history of the modern Olympics. In the Western legs of the torch relay, protesters tried to interrupt the relay and, on several occasions, doused the torch's flame. The largest and most violent protests were in the United States, Britain and France. The protests in these countries stood in stark contrast to the relatively minor problems that torch bearers faced in Latin America, Africa and Asia. The difference in the responses in different regions to the torch relay highlights the competing audience paradigms and, we argue, speaks to the relative legitimacy, reach and influence of Western-based NGOs and civil society groups across the globe.

A *New York Times* article explained: 'The torch ceremonies have focused attention on causes that have languished on the world's back burner for decades'. The article continued, describing the situation in Paris:

> [H]uman rights organizations like Amnesty International and press freedom groups like Reporters Without Borders protested side by side with representatives of a banned underground Chinese democracy party, Taiwan nationalists and proponents of independence for Uighurs, a Muslim minority in western China... The range of China's opponents was so thoroughly covered that it included a protest by Amnesty International on behalf of a blind Chinese human rights lawyer who is in prison in Beijing.[26]

This article is representative of American coverage, noting the variety and number of protest groups, but without delving into any critical coverage of the legitimacy of the various groups' motives. The legitimacy of China's intentions, on the other hand, was routinely questioned. For example, in an article entitled 'The Relay of Fire Ignited by the Nazis', *New York Times* contributor Edward Rothstein pointed to the origin of the torch relay in the 1936 Olympics, making a clichéd connection between the so-called Nazi Olympics and Beijing. He continued by questioning China's true motives in constructing the most ambitious relay in history:

> Now, despite China's attempt to put a smiley face on the torch relay – 'Light the Passion, Share the Dream' says the Chinese Web site (see torchrelay.beijing2008.cn/en) – the Tibetan protests have laid bare its nationalist essence. There are reasons why the Chinese wanted a route that invoked glory (by touching Everest's peak) and power (by passing through Taiwan).[27]

Numerous reporters and commentators in American media outlets ran stories that contained similar biases and hostility towards China. The most infamous of which was CNN's Jack Cafferty, who called the Chinese 'thugs and goons' and described Chinese products as 'junk' during a report on the torch relays. The Chinese foreign ministry demanded an apology from CNN, stating that Cafferty's comments reflected his 'ignorance and hostility towards China'. In CNN's subsequent apology, the broadcaster explained that 'Cafferty was offering his "strongly held" opinion of the Chinese Government, not China's people'.[28] The distinction between the Chinese government and the Chinese people in CNN's apology is particularly interesting because it was relatively rare in both the materials constructed by NGOs and civil society groups and in American media coverage. As the protests continued along the torch route, this important, but always underemphasized, distinction was further muddied by an explosion of Chinese nationalism.

On 7 April 2008, the disabled torchbearer Jin Jing was carrying the torch through Paris when she was attacked and almost thrown from her wheelchair. The official Beijing Olympics website for the torch relays described the incident:

> Carrying the torch on the new course along the Seine River, Jin demonstrated great valor when a 'pro-Tibet independence' activist, attempting to disrupt and sabotage the torch relay, reached for her wheelchair and lunged toward her. Without concern for her own safety, Jin did her best to protect the flame, her face exhibiting courage and pride in spite of the chaotic situation. In that moment, it was easy to see why her friends call her the 'smiling angel in a wheelchair'.[29]

The above quote uses quotation marks in identifying Jin's attacker as a pro-Tibet protester, implicitly calling the motives of the attacker into question. This and other similar tactics were employed by BOCOG, the Chinese government and the Chinese media throughout the torch relay. China's *English People's Daily Online* went further, covering a Xinhua story about an international conspiracy network that had been plotting to 'tarnish the Olympics'.[30] The selective Chinese coverage of torch relay protests in the West, which highlighted CNN as an example of Western anti-China bias and Jin as a sympathetic hero, triggered a series of dramatic protests in China against CNN and the West. After the particularly violent events during the protests in Paris, the French grocery store Carrefour became a locus of protest activity in China.[31]

In the United States, diasporic Chinese held counterdemonstrations at the torch relays and at universities across the country. *The New York Times* reporter Shaila Dewan wrote: Chinese students 'have been forced to confront an image of their homeland that they neither recognize nor appreciate... Chinese students, traditionally silent on political issues, have begun to lash out at what they perceive as a pervasive anti-Chinese bias'. The report quotes student Chou Wu, who said: '"We thought Western media is very objective... and what it turned out is that Western media is even more biased than Chinese media. They're no better, and even more, they're against us.'[32]

As the protests in China and by members of the Chinese diaspora continued in late April and May 2008, the focus moved from specific issues to a general anti-Western agenda, which unnerved China's Communist Party, who worried the public anger would 'spin out of control'.[33] The torch relay, intended as a soft power overture that would demonstrate China's Peaceful Rise intentions and showcase the country's industriousness, had instead intensified tensions between China and the West. Unfortunately, the ineffective and late response of the Chinese government to the anti-West protests in China and across the world failed to reign in public displays of angry Chinese nationalism. Thus, the aim to use the Olympics as a vehicle for introducing the idea that a viable alternative to the West, which could also prosper in harmony with the West in a globalizing world, was deterred before the Games had even begun.

As discussed earlier, soft power is dependent on the predispositions of the receiving audience. Although we contend that the Chinese government made serious mistakes during this phase of the preparatory period, it should be emphasized that the destructive impact of the torch relay on China's global diplomacy efforts could have been contained by a more responsible use of the media by Western NGOs and civil society groups. Instead of treating the torch relay as an opportunity for dialogue, these groups allowed their causes to be integrated into a growing anti-China movement in the West, one that had been fuelled by everything from America's growing public debt to China to concerns about tainted toys and toothpaste. Working within an existing media frame is easier than constructing a new one. However, by doing this and by not engaging in any significant outreach attempts to the Chinese people, NGOs and civil society groups hurt their own causes by stifling dialogue and allowing nationalist sentiment in China to blossom into a generalized anti-West movement. Further, despite their heavy media presence, there was little attempt to problematize the messaging of media figures, such as Jack Cafferty, who openly connected the messaging of the groups involved in the torch relay protests to what could best be called unrelated fears about China.

Ultimately, the soft power potential of the torch relay was foiled by a nationalist zeal in China that had been stoked by Western NGOs and civil society groups and that was poorly managed by the Chinese government and Olympic organizers. Further, the negative ramifications of the Olympic torch's procession through the West are still being felt. Organizers of the Vancouver 2010 Winter Olympics and the 2012 London Olympics announced that their torch relays would not include international legs. In March 2009, the IOC introduced a ban on future international torch relays.[34] And just months after the Games, a 2009 BBC World Service survey of global opinion, found a 'polarizing trend seems to be appearing in relations between China and the West', with negative views of the United States in China rising from 46% to 58% and positive views of France dropping 'from 64% to 44% – perhaps in reaction to French demonstrations regarding the Tibet issue'.[35]

Preparatory period two: the Sichuan earthquake (May–July 2008)

Perversely, an earthquake in the Sichuan province of China on 12 May 2008 accomplished many of the public diplomacy goals that the torch relay had failed to do. The Olympics were discursively connected to the earthquake almost immediately: 'In Beijing, officials announced a three-day mourning period during which the ceremonial relay of the Olympic torch, which has been traveling through China, would be suspended.'[36] Olympic organizers continued to make explicit connections between the two events through the Olympics, the most poignant of which was during the Parade of Nations in the opening ceremony when Chinese basketball legend Yao Ming walked hand-in-hand with Lin Hao, a 9-year-old boy who had been praised for rescuing classmates during the earthquake.

The effort to maintain this connection was important as the tragic event had reframed China in the American media in at least two ways. First, the earthquake, which happened during the torch relay, focused the Chinese people's attention on the tragedy and relief efforts. Relief efforts stemming from both China and actors in the international community highlighted a common humanity, challenging the continuing resonance of the Carrefour and other anti-Western protests. The sudden spike in xenophobic nationalism ebbed in China at the exact same moment as images of the earthquake's devastation, the wounded and dead, and everyday Chinese heroes reached global audiences. Eric Reeves, one of the main actors in the effort to link China to the genocide in Darfur, expressed frustration that years of NGO and civil society work would likely become muted and possibly ineffective against the grisly backdrop of the May earthquake. As Harvey Araton wrote in *The New York Times*:

> Reeves is right: the horror in Sichuan Province could well foster a lasting belief that the Chinese people have been through enough. Activists will have a daunting call to make: lose the long-awaited-for stage of what Reeves and others have been calling the Genocide Olympics, or pour salt in China's wound?[37]

Indeed, those few Western actors who continued to actively pursue the narratives of the torch relay protests faced public criticism and humiliation. Perhaps the most notorious example was Sharon Stone, who lost a contract with Christian Dior after suggesting that 'the recent earthquakes in Sichuan Province were karmic retribution for Beijing's treatment of Tibet'.[38]

International actors praised the Chinese government for its management of rescue and relief operations. Western and American media compared the responses of China and Myanmar to the large scale disasters that devastated parts of their respective countries in May 2008. This was encouraged by world leaders, including the United Nations Secretary General, whose 'actions and comments seemed to invite comparisons between the responses of the two countries'. The Chinese government was especially commended for allowing Chinese and international journalists to provide uncensored coverage of the earthquake. China's relatively open coverage helped international and domestic relief efforts through providing a clearer scope of the earthquake's ramifications and the survivors' needs. Quoting Shin Anbin, a media studies professor at Tsinghua University in Beijing, *The New York Times* suggested that 'the Olympics were pushing China to experiment with a greater degree of openness. "This is the first time the Chinese media has lived up to international standards", [Shin] said.'[39]

We suggest Shin's comment about China and international standards provides a useful insight into the relationship between soft power and the Olympics for periphery nation-states such as China. During the torch relays, China presented a self-constructed and, arguably, unapologetic version of itself to the world. Further, China appeared to be inviting the notion that the country could be understood as an alternative to existing Western norms of so-called global civil society. As a periphery nation offering an alternative narrative of progress and a different set of aspirational internationalist goals, it was trounced. In the aftermath of the earthquake, which had been discursively linked to the Beijing Olympics, China was commended for adapting its responses to emergency situations and following a set of international rules constructed by Western actors. These rules, which are inherently normative, are rarely questioned in Western societies. Instead, the prevailing assumption is that if a nation-state does not blindly follow the rules, this is evidence of that nation-state's lack of progress or its deceitfulness. By linking the Beijing Games to China's new appreciation for international standards, the Olympics once again appeared, at least temporarily, to have at least partly fulfilled its graduation and rehabilitation function.

We argue that this was enormously problematic for China and could have a dangerous influence on future periphery Games hosts. The correlation of China's relative power to attract, a key component of soft power, and the vacillation of American media framing of the nation-state as a frightening and nationalistic rising power and as a sympathetic ward of so-called global civil society, calls the soft power potential of peripheral nations into question. We assert that a peripheral state's soft power rise in the global comity of nations may only be possible if it assimilates the socio-political and cultural norms of hegemonic core states. The evidence analysed from the American media coverage of the two phases of Beijing 2008's preparatory period supports this assertion.

The Olympic Games: giving familiar discourses new power (August 2008)

As the effects of the earthquake became less immediate, NGOs and civil society groups began their counter-narrative campaigns again. Mia Farrow, for example, hosted a webcast of an alternative Olympics from Darfur during the first week of the Olympic Games.[40] However, the spectacle of the opening and closing ceremonies in Beijing and the triumphs of athletes such as Michael Phelps and Usain Bolt captured the imagination of American broadcasters and journalists, subduing the influence of the counter-narratives. This was compounded by the fact that there were no major 'trigger events' during the Games, such as mass protests or other major political scandals in Beijing. Indeed, we contend that the influence of NGOs and civil society groups climaxed during the torch relays. However, this is not to suggest that the work of these groups did not influence how the Games were framed in the United States. In this section, we briefly analyse key controversies during the Games and suggest that the way they were framed in the American media relied on familiar discourses that NGO and civil society groups had, perhaps inadvertently, given new power.

The 8 August opening ceremonies, with over 15,000 performers directed by Zhang Yimou, were the most extravagant and expensive in history. Writing about the opening ceremony, *The New York Times*'s Jim Yardley noted: 'there was also a message for an uncertain outside world: Do not worry. We mean no harm.'[41] In the United States, this message was not clearly received. As Irwin Tang observed, 'the specter of "Asiatic hordes" was invoked during the opening ceremonies, when American commentators intimated that 2008 Chinese men banging on traditional drums was "intimidating'".[42] The response on NBC was not unique. A reviewer in *The USA Today*, using yet another allusion to the 1936 Games, also expressed concern about the drumming portion of the show:

> [There] were a few moments that came across as sort of Albert Speer meets *Star Wars*. As memorable and impressive as that opening, pounding, screaming drum corps may have been, it was also the least welcoming 'welcome' ever recorded – and having the drummers smile during it just made it seem odder and a bit chilling.[43]

Initial responses to the show were mixed between those who were impressed by the extraordinary spectacle and those who viewed it more as Shock and Awe. *New York Times* columnist David Brooks suggested that the opening ceremony 'was part of China's assertion that development doesn't come only through Western, liberal means, but also through Eastern and collective ones'.[44] Building on Brooks, we suggest that it is for this reason that, like the torch relays, the opening ceremonies were progressively discredited in the American media.

In the days following the opening ceremony, controversial stories about the it began to circulate in the United States. Sam Eifling, writing in the *Columbia Journalism Review*, suggested 'the swell of sour press about the Olympics may have begun with a couple of crooked teeth', referring to the scandal around the young Lin Miaoke who lip-synched a song sung by 7-year-old Yang Peiyi. China's official explanation, that Yang was allegedly not beautiful enough and thus replaced because 'for the national interest ... the child on camera should be flawless in image, internal feeling and expression',[45] was greeted with outrage in the American media. Explanations of Sinologists and other experts, who suggested that the incident was an apt illustration of important cultural differences between the expectations of an individualistic Western audience and the intentions of producers from a society where working together to create the best possible outcome was the norm, led to further foment. This, in turn, prompted a spirited media dissection in the United States and the West about precisely what Brooks had identified in the above quotation, the merits of China's assertion about Eastern and collective socio-cultural and political approaches.

We contend that the media flurry about the lip-synching did not progress into new or self-reflective territory. Instead, it reignited Cold War rhetoric that pitted the apparently obvious benefits of neo-liberalism against the dubious outputs of collectivist societies. Further, Western commentators continuously tried to take the moral high-ground, arguing that China's collectivism was inhumane. Sympathetic portrayals of both girls as victims of a nefarious Chinese Communist Party were supplemented by stories about Chinese performers who were forced to wear adult nappies so that they could perform during the four-hour opening ceremony without taking a break. As in the Cold War, collectivism was implicitly framed as exploitative, where individuals were forsaken for the glory of the nation-state.

This type of rhetoric was also common in those events where Chinese and American athletes competed head-to-head. During the Cold War, American national anxiety about a perceived 'muscle gap' between the United States and the Soviet Union 'led not only to an "arms race" but also to an entire "body race" in that citizens' bodies and the body politic were seen as weapons of geopolitical struggle'. In response to 'muscle gap' fears, president John F. Kennedy 'established the President's Council on Youth Fitness to counter a "growing softness, our increasing lack of physical fitness", which, he said, constituted "a threat to our security".' Reports of 'a comprehensive Chinese medal harvest program called Project 119' and the rigorous, almost inhuman, training of Chinese athletes abounded in the American media during the 2008 Games and, at least to *The New York Times* contributor Harvey Araton, 'sounded a bit too much like Cold War rhetoric'.[46]

Rhetoric about the production of gold medal winners also moved into the familiar Cold War territory of concerns about cheating. Questions about the ages and, therefore, legitimacy of the gold-winning Chinese gymnasts were a major focus of NBC and other American media outlets. We suggest that attempts to make Chinese accomplishments during the Games suspect, from questions about the young gymnasts to accusations about the authenticity of an opening ceremony that included lip synching and digitally animated fireworks, can be read as the continuation of the *Made in China* critique.[47] This critique extends the existing stereotypes about poorly constructed, mass produced and cheap Chinese goods to multiple aspects of China. In the case of the Olympic Games, this critique was extended to portray both Chinese showmanship and Chinese athletes as mass produced fakes.

As the Games came to a close, *The New York Times* ran an editorial, 'Beijing's Bad Faith Olympics', in which it was suggested that 'the final gold medal – for authoritarian image management – can already be safely awarded to China's Communist Party leadership'. Others, such as the *Columbia Journalism Review,* referred to the Games as 'China's Potemkin Olympics'.[48] While there is no denying that China's overt and too-transparent image control efforts hindered any soft power gains during the Games, we contend that the hostility and suspicion that followed even the smallest controversies was partly due to the agenda-setting effects of Western NGOs and civil society groups in the preparatory period. As we argued earlier, these actors made little attempt to differentiate their causes and messaging from the existing wave of anti-China sentiment in the West. Instead, these groups allowed their messaging to be co-opted by this existing media frame and thus it became increasingly difficult to distinguish fear-induced anti-China tirades from the legitimate concerns raised by NGOs and civil society groups. During the Games, we saw how the reiteration of clichéd Cold War imagery and the extension of a prejudiced *Made in China* critique, both given a new patina of morality by an NGO and Western civil society aided anti-China critique, combined to aid the Othering of Chinese athletes, performers, audiences and citizens. We contend that the rabid nationalist response to the torch relay protesters by Chinese demonstrators tainted China's Olympic 'coming out' party as it was only too easy for Western audiences and the American media to connect the unofficial and official displays of nationalism surrounding the Games.

In a *New York Times* story on the Chinese gymnasts, it was suggested that the IOC, 'so heavily invested in a Games China can be proud of, said it would not investigate' the scandal.[49] Indeed, there were accusations throughout the Games period that Western actors, from the IOC to NBC, were complicit in China's soft power strategy throughout the Games. As we argued earlier in this essay, Olympics-related soft power can be understood as cooperative soft power. Ideally, the notion that the IOC or major broadcasters would aid in the construction of a successful Games that, in turn, would give a nation-state further soft power, should not be controversial. In the Beijing 2008 case, however, this was a major point of contention. Again, we suggest that this can be attributed to China's murky status as both a peripheral and powerful nation-state. It is one thing to help a less powerful peripheral nation on their road to Olympics-aided graduation or rehabilitation. It is quite another to be an enabler of a nation-state that tries to present a soft power message that promises harmony, but that, at the same time, presents its own soft rise as evidence that international harmony need not be synonymous with global conformity.

Case study 2: Sino-Japanese relations and the interaction of soft power and nationalism

Beijing 2008: overcoming or containing long-term antagonisms?

We suggest that Japan is a particularly interesting case to examine how the interplay of public diplomacy and nationalism results in different responses from different audiences. On the one hand, Japan has been a member of the global comity of nations since the nation's defeat in the Second World War. Indeed, the Tokyo Olympics are routinely offered as an example of how the Olympics functions as a rehabilitation tool. Moreover, Japan is also a major power in Asia, where the effects of China's rise are arguably more dramatic and more direct. Further, Japan and China, geographically close to one another, have a long history of antagonism. Thus, we contend that the response of Japan's media to China's soft power manoeuvres in the two phases of the preparatory period and during the Games would be both unique from that of the United States and the rest of the West and would provide important insights about the relationship between the two countries. Although China did not and, given the global nature of contemporary media, could not deter from its international Olympics messaging, it was able to augment this strategy with specific initiatives that would speak to ongoing Sino-Japan issues.

In this case study, our analysis was primarily informed by articles published in The *Beijing News* and *Global News*. The *Beijing News* represents the views of Chinese reformers with a relatively open world view, while the *Global News*, the major income source of the influential Party mouth-piece, *People's Daily*, is famous for publishing columns and reviews with strong Chinese nationalism sentiments. These two newspapers are popular in Beijing and other big cities. The latter mainly reports international news, while the *Beijing News* had a special section covering the Beijing Olympics and international news. Most of the articles which were published in offline newspapers are also available on their news website. Overall, our analysis suggests that China had much clearer objectives and attempted to adopt a much more cooperative approach with Japan, although this did not necessarily result in an intended positive outcome. According to a survey jointly conducted in June and July 2008 by the Japanese non-governmental organization Genron NPO and the *China Daily*, China's state-owned English language newspaper, nearly 70% of Japanese were pessimistic about future relations with China.[50] While nearly 80% of the Chinese respondents believed that summits between Prime Minister Yasuo Fukuda and President Hu Jintao in May 2008 helped improve bilateral ties, only 20% of Japanese respondents felt the same way. Further, more than 80% of Japanese respondents said they would not visit China because of food safety and hygiene concerns. Not only did this survey demonstrate the fact that the Japanese were more pessimistic about the future of Sino-Japan relations than the Chinese were, it also demonstrated that China had a much more challenging soft power task to handle – the rehabilitation of the everyday image of China – than simply overcoming political rivalry.

The complexity of Sino-Japan relations are periodically intensified by different disputes, some of which are linked to historical issues, but also some of which are based on current conflicts of interest between the two Asian powers. These disputes often become a source of Chinese or Japanese nationalistic sentiments towards each other. If we put the core of the historical disputes between China and Japan in a historical context, China's nationalistic anger about Japan is largely based on the lack of consensus or reconciliation by Japan regarding apologies to Chinese war victims and China's continuing lack of forgiveness for Japan's brutal past. As the Western media have noticed, the majority of the Chinese public remains 'bitter about the massacre of 300,000 Chinese civilians in Nanjing in 1937, as well as numerous allegations of human rights abuses before and during the war'.[51] For them, the Chinese victims and their families deserve a sincere apology – an equivalent to what Germany did after the Second World War – from Japan. When China's official demand for a 'written apology' from Japan was repeatedly emphasized by the former president Jiang Zemin during his visit to Japan in 1998, not only was Jiang's request rejected, but also criticisms were raised in Japan. The Japanese public reacted negatively towards Jiang's request, 'concluding that no matter how much apologising or economic assistance the Chinese got from Japan, Beijing cynically intended to keep playing the guilt card to gain further concessions'. 'Noting the adverse reaction to Jiang's visit', Chinese Communist Party leaders 'reportedly decided to press the history issue less strongly to prevent the relationship from deteriorating further'. It also subsequently forced China to adopt 'new thinking' about how to deal with Japan in order to create a better environment for improved relations in the twenty-first century. China's 'new thinking' is now abstractly simplified by the 'current slogan for relations with Japan': 'taking history as a mirror while looking toward the future'. The underlying meaning of the slogan is that 'China desires to move from stagnation towards substantially improved political relations, but insists that the Japanese meet a minimum standard of avoiding what the Chinese consider behaviour that is blatantly offensive to Chinese sensibilities'.[52]

Further, the 'sincerity' of any apology would also be judged by the Chinese based on two related issues: the first is the question of whether Japanese officials would stop their visits to the Yasukuni Shrine for the War dead, and the second is whether the Japanese Army's massacre of Nanjing is documented accurately and in detail in Japanese textbooks. The former Prime Minister Junichiro Koizumi's visit to the Yasukuni war shrine in 2002 was therefore considered as a serious rejection of China's demand for actions that would be in synch with an apology. This aroused anger in the Chinese public who turned up to massive anti-Japan protests.[53] As for the Japanese history textbooks, David McNeill found that a 1993 version of a standard Japanese history textbook (*Nihonshi*), as well as more recent versions of other textbooks, did not use the term 'Nanjing Massacre'. Instead, these textbooks referred to it as the 'Nanjing Incident', with no more than a couple of sentences of explanation. Further, in the Japanese History Section of the Kodansha Encyclopaedia of Japan, there is only one page on the Pacific War without any mention of Nanjing.[54]

In addition to the historical issues discussed above, between China as an emerging power and Japan as an existing power in Asia, there have been conflicting interests over territory and trade-related issues. China and Japan still 'disagree over the demarcation of the East China Sea between the Ryukyu Island chain and the Chinese coast'. When China 'began building an undersea pipeline out to gas fields that lie partly within an area of the East China Sea that Japan claims as part of its exclusive economic zone', Japan responded by 'charter[ing] a Norwegian research ship to map a section of the bottom of the East China Sea'. Subsequently, in 2005 anti-Japan and anti-Japanese protests and boycotts of Japanese products took place in Shanghai, Guangzhou, Shenzhen and other cites in China. Moreover, the 'unresolved issue of the Senkaku/Diaoyu Islands, which both Japan and China claim to own, periodically causes a minor crisis in Sino-Japan relations'. The tension is mainly triggered by 'ostensibly private activists, whose actions force both governments to reassert their conflicting claims'; for example, 'in 2003 and early 2004 Chinese activists made four attempts at a symbolic landing on the islands, which lie in the East China Sea roughly halfway between Okinawa and the Chinese coastal city of Fuzhou'.[55]

In addition, a recent food scandal in which the dumplings imported into Japan from China were found to contained pesticides and subsequently sickened nearly 200 Japanese added to the tension. The poisonous dumplings caused Japanese public concern over the

Chinese-made food safety in Japan and had a negative impact on the Sino-Japan relations.[56] The concern over food safety was also reflected in the opinion polls conducted by NPO and *China Daily* in 2008, as mentioned earlier.

Public opinion particularly as reflected by internet users, or *netizens*, has for years contained nationalist views and even hate speeches, leading to 'verbal confrontations' between Chinese and Japanese nationalists in recent years. In China the newspaper *Global News* and the online forum *Qiangguoluntan* (both of which are run by *People's Daily* and are famous for the dissemination of anti-Japanese and Chinese nationalistic sentiments) are routinely and extensively quoted in China and Japan's major media. Xenophobic views and nationalist words are quoted directly in order to boost readership and ratings. For example, some 'verbal confrontations' led to riots in the aftermath of football matches between the two national teams in the Asia Cup in 2004. The riots caused serious concern in the Japanese media, as both officials and members of the public began to question China's legitimacy as the host of the Beijing Olympics.[57]

Chinese authorities were aware of the fact that it was necessary to manage extreme forms of Chinese nationalism during the Beijing Olympics, particularly to control the string of anti-Japan and anti-Japanese sentiments. This can partly be attributed to the lessons learned from previous outbreaks of nationalistic anger in the two neighbouring countries. Nationalistic anger had been believed to be fuelled by both sides' sensationalist domestic media coverage, often held to be at the expense of bilateral relations. Therefore, Sino-Japan relations were chosen to be one of the chief public diplomacy objectives to handle before and during the Olympic Games. This was seen as essential to accomplish China's goal to project an 'open and friendly image' to the outside world.[58]

Japan had similar concerns over anti-Chinese feelings among their population. Anti-Chinese sentiments were 'inflamed by televised images of Chinese demonstrators hurling stones at the Japanese embassy in Beijing, and reports of attacks on Japanese restaurants and on Japanese citizens at the time of the protests'.[59] Japan had its own soft power objective too, namely projecting an image of itself as a civilized and progressive country during the Beijing Olympics. This was all the more important given Tokyo's bid for the 2016 Olympics.

Strategic considerations led both China and Japan to try and warm bilateral relations, which had cooled down significantly since 2005. According to Qiu Zhenhai, a current affairs commentator on Hong Kong-based Phoenix Satellite Television, Hu's 2008 visit to Japan was seen as a good opportunity for China to repair negative images of China. It seemed particularly urgent and necessary given that Japan was becoming more inclined to agree with the Western critical views about China's handling of the Tibet riots.[60] The May 2008 earthquake in south-west China directed international attention to Chinese victims and made the visit of the Chinese President Hu Jiantao to Japan somewhat less important as it had become a less appealing story for the media. However, it remains important to note that Hu's visit to Japan had been planned as a media event, which took place just before the opening ceremony of the Beijing Olympics. This can be read as evidence of China's plans to eliminate some of the negative effects of the global controversy over China's legacy as a host country.

Common concerns came up with certain joint efforts in order to avoid diplomatic embarrassments to the Chinese and Japanese leaders, who were ready to meet before as well as during the Olympics. The leaders of the two nation-states shared concerns about how to influence media coverage of the extreme nationalism of the respective countries, which was all too often based on hostility against each other. As Chinese media outlets remain state-owned within the still centralized propaganda system, it theoretically should have been relatively easier for Chinese authorities to implement a nationalism management strategy, compared with the free media in a democratic Japan. However, in both Japan and China nationalistic comments on each other were and still are a selling point for domestic media consumption. This inevitably posed more challenges to any kinds of nationalism management, hindering public diplomacy efforts. This also raised a question about the sources and causes of the widely spread nationalistic sentiments in the two countries. From the Chinese perspective, certainly there are historical reasons behind the complicated Sino-Japan relations and current unsolved national interest conflicts between the two countries. Moreover, there has been a tendency of the rise of Chinese nationalism along with the country's continuing economic growth in the past few decades. The negative impact of Chinese nationalistic sentiments tends to be hidden, particularly when they are mobilized and aroused by the national pride for 'serving the glory of the country'. In these circumstances, nationalism is difficult to separate from patriotism. Yet, when it comes to the relations with Japan, hidden sentiments emerge that are based on the complex emotions associated with the sense that China was humiliated by Western and Japanese imperialists during a period of over 100 years (1840–1945). These complicated components of Chinese nationalism vis-à-vis China are particularly difficult to manage or contain.[61] For example, annual 'patriotic education' campaigns and the particular framing of history in Chinese school texts have only served to enhance a sense of humiliation and injustice for generations of Chinese. Thus, we suggest that while the management of nationalism during the short period of the Games in August 2008 was possible, it could be argued that it was ultimately little more than a temporary containment strategy. As for the longer term, the best BOCOG and the Chinese Community Party could hope to do was lay initial groundwork for permanent change.

Furthermore, we suggest that although a clear soft power objective towards Sino-Japan relations was put into practice, it did not make substantial changes to the way in which the authoritarian Chinese government dealt with their domestic media. As usual, forceful administrative orders were passed to the media managers of each state-owned news organization long before the opening ceremony. The orders came from different directions, including the Party's propaganda authorities as well as officers who were in charge of sport issues. One of the major outcomes of this kind of forced implementation of control over how Chinese nationalism would be covered is that *all* media outlets, particularly newspapers, had to cover issues related to Japan and the Japanese in a similar way. The major evidence of this trend can be found in the difference between the *Beijing News*, which is traditionally more international and positive about Japan in its daily coverage, and the *Global News*, which enjoys popularity among Chinese nationalists and whose anti-Japan bias disappeared during the Beijing Olympics only to be revived in the aftermath of the Games. To a large extent, it was hoped that governmental editorial control and censorship would have an immediate and direct effect on the long-held opinions of *Global News* readers during the Games. Beyond the *Global News*, all Chinese media outlets were required to carry positive stories about Sino-Japan relations and Japanese athletes and visitors. They were also expected to document their positive comments on Beijing, Olympic venues, the host's organization, the Chinese audience and friendship between Japanese and Chinese athletes.

As we suggest, this examination of Sino-Japan relations offers a unique opportunity to gain a better understanding of the relationship between engendering soft power in Japan and with Japanese audiences, and the management of nationalism around the Olympics. Moreover, it reveals the limitations to these efforts if they are not part of a long term strategy and are not followed by further action. Despite government attempts to control how the traditional media in China covered Japan during the Olympics, both new media and the long-term agendas of the traditional media stymied this initiative. Instead of public diplomacy efforts exerting control over the media in 2008, the media, both new and old, demonstrated that they had an influence on public diplomacy efforts, which tended to be negative, especially given intensified media competition and the relationship of anti-China or anti-Japan stories to audience sizes for media outlets in the respective countries.

Preparatory period one: the torch relays (April–May 2008)

The Japanese leg of the torch relay in Nagano in April was little different from the torch relays that took place in Europe and North America. The torch relay in Japan was also accompanied by some NGO protests, such as Pro-Tibet groups and Reporters Sans Frontières. In Japan, however, these groups were joined by Japanese right-wing groups and nationalists who clashed with Chinese supporters. Injuries and arrests occurred. The chaotic process was similar to what had happened in Paris, London and San Francisco. As the torch relay was just days ahead of Chinese president Hu Jintao's visit to Japan, both Japanese and Chinese officials did not want embarrassing incidents during the torch relay to create tensions between Japan and China. Both the Chinese and Japanese media tried to emphasize how much effort the Japanese hosts, particularly the local police, had put into ensuring the security of the torch relay. For example, the *Global News*'s website quoted the Japanese publication *Keyodo*'s story about the torch relay, showcasing a multiplicity of Japanese voices on the relay.[62]

Ultimately, however, the torch relay in Japan did not help China to project a better image of itself to the Japanese. Further, unpleasant scenes were documented by some Chinese newspapers, news websites and online forums. This kind of media coverage by the Chinese media further fuelled Chinese nationalistic sentiments, which were widely expressed in some popular online forums, such as Qianghualuntan. Online discussions in this website were dominated by extreme nationalistic views and even verbal insults, which were then translated into Japanese by journalists and academics. Some Japanese newspapers began to question whether Chinese students overseas were mobilized by the Chinese government to join the massive counter-protests in Japan.[63]

Still, it is important to note that during this period there were more sensitive issues than the torch relay itself, which could provoke nationalist anti-Japan or anti-China sentiment in the respective states. Apart from the historical issues discussed earlier, there were more recent territorial disputes between China and Japan over the area of the East China Sea, which is rich in oil and gas resources. In addition, tensions relating to Chinese-made contaminated dumplings added to the hostilities between the two countries. Therefore, the impact of the torch relay on the Sino-Japan relationship, while important, should not be exaggerated.

Preparatory period two: the Sichuan earthquake (May–July 2008)

As with the wider world, the earthquake that hit south-west China in May 2008 became a turning point in Olympics-related Sino-Japan relations after the Chinese government agreed to accept aids and rescue teams from Japan. On 15 May 2008, Japan became the first country whose offer of a rescue team was accepted by China. However, the Chinese government did not immediately accept Japan's offer to use its military force to deliver tents and blankets to the earthquake zone due to concerns about possible Chinese nationalistic reactions. One of the most popular newspapers in Japan, *Asahi Shimbun*, published an article on 31 May that expressed Japan's understanding of the Chinese hesitance to receive military aid from a former 'enemy' and showed its respect to the way in which China preferred to be helped by Japan during this crisis. In response to Japan's attitude, *China Youth Daily*, which aims to promote ties between Japanese and Chinese young people, commented on *Asahi Shimbun*'s article. A few left-wing Japanese newspapers praised rescue teams, labelling them a bridge for mutual understanding between the Japanese and Chinese. On 16 May, the fourth day of earthquakes in Wenchuan, a news story about the arrival of the Japanese rescue team in China became the lead story in a number of Japanese broadsheets such as the *Daily Yomiuri*, *The Mainichi Daily News*, *The Sankei Shimbun* and even some tabloids in Japan. Japan's national broadcaster, NHK, gave information on how to donate to relief efforts in China. In China, the media expressed gratitude to the Japanese rescue teams and relief efforts. And in Japan, the newspaper *Sankei Shimbun* filed reports about the numerous thank you messages left to the Japanese on the discussion boards of the Qiangguoluntan forum. Coverage of this phenomenon was translated into Chinese and received positive feedback from Chinese viewers.[64] Such interactions between the media and the public appeared to work better than official contacts alone.

During this period, the threatening image of China as a country of extreme nationalism was replaced by an image of a victim suffering from a serious natural disaster. China's prompt responses to outside aid gave a soft touch to its old image of being inward looking and refusing to accept any criticism or aid from the larger international community. However, as a Chinese communication scholar based in Shanghai pointed out, the openness and transparency that the Chinese government attempted to project during the earthquake may have only been an aberration, as it is still too early to be considered a permanent change of policy.[65] Rather, it should be merely considered a programmatic response of the government in order to improve its public image, which was seriously damaged by its controversial approach in handling the riots in Tibet and an unsuccessful presentation of itself to the world during the torch relays.

The Olympic Games: testing emerging discourses (August 2008)

When the Games began, the Chinese Community Party's propaganda department and the General Administration of Sport in China took a joint action to serve what had been termed the 'Big Olympics' project. One of the major early aims of this project was to ease Chinese nationalism by avoiding overemphasizing the victories of Chinese teams. More specifically, the Chinese media were encouraged to promote a new discourse of friendship and commonality between China and Japan, following the official line 'taking history as a mirror and looking forward to the future', a phrase which reappeared in many newspapers just before the opening ceremony.[66] At this stage, the soft power strategy focussed on controlling the media to advance unofficial and cultural ties between China and Japan.

Hybrid public icons were selected to represent a new hybrid Sino-Japanese identity that would hopefully symbolize Sino-Japan reconciliation despite the continuing disputes between the two countries outside the Olympics sports venues. Ai Fukihara, a young Japanese female table tennis player, and Masayo Imura, the Japanese coach of the Chinese Olympics synchronized swimming team, were chosen to highlight emerging Sino-Japan ties. Ai was born in Japan and studied table tennis in China. The Chinese media teased Ai in a friendly manner, suggesting that 'she was born in Japan but made in China'. Ai also played table tennis with China's president Hu during a trip to Japan in advance of the Olympics. Given the Chinese nickname, 'Ceramic doll' (*ci wa wa*), Ai was treated like a celebrity in China. She was photographed in a crowd of fans and journalists soon after her arrival in

Beijing for the Games. She was also chosen to be the Japanese flag bearer at the opening ceremonies, a clear symbolic message from both governments that a new era in Sino-Japanese relations should begin. After Ai lost the match with the famous Chinese player Zhang Yining, the *Beijing News* issued an article quoting Ai saying that she felt like she was playing at home when playing in Beijing because so many Chinese fans cheered for her.[67]

Masayo Imura, 'known as the godmother of Japanese synchronised swimming', was praised by Chinese media for coaching the Chinese team, 'a mission once unthinkable'. Appointing her the coach of the Chinese team was explained by a combination of 'the attempt to tap into her experience for success in the pool' and the aim 'to promote Imura as an icon for Sino-Japanese reconciliation'. In an article published by the *Beijing News* on 23 August Masayo was praised again for her contribution to the Chinese team. This article also mentioned the great pressure that Masayo felt in Japan for coaching the Chinese swimmers. According to the article, Masayo was criticized in Japan for leading the Chinese team, which defeated the Japanese during the Asian Games in Doha in 2006. After Russia and Spain, China and Japan are considered the major contenders in this sport. However, this article did not mention the fact that Masayo was labelled as a 'traitor' by some Japanese media.[68] The hostility experienced by Masayo at home suggests that this hybrid public icon was not easily accepted, even though her history in this role dated back to at least 2006.

In addition to the promotion of hybrid public icons, there were news stories addressing mutual understanding and cultural commonalities between China and Japan. In a *Global Times* article titled 'Japanese Understood China's Olympic Complex Most', Geng Xin, the Assistant Director of the Institute of Japanese JCC New Japan, suggested that in comparison with Europeans and Americans, the cultural commonality between China and Japan helped the Japanese understand China's desire to host the Olympics better. He also addressed the differences in how both protesters and China's supporters were treated during the torch relay in Japan compared to how they were treated in Europe and North America.[69] The differences, as suggested by the scholar, include a better understanding of Chinese sentiments, the politer approach of the local police towards Chinese students, and the tougher approach adopted for those who attempted to stop the torch relay.

Similarly, a *Global Times* story published on 9 August about how the world reported and discussed the opening ceremony stated that an NHK commentator in the live TV broadcast of the ceremony promptly and accurately interpreted the meaning of 'Confucius words' read out by Chinese dancers as well as the meaning of the Chinese character '和' (Harmony) shown on the screen.[70] The underlying meaning of this article was that the Japanese had a better understanding of Chinese culture than media commentators from other nation-states, again reinforcing the notion of a special relationship between China and Japan.

Another approach to soft power vis-à-vis Japan was also pursued, although due to its subtle nature, it was not as clearly linked with the Olympics as the promotion of hybrid public icons and stories focusing on commonalities between the two nation-states. This approach involved some nascent attempts to emphasize Asian unity during the Olympics. For instance, the *Global Times* article 'Asians are Pride of Olympics Medals' suggests that both China's and Japan's victories, along with those of other Asian nation-states, should be interpreted as contributing to Pan-Asian success and that the whole of Asia should act together in order to compete with Europe and North America in sport.[71]

In addition to these laudatory articles praising commonality, there were articles that covered concerns over food safety in China. For example, on 21 August the *Global Times* quoted a news story released by Kyodo on the 19th, which reported how the Chinese government took serious action to ensure the safety of the food provided in the Olympic village in order to ease previous concerns caused by the contaminated dumplings imported from China. In addition, in the middle of the Games, there were some reports on the decision made by the former Japanese Prime Minister Fukuda to not visit Yasukuni Shrine in Japan on 15 August. An article titled 'Fukyda is Not Going to Visit the Shrine on August 15' released by Xinhua News Agency appeared in the *Beijing News* issued on 6 August. Clearly, the *Beijing News,* just like other Chinese newspapers, had to follow Xinhua's line on this politically sensitive issue. On the one hand, this article quotes Fukuda speaking to the Japanese media which clearly indicated his attitude towards the Shrine and the improved relations between China and Japan; on the other hand, it emphasized the consequences of visits by Fukuda's predecessor on the tense relations between China and South Korea. *Global News* also released a feature on the day after the 63rd anniversary of Japan's surrender in the Second World War that was about Fukuda's decision to not visit the Shrine again.[72] The article also covered the ceremonies held in South Korea, as if to frame the issue as less relevant to China in order to avoid provoking Chinese nationalistic sentiments. Ultimately, however, Fukuda's decision upon the 63rd anniversary of Japan's surrender in the Second World War was largely overshadowed by the coverage of the Games.

Overall we found that, unlike in the United States where old discourses were given new power, the Beijing Olympics were used by both the Chinese government and the Japanese government to test emerging discourses. As we have suggested, however, these emerging media discourses faced enormous pressures from the existing expectations of audiences used to the agendas of publications such as the *Global News* and from a new media landscape that the Chinese government has more difficulty controlling. Nevertheless, we contend that the stories of Ai, the table tennis player, and Masayo, the swim coach, can be read as successful future-oriented soft power narratives that both supplement other public diplomacy efforts to emphasize a common history and culture and, perhaps more importantly, demonstrate how a common future could be built.

Conclusion

The Olympics, as a global media event, provided China with public diplomacy opportunities and challenges. Our comparative analysis of how the interaction of Chinese nationalism and soft power strategies was covered by the media in the United States and Japan indicates that the 2008 Beijing Olympics did not make any major public diplomacy breakthroughs. In general, a negative predisposition to China in both nation-states, combined with overly transparent and unsophisticated Chinese image control tactics, limited the soft power potential of the Games.

Our findings suggest that in the United States the Beijing Olympics may have actually had a detrimental impact on China's image, with the Olympic spotlight highlighting China's refusal to conform to the norms of Western civil society. We have suggested that the Olympic Games were a poor vehicle for China's attempt to fashion itself as an exemplar of an alternative to American and Western notions of progress, given how steeped the IOC is in Western conceptions of internationalism. Further, we have argued that this poorly chosen vehicle was made all the more problematic by the influence of NGOs and civil society groups, whose multiple agendas were swallowed by a larger anti-China narrative that existed in the United States prior to the Games. Ultimately, the messaging of NGOs and civil society groups gave new power to the already growing American anti-China narrative. This anti-China narrative was further fuelled by protests in China and by members of the Chinese diaspora who were angered by what they saw as a hijacking of China's 'coming out' party. Although the May 2008 Sichuan earthquake seemed to cool the influence of both pro- and anti-China activists, this proved to be a temporary reprieve. As the Beijing Games progressed in August 2008, evidence of the lasting negative influence of the torch relay controversy appeared in negative American media coverage of China's efforts during the opening ceremonies and key athletic competitions. Ultimately, the Olympic Games, which had been a space for Cold War battles, once again provided a platform for an ideological battle, this time between the normative Western forces of a self-defined global consensus and a nation-state claiming status as a leader of an alternative to that so-called consensus. In the United States, at least, the battle was over before it began, as NGO and civil society groups promoted media messages that reassured American audiences that they were on the side of the righteous, and as Chinese nationalism, climaxing in xenophobic protests in the spring of 2008, cast a dubious shadow over any alternative soft rise narrative that emerged from China.

Our analysis of the soft power influence of the Olympic Games on Japan indicates that China did realize some limited public diplomacy goals. During the Japanese leg of the torch relay, the negative response, although somewhat muted, was similar to that in North America and Europe. And, the earthquake became a turning point in China's relationships with Japan, as it did with much of the rest of the world. However, the mutual respect that came out of the earthquake's aftermath was particularly powerful in the relationship between China and Japan, usurping the well-planned China-Japan summit as a key moment in the recent thawing of relations between the two nation-states. During the Olympic Games in August, a new discourse about hybrid Japanese-Chinese identity began to emerge around key figures such as Ai Fukihara and Masayo Imura. This and other new discourses of shared identity and a shared future were based on what appears to be a growing appreciation of cultural similarities between China and Japan. However, the influence of this nascent discourse on soft power efforts beyond the Beijing Olympics has yet to be tested. It is essential to remember that the apparent August reprieve in tensions between the two nations was largely the result of a temporary administrative decision to control and construct Chinese media coverage of Japan. Therefore, it will be important to gauge the long-term viability of these emerging narratives and ask whether the short term soft power strategies of the Beijing Olympics will be enough to combat nationalisms that have, to a large extent, been premised on centuries of historical tensions between the two countries.

As the Olympic spotlight shines on future Games hosts, we believe it is important to ask questions about the role of the Games in the larger arena of contemporary public diplomacy. While the Beijing Olympics did allow China and Japan to explore new approaches to mutuality, the global reach of the Games meant that China, as the host nation, was expected to cooperate with other stakeholders in the Olympics Family to construct a generalized and benign Games narrative that would resonate with global audiences. We contend that Games narratives, as products of what we've termed cooperative soft power, remain too general for different and nuanced applications to multiple nation-states. We suggest, for example, that Olympics-related positive outcomes in Sino-Japanese relations were relatively small and could probably have been accomplished via vehicles other than the Olympic Games. Indeed, we are tempted to ask whether the advances in Sino-Japanese relations happened because of the Games or in spite of nationalisms excited by the Games. Further, we contend that despite the apolitical pretences of the IOC, the internationalist ideology of Olympism, which Games' messaging is expected to promote, contributes to the continued hegemony of Western norms. As our analysis of the American response to Beijing's attempt to produce different Olympics messaging that challenged Western hegemony indicates, periphery host-nations are likely to expose themselves to condemnation for such behaviour. Given China's relatively modest public diplomacy successes in bilateral relations with Japan and its multilateral public diplomacy failures with the United States and other Western nation-states, we contend that the Olympic Games was a poor vehicle for extending China's *Charm Offensive* and we suggest that the Beijing Games should be studied closely as a cautionary example by future non-Western *or* periphery hosts who are considering bidding for the Olympics

Notes

1 Nielson Wire, 'Beijing Olympics Draw Largest Ever Global TV Audience'. September 5, 2008. http://blog.nielsen.com/nielsenwire/media_entertainment/beijing-olympics-draw-largest-ever-global-tv-audience; Wurtzel, 'NBC's Billion-Dollar Research'.
2 Cull, 'The Public Diplomacy', 126.
3 'BBC World Service Poll: Views of China and Russia Decline in Global Poll'. BBC World Service, February 6, 2009. http://news.bbc.co.uk/2/shared/bsp/hi/pdfs/06_02_09bbcworld servicepoll.pdf.
4 Ibid.; Kurlantzick, *Charm Offensive*.
5 Nye, *Soft Power*, 11.
6 Dayan and Katz, *Media Events*.
7 MacAloon, 'Olympic Games'.
8 deLisle, 'One World', 31.
9 Anderson, 'Western Nationalism'. Also see for example: Alison, 'Sport and Nationalism'; Bairner, 'Sport and the Nation'; Miller *et al.*, *Globalization and Sport*.
10 Kevin Eason, 'American Refuses to Accept Defeat in the Medal Count'. *Times Online*, August 25, 2008. http://www.timesonline.co.uk/tol/sport/olympics/article4599875.ece.
11 Anderson, *Imagined Communities*; Hobsbawm, *Nations and Nationalism*.
12 Ang, *Living Room Wars*, 146.
13 Human Rights Watch, for example, released a *Reporters Guide* for activist-reporters who planned to travel to Beijing in 2008. The guide is available online: 'Human Rights Watch Reporter's Guide to Covering the Beijing Olympics'. http://china.hrw.org/files/HRW_Beijing_Olympics_Reporters_Guide.pdf.
14 Students for a Free Tibet, 'Tibetan-Canadian Observer Detained in Beijing Hours before Olympics Countdown Celebration'. August 3, 2007. http://www.studentsforafreetibet.org/article.php?id=1103.
15 Price, 'On Seizing the Olympic Platform'.
16 Smith, '2008 Summer Games'; Girginov, 'Creative Tensions'.
17 Wasserstrom, 'Dreams and Nightmares'.
18 Henry and Al-Tauqi, 'The Development', 356.
19 Black and Van Der Westhuizen, 'The Allure'.
20 Quoted in Finlay, 'Toward the Future', 383.
21 deLisle, 'One World'; Girginov, 'Creative Tensions', 899; Ren, 'Embracing Wushu'.
22 Wang, 'Public Diplomacy', 265.
23 Economy and Segal, 'China's Olympic Nightmare'.
24 Quoted in 'IOC "Surprised" by Tibet Unrest'. *Tibet News Digest*, December 31, 2008. http://www.tibetinfonet.net/content/news/10906.
25 Close, Askew and Xu, *The Beijing Olympiad*; K. Bennhold and E. Rosenthal, 'As Olympic Torch Visits Paris, Protests and Scuffles Follow', *The New York Times*, April 8, 2008, A6.
26 Bennhold and Rosenthal, 'As Olympic Torch Visits Paris', A6.
27 Rothstein, 'The Relay of Fire Ignited by the Nazis', E1.
28 Mostrous, 'CNN Apologises to China over "Thugs and Goons" Comment by Jack Cafferty'.
29 'Torchbearer Exhibits Courage in Paris'. Beijing Organizing Committee for the Games of the XXIX Olympiad, April 8, 2008. http://torchrelay.beijing2008.cn/en/journey/paris/news/n214297268.shtml.
30 Xinhua News Agency, 'Dalai Coterie's Conspiracy Aimed at Sabotaging Olympics, Seeks Tibet Independence'.
31 'Beijing's Bad Faith Olympics', *The New York Times*, August 23, 2008, A8.
32 Dewan, 'Chinese Students in the U.S. Fight "Biased" View of Home', A1.

[33] Economy and Segal, 'China's Olympic Nightmare'; see also Jacobs and Wong, 'As the Search for Survivors Scales Back, an Air of Hopelessness Descends', A10.

[34] Zinser, 'I.O.C. Bars International Torch Relays'.

[35] BBC World Service, 'BBC World Service Poll'.

[36] Jacobs and Wong, 'As the Search for Survivors Scales Back', A10.

[37] Araton, 'Stepping off Soapbox as China Mourns', D1.

[38] Jolly, 'Dior Drops Actress From Ads After China Remarks', C8.

[39] French, 'U.N. Leader Praises China's Response to Quake', A8; Jacobs, 'A Rescue in China, Uncensored'.

[40] The Darfur Olympics webcast is available online: 'The Darfur Olympics: August 8–15th, 2008'. http://www.darfurolympics.net/dayone.php.

[41] Yardley, 'China's Leaders Try to Impress and Reassure World'.

[42] Tang, 'Eyes Pulled Back, the Chinese Look Intimidating'.

[43] Bianco, 'Review: Opening Ceremony Rewrote the Record Books'.

[44] Brooks, 'Harmony and the Dream', A21.

[45] Eifling, 'China's Potemkin Olympics', quoted in Yardley, 'In Grand Olympic Show, Some Sleight of Voice', A1.

[46] Montez De Oca, 'As Our Muscles Get Softer', 149; Miller, *Sportsex*, 30; Araton, 'Earthquake Shifts Tone of Games'.

[47] Humphreys and Finlay, 'New Technologies'.

[48] *New York Times*, 'Beijing's Bad Faith Olympics', A8; Eifling, 'China's Potemkin Olympics'.

[49] Araton, 'Athletes Only as Old as China Says They Are'. The IOC later investigated the scandal. The investigation was not able to substantiate claims about the underage gymnasts.

[50] Reported by the BBC Chinese Service, 'Opinion Polls show Big Disagreement in what Japanese and Chinese Publics think about Each Other' (in Chinese), September 9, 2008. http://news.bbc.co.uk/chinese/simp/hi/newsid_7600000/newsid_7607000/7607020.stm.

[51] 'Chinese Riot after Japan Victory', BBC World Service, August 7, 2004. http://news.bbc.co.uk/1/hi/world/asia-pacific/3541380.stm

[52] Feng, 'The Causes and Symptoms of Sino-Japan Historical Problems' (in Chinese), May 12, 2005. http://theory.people.com.cn/GB/ 40536/3383248.html; Roy, 'The Sources', 195.

[53] BBC World Service, 'China Protests at Japanese Shrine Visit', April 23, 2002. http://news.bbc.co.uk/1/hi/world/asia-pacific/1946389.stm.

[54] McNeill, 'Media Intimidation in Japan'.

[55] Roy, 'The Sources', 198; Penney, 'China Comparisons'; Zhou, *Cheering up for China*, 199.

[56] Ueno and Hirokawa, 'China Pesticide-Tainted Dumplings Poison 175 Japanese', February 1, 2008. http://www.bloomberg.com/apps/news?pid=20601087&sid=aymCD4ZxVaLE&refer=home.

[57] Feng, 'The Causes and Symptoms of Sino-Japan Historical Problems'; Curtin, 'Sea of Confrontation: Japan-China Territorial and Gas Dispute Intensifies', October 26, 2005. http://www.nautilus.org/aesnet/2005/OCT2605/JF_ChinaSea.pdf; Lin, 'An Analysis'; Penney, 'China Comparisons'; K. Yoshikazu, 'Do We Still Need Diplomacy?' (in Chinese), February 13, 2009. http://www.ftchinese.com/story.php?storyid=001024654; 'China's Olympic Hopefuls Go for Gold', *BBC World Service*, August 5, 2007. http://news.bbc.co.uk/1/hi/world/asia-pacific/6918060.stm.

[58] Song, *A Study on Olympics*; Zhou, *Cheering up for China*; Curtin, *Sea of Confrontation*; Lin, 'An Analysis'; Penney, 'China Comparisons'.

[59] Penny, 'China Comparisons', 15.

[60] Qiu, 'Why is Hu's Visit to Japan Highly Sensitive' (in Chinese), April 22, 2008. http://blog.ifeng.com/article/1408452.html.

[61] Song, *A Study on Olympics*, 101–3.

[62] 'Each Torchbearer will be Encircled by Five Riot Police Force Members in Japan' (in Chinese), *Global News* (or Huanqiu Online), April 24, 2008. http://world.huanqiu.com/roll/2008-04/97714.html.

[63] 'Japanese Rightists Beat Chinese Students in Japan During the Torch Relay' (in Chinese), *Global Times* (or Huanqiu Online), April 26, 2008. http://world.huanqiu.com/roll/2008-04/98799_5.html; Zhang, 'Chinese Student's Analysis of Japanese Media's coverage of the Japanese Leg of Torch Relay' (in Chinese), May 8, 2008. http://www.zaobao.com/special/forum/pages6/forum_jp080508.shtml.

[64] *Associated Press*, 'Report: Japan Won't Use Military to Deliver Aid: Amid Unease in China, Former Enemy Ditches its Plan for Quake Relief', May 29, 2008. http://www.msnbc.msn.com/id/24871606//; Pei, 'Were the "Rumours" about Japan's Plans to Use Military Force to Deliver Aid to China True?'; *Beijing Daily*, 'This is a Better Sino-Japan Diplomacy' (in Chinese), May 22, 2008. http://www.beijingdaily.com.cn/sdbd/200805/t20080522_460526.htm; *Kyodo Chinese Service*, 'Olympics Stories Hub' (in Chinese), 2008. http://china.kyodo.co.jp/modules/fsStory. The Kyodo Chinese News Service featured a series of Olympic Stories during the Games on a central website: http://china.kyodo.co.jp/modules/fsStory.

[65] This Chinese communication scholar preferred to stay anonymous for this essay.

[66] Song, *A Study on Olympics*, 170–1; *People's Daily (Overseas Edition)*, 'The 30th Anniversary of the Signing of the China-Japan Treaty of Peace and Friendship' (in Chinese), August 5, 2008. http://news.xinhuanet.com/world/2008-08/05/content_8956889.htm.

[67] *Xinhua Daily Telegraph*, 'One Ai Fukyhara is Not Enough' (in Chinese), April 9, 2006. http://news.xinhuanet.com/mrdx/2006-04/09/content_4401858.htm; Min, '"Ceramic Doll" was Carried to Bus', A20; Zhao, 'Playing with Zhang Yining: "I only tried what I could"', A22.

[68] Zhou, 'Foreign Coaches Drive China's Success'; Zhang, 'The Godmother of Synchronised Swimming Masayo Imura: "Martial Arts are Very Cool"', A25; Heller, 'An Expat Coach's Olympic Game Plan', August 1, 2008. http://features.csmonitor.com/backstory/2008/08/01/qbastian/.

[69] Geng, 'Japanese Understood China's Olympic Complex Most', 14.

[70] 'The Whole World is Enjoying this Moment' (in Chinese), *Global Times*, August 9, 2008, 1–2.

[71] 'Asian are Pride of Olympics Medals' (in Chinese), *Global Times* (or Huanqiu Online), August 13, 2008, 7.

[72] 'Japan and South Korea are Celebrating 8/15' (in Chinese), *Global Times*, August 15, 2008, 3.

References

Alison, L. 'Sport and Nationalism'. In *Handbook of Sports Studies*, edited by J. Coakley and E. Dunning, 344–55. London: Sage, 2000.

Anderson, B. *Imagined Communities: Reflections on the Origin and Spread of Nationalism*. London: Verso, 1991.

Anderson, B. 'Western Nationalism and Eastern Nationalism: Is There a Difference that Matters?'. *New Left Review* 9 (2001): 31–42.

Ang, I. *Living Room Wars*. London: Routledge, 1996.

Araton, H. 'Athletes Only as Old as China Says They Are'. *The New York Times Online*, August 13, 2008. http://www.nytimes.com/2008/08/13/sports/olympics/13araton.html?scp=2&sq=Araton&st=Search.

Araton, H. 'Earthquake Shifts Tore of Games'. *The New York Times Online*, May 23, 2008. http://www.nytimes.com/2008/05/23/sports/olympics/23araton.html.

Araton, H. 'Stepping off Soapbox as China Mourns'. *The New York Times*, May 23, 2008.

Bairner, A. 'Sport and the Nation in the Global Era'. In *The Global Politics of Sport*, edited by L. Allison, 87–100. London: Routledge, 2005.

Bianco, R. 'Review: Opening Ceremony Rewrote The Record Books'. *The USA Today*, August 9, 2008. http://www.usatoday.com/life/television/reviews/2008-08-09-opening-ceremony-review_N.html.

Black, D., and J. Van Der Westhuizen. 'The Allure of Global Games for 'Semi-peripheral' Polities and Spaces: A Research Agenda'. *Third World Quarterly* 25, no. 7 (2004): 1195–214.

Brooks, D. 'Harmony and the Dream'. *The New York Times*, August 12, 2008.

Close, P., D. Askew, and X. Xu. *The Beijing Olympiad: The Political Economy of a Sporting Mega-Event*. London: Routledge, 2007.

Cull, N. 'The Public Diplomacy of the Modern Olympic Games and China's Soft Power Strategy'. In *Owning The Olympics: Narratives of the New China*, edited by M. Price and D. Dayan, 117–44. Ann Arbor, MI: The University of Michigan Press, 2008.

Dayan, D., and E. Katz. *Media Events: The Live Broadcasting of History*. Cambridge, MA: Harvard University Press, 1992.

deLisle, J. 'One World, Different Dreams: The Contest to Define the Beijing Olympics'. In *Owning The Olympics: Narratives of the New China*, edited by M. Price and D. Dayan, 15–66. Ann Arbor, MI: The University of Michigan Press, 2008.

Dewan, S. 'Chinese Students in the U.S. Fight "Biased" View of Home'. *The New York Times*, April 29, 2008.

Economy, E., and A. Segal. 'China's Olympic Nightmare'. *Foreign Affairs*, July/August, 2008. http://www.foreignaffairs.com/articles/64447/elizabeth-c-economy-and-adam-segal/chinas-olympic-nightmare.

Eifling, S. 'China's Potemkin Olympics'. *Columbia Journalism Review*, August 22, 2008. http://www.cjr.org/behind_the_news/chinas_potemkin_olympics.php.

Finlay, C. 'Toward the Future: The New Olympic Internationalism'. In *Owning The Olympics: Narratives of the New China*, edited by M. Price and D. Dayan, 375–90. Ann Arbor, MI: The University of Michigan Press, 2008.

French, H. 'U.N. Leader Praises China's Response to Quake'. *The New York Times*, May 25, 2008.

Geng, Z. 'Japanese Understood China's Olympic Complex Most'. *The Global News*, August 17, 2008.

Girginov, V. 'Creative Tensions: "Join in London" Meets "Dancing Beijing" – The Cultural Power of the Olympics'. *The International Journal of the History of Sport* 25, no. 7 (2008): 893–914.

Henry, I., and M. Al-Tauqi. 'The Development of Olympic Solidarity: West and Non-West (Core and Periphery) Relations in the Olympic World'. *The International Journal of the History of Sport* 25, no. 3 (2008): 355–69.

Hobsbawm, E. *Nations and Nationalism since 1780*. Cambridge: Cambridge University Press, 1990.

Humphreys, L., and C. Finlay. 'New Technologies, New Narratives'. In *Owning The Olympics: Narratives of the New China*, edited by M. Price and D. Dayan, 284–306. Ann Arbor, MI: The University of Michigan Press, 2008.

Jacobs, A. 'A Rescue in China Uncensored'. *The New York Times Online*, May 14, 2008. http://www.nytimes.com/2008/05/14/world/asia/14response.html?pagewanted=1&_r=3.

Jacobs, A., and E. Wong. 'As the Search for Survivors Scales Back, an Air of Hopelessness Descends'. *The New York Times*, May 19, 2008.

Jolly, D. 'Dior Drops Actress From Ads After China Remarks'. *The New York Times*, May 30, 2008.

Kurlantzick, J. *Charm Offensive: How China's Soft Power is Changing the World*. New Haven, CT: Yale University Press, 2007.

Lin, X. 'An Analysis of the Changes to Japanese Media's Coverage of China'. (in Chinese) *World Economics and Politics* 10 (2006): 1–13. http://www.iwep.org.cn.

MacAloon, J. 'Olympic Games and the Theory of Spectacle in Modern Societies'. In *Rite, Drama, Festival, Spectacle*, edited by J. MacAloon, 241–80. Philadelphia, PA: Institute for the Study of Human Issues, 1984.

McNeill, D. 'Media Intimidation in Japan: A Close Encounter with Hard Japanese Nationalism'. Discussion Paper published in *Electronic journal of contemporary Japanese Studies*, 2001. http://www.japanesestudies.org.uk/discussionpapers/McNeill.html.

Miller, T. *Sportsex*. Philadelphia, PA: Temple University Press, 2001.

Miller, T., G.A. Lawrence, J. McKay and D. Rowe. *Globalization and Sport*. London: Sage Publications, 2001.

Min, H. '"Ceramic Doll" Was Carried to Bus' (in Chinese). *Beijing News*, August 8, 2008.

Montez De Oca, J. 'As Our Muscles Get Softer, Our Missile Race Becomes Harder: Cultural Citizenship and the "Muscle Gap"'. *Journal of Historical Sociology* 19, no. 3 (2005): 145–72.

Mostrous, A. 'CNN Apologies to China over "Thugs and Goons" Comment by Jack Cafferty'. *Times Online*, April 16, 2008. http://www.timesonline.co.uk/tol/news/world/article3756437.ece.

Nye, J. *Soft Power*. New York: Public Affairs, 2004.

Pei, J. 'Were the "Rumours" about Japan's Plans to Use Military Force to Deliver Aid to China True?' (in Chinese). *China Youth Daily*, June 2, 2008. http://world.people.com.cn/GB/14549/7328296.html.

Penney, M. 'China Comparisons: Images of China in Japanese Popular Non-Fiction'. *Graduate Journal of Asia-Pacific Studies* 4, no. 2 (2006): 15–28.

Price, M. 'On Seizing the Olympic Platform'. In *Owning The Olympics: Narratives of the New China*, edited by M. Price and D. Dayan, 86–116. Ann Arbor, MI: The University of Michigan Press, 2008.

Ren, H. 'Embracing Wushu: Globalization and Cultural Diversification of the Olympic Movement'. In *Owning The Olympics: Narratives of the New China*, edited by M. Price and D. Dayan, 307–19. Ann Arbor, MI: The University of Michigan Press, 2008.

Rothstein, E. 'The Relay of Fire Ignited by the Nazis'. *The New York Times*, April 14, 2008.

Roy, D. 'The Sources and Limits of Sino-Japanese Tensions'. *Survival* 47, no. 2 (2005): 191–214.
Smith, B. '2008 Summer Games: Beijing's Image Campaign'. Paper presented at the 2007 annual meeting of the International Communication Association, San Francisco, California, May 25, 2007.
Song, J. *A Study on Olympics Pursuing Peace* (in Chinese). Beijing: Beijing Sports University Press, 2007.
Tang, I. 'Eyes Pulled Back, the Chinese Look Intimidating'. *Asian Week*, September 5, 2008. http://www.asianweek.com/2008/09/us/eyes-pulled-back-the-chinese-look-intimidating.
Wang, Y. 'Public Diplomacy and the Rise of Chinese Soft Power'. *The Annals of the American Academy of Political and Social Science* 616 (2008): 257–73.
Wasserstrom, J. 'Dreams and Nightmares: History and U.S. Visions of the Beijing Games'. In *Owning The Olympics: Narratives of the New China*, edited by M. Price and D. Dayan, 163–84. Ann Arbor, MI: The University of Michigan Press, 2008.
Wurtzel, A. 'NBC's Billion-Dollar Research Lab: 8 Audience Lessons We Learned From Beijing'. The 2008 Robert Lewis Shayon Lecture at the Annenberg School for Communication, Philadelphia, PA, November 1, 2008.
Xinhua News Agency. 'Dalai Coterie's Conspiracy Aimed at Sabotaging Olympics, Seeks Tibet Independence'. *English People's Daily Online*, July 3, 2008. http://english.people.com.cn/90001/90776/6441615.html.
Yang, J. 'Of Interest and Distrust: Understanding China's Policy Towards Japan China'. *An International Journal* 5, no. 2 (2007): 250–75.
Yardley, J. 'In Grand Olympic Show, Some Sleight of Voice'. *The New York Times*, August 13, 2008.
Yardley, J. 'China's Leaders Try to Impress and Reassure World'. *The New York Times Online*, August 9, 2008. http://www.nytimes.com/2008/08/09/sports/olympics/09china.html?page wanted = 1&sq = Opening&st = Search&scp = 2.
Zhang, B. 'The Godmother of Synchronised Swimming Masayo Imura: "Martial Arts are Very Cool"' (in Chinese). *Beijing News*, August 23, 2008.
Zhou, M. 'Foreign Coaches Drive China's Success'. *The South China Morning Post Online*, August 23, 2008. http://postphoto.scmp.com/Article.aspx?id=3261&section = latestnews.
Zinser, L. 'I.O.C. Bars International Torch Relays'. *The New York Times Online*, March 28, 2009. http://www.nytimes.com/2009/03/28/sports/othersports/28torch.html.

Human rights and the Olympic Movement after Beijing

Bruce Kidd

Faculty of Physical Education and Health, University of Toronto, 55 Harbord St., Toronto, Ontario M5S 2W6, Canada

It was the Olympic Movement and the IOC, not China, which received the harshest criticism for the abuse of human rights and athletes' rights during the year of the Beijing Olympics. The IOC appeared complicit in the Chinese Government's crackdown on open protest and public dissent, and it contributed to a deep chill among athletes and coaches before and during the Games. It suffered serious blows to its moral authority and legitimacy as a humanitarian organization as a result. This essay places the human rights debates precipitated by the Beijing Olympics in the context of Olympic history, and discusses their implications for the future of the Olympic Movement. I argue that while the IOC never previously made adherence to human rights a monitored standard for admission into the Olympic Movement, nor a condition for staging its Games, it should now do so, and will recommend several measures that should be taken.

Introduction

Human rights and athletes' rights took a beating during the Beijing Olympics. Although China has become a much more open and prosperous society in recent years, in the build-up to the Games the government repeatedly cracked down on open protest and public dissent. Amnesty International and Human Rights Watch documented forced removals of inner-city residents to clear the ground for Olympic construction and forced removals of minority workers from the city; the increased arrest, detention and harassment of critics, including those brave enough to apply to speak at 'protest zones'; and repeated violations of media freedom for Chinese and international media, including Olympic-accredited journalists. During the Games, websites were blocked on the internet.[1] Between 2004 and 2008, Amnesty International monitored four categories of human rights abuse – censorship of the Internet, arbitrary detention, abusive treatment of those in detention and the use of the death penalty. On the eve of the Olympics, it concluded:

> Notwithstanding some important legislative and institutional reforms ... on balance the Chinese authorities have so far failed to fulfil their own commitments to improve human rights. In fact, the authorities have used the Olympic Games as pretext to continue, and in some respects, intensify existing policies and practices which have led to serious and widespread violations of human rights. Within the core areas monitored by Amnesty International, the only sign of significant reform is with regard to the application of the death penalty and the ability of foreign media to cover news stories in China. While these reforms are welcome, they have both been beset by structural weaknesses and a failure to make them fully operational in practice.[2]

On the eve of the Paralympics, Sophie Richardson, Asia advocacy director of Human Rights Watch, said that:

> The Chinese government deserves praise for enacting laws and ratifying the Convention on the Rights of Persons with Disabilities. But so far these protections have meant little to persons with disabilities and their advocates in China who struggle to promote their rights and, in particular, to fairly compete for employment.[3]

Athletes and other members of the Olympic Family felt a similar chill. While they were well treated materially in Beijing, they felt under enormous pressure to bite their tongues on the issues swirling around the China and the Games. They received little support from the Olympic leadership; at best, the messages were contradictory. In April 2008, at a meeting of the Association of National Olympic Committees (ANOC) in Beijing, International Olympic Committee (IOC) President Jacques Rogge told a news conference that 'freedom of expression is a basic human right', but at the very same meeting, ANOC president Mario Vazquez Rana said that athletes 'should be given some guidance on where their freedom ends'. Two days later in Calgary, Canadian IOC member Richard Pound told Canadian athletes to 'shut up or stay home'.[4] US Olympic speed skating champion Joey Cheek, a member of Team Darfur that sought to raise the awareness about the genocide and the Chinese government's close ties to the government of Sudan, was denied a visa to attend the Games.[5] Press commission chair Kevin Gosper was forced to admit that the IOC had acquiesced in the blocking of Internet sites.[6]

In these circumstances, Rule 51.3 of the *Olympic Charter* – 'No kind of demonstration or political, religious or racial propaganda is permitted in any Olympic sites, venues or other areas' – became a big stick. Canadian aboriginal athlete Monica Pinette, who had proudly worn her Métis sash in the opening ceremony in Athens, was ordered to leave it in her suitcase in Beijing.[7] Kathy Freeman, who so movingly inspired the spirit of reconciliation in Australia by carrying the aboriginal and Australian flags together during her victory lap in Sydney, would never have been allowed to do that in Beijing. Despite the well-known activism and support for progressive causes of athletes throughout the world, I know of only three athletes – Italian fencer Margherita Granbassi, boxer Clemente Russo and kayaker Josefa Idem – who spoke out on issues of social justice during the Games.[8] Others, such as Polish weightlifter Szymon Kolecki, who shaved his head in solidarity with the Tibetans, limited themselves to silent protest.[9] Neither the IOC Athletes' Commission nor any national athletes' association made an effort to defend athletes' rights. Canadian rower Ian Bramwell, who chairs the Athletes' Council of the Canadian Olympic Committee, counselled his fellow athletes to abide by the restrictions imposed by the IOC and COC.[10] Despite their pledges of corporate social responsibility, including the affirmation of human rights, the 12 TOP ('The Olympic Partner') sponsors refused comment.[11]

It was the IOC and the Olympic Movement – not China – that received the bulk of the criticism for these abuses, contradictions and silences. In Canada, three journals that rarely agree on editorial policy were unanimous in their condemnation. The *National Post* proclaimed 'A Black Eye for the IOC', while the other pan-Canadian English-language daily, *The Globe and Mail* editorialized: 'For China to break its promise (to improve human rights) is galling but not surprising. For the IOC to effectively participate in Chinese censorship casts the Olympic Movement into dispute.' The English-Canadian weekly *Maclean's* editorialized: 'Granted, the Olympics are not about politics but since when was silence and injustice an Olympic ideal?'[12] By cowering before the Chinese, the IOC seemed to undermine the very 'placement of sport at the service of the harmonious development of man (and) the preservation of human dignity' that lies at the very heart of the Olympic Charter, seriously damaging the legitimacy and moral integrity of the entire Movement.

How will the Beijing Olympics affect the long struggle for human rights in sport and throughout society? What lessons should be drawn for the realization of athletes' rights? This essay places the human rights debates precipitated by the Beijing Olympics in the context of Olympic history, and discusses their implications for the future of the Olympic Movement. I will argue that while the IOC never previously made adherence to human rights a monitored standard for admission into the Olympic Movement nor a condition for staging its Games, it should now do so. I am a member of both the Canadian Olympic Committee and Amnesty International. While a member of Toronto's bid committee for the 2008 Olympics, I always defended Beijing's right to stage the Games. During the boycott debates in the early months of 2008,[13] I consistently argued against any form of withdrawal, either from the opening ceremonies or the Games. But I believe it is time for the Olympic Movement to step up its support for human rights, and will recommend several measures that should be taken.

An ambiguous history

Many of the attacks on China's record were opportunistic and hypocritical. 'Two wrongs don't make a right', but few critics acknowledged that other Olympic cities have bulldozed neighbourhoods and parks to build facilities and forced minorities out of town. On the eve of the opening ceremonies at the 1976 Games in Montreal, for example, the city tore down an award-winning arts installation drawing attention to the block-busting tactics of developers, and told activists, gays and lesbians to get out of town.[14] Many of the sharpest media criticisms of China's human rights record came from the United States, where capital punishment is still practised, minorities disproportionately imprisoned (one in three black males between the ages of 18 and 30 are in the criminal justice system, ten times the rate for whites in the same age cohort), and under President Bush, international detainees were held without due process at Guantanamo Bay.[15] As the essay by Christopher Finlay in this volume illustrates, many of the attacks rehashed out-of-date Chinese stereotypes. Moreover, the bellicose statements at the time of the international Olympic torch relay by western leaders such as German chancellor Angela Merkel and French president Nicolas Sarkozy belied their governments' support of the United Nation's resolution the previous October 'to use sport as an instrument to promote peace, dialogue and reconciliation in areas of conflict during and beyond the Olympic Games period'.[16]

Moreover, despite the promise of Beijing vice-mayor Liu Jingmin and Olympic leaders Juan Antonio Samaranch, Jacques Rogge and Hein Verbruggen at the time the 2008 Games were awarded to Beijing that human rights would be strengthened as a result, it was not a contractual condition of those Games. In fact, it has never been a condition for membership in the IOC, the recognition of an NOC, nor for the awarding of the Games to demonstrate an exemplary record of human rights. During its first century, the IOC shied away from anything other than its own personal networks for the recruitment of IOC members, and a modest organizational requirement for NOCs and host cities. Its overarching strategy has been to 'fill up the tent', i.e. to create a worldwide movement. It has therefore recognized NOCs and awarded and presided over Games without regard to form of government, social and economic policies and practices, and international behaviour. Such an approach has led it to turn a blind eye to the human rights abuses carried out by host governments, the most horrendous of which was the massacre of several hundred peaceful demonstrators prior to the 1968 Olympics in Mexico.[17] It has left the IOC vulnerable to accusations that it practises 'amoral universalism' and prefers to partner with authoritarian regimes to stage the Games.[18] On the other hand, such a strategy is not just *realpolitik*, but a deliberate corollary to its goal of enhancing intercultural communication and exchange in a diverse, often divided world. 'To ask the peoples of the world to love each other is merely a form of childishness', wrote Pierre de Coubertin in the well-known expression of this logic. 'To ask them to respect each one another is not in the least utopian, but in order to respect one another it is first necessary to know one another.'

It would be impossible to realize the intercultural dialogue it seeks to encourage, goes the argument, if the IOC limited membership to those of like-minded views. There are profound differences in political and social systems among the states and national communities in the world. Even when the United Nations proclaimed the Universal Declaration on Human Rights in 1948, in what was perhaps the last achievement of the coalition that emerged victorious in the Second World War, the signatories placed signi-ficantly different emphases on what it meant, with the liberal-democratic countries stressing the protection of individual freedoms and the socialist countries the obligations of states to fulfil the basic human needs of all citizens. In subsequent years, with the entry of the newly independent countries from the global south into the Olympic Movement, the diversity of political and cultural values and practices further increased. The low threshold ensured an accessible tent. Moreover, for most of the twentieth century, there was wide international consensus around the principle of non-intervention in the domestic affairs of nation states.

To be sure, the contending interests and ideologies of the day have always buffeted the IOC as they did in 2008. There have been intense politics around many NOCs and Games, and the IOC has often been forced to respond. Following the First World War, the IOC was persuaded to suspend the NOCs from the 'aggressor nations' of Austria, Germany and Hungary from the 1920 and 1924 Olympics. It faced a worldwide boycott campaign against the 1936 Olympics in Nazi Germany. In the period since the Second World War, the Olympic Movement has experienced fierce debates about the recognition of NOCs from Israel and Palestine, the Soviet Union, the two Germanys, the two Koreas, China and Taiwan, apartheid South Africa and the breakaway state of Rhodesia, and formal boycotts against the 1976, 1980, 1984 and 1988 Olympics. Each of these issues challenged the assumptions of non-intervention, and drew the IOC willy-nilly into the politics and calculations of human rights. In 1936, the IOC forced the Nazi organizers to remove anti-Semitic signs and banners from Garmisch-Partenkirchen, the site of the Winter Olympics, and Berlin, admit all duly IOC-credentialed participants, and place token Jews on the Germany teams. While these modest conditions did not satisfy the opponents of those Games, let alone prevent the saturation with Nazi propaganda, they did establish important precedents that stood the IOC in good stead in future games, particularly during the Cold War when some western governments sought to exclude athletes and coaches from countries like the German Democratic Republic that they did not formally recognize from participating in Games within their borders.

Perhaps the most instructive example comes from the long struggle against apartheid sport. Initially, the IOC's response to the international campaign was lukewarm. Although it suspended the apartheid-supporting National Olympic Committee of South Africa in 1963 and expelled it in 1970, it did not play an active role in monitoring and enforcing the international moratorium until after the African-led boycott of the 1976 Olympics in Montreal. But then it did, contributing significantly to the legitimization of the moratorium and its increasing effectiveness. In 1980, while standing up to the US-led boycott of the Moscow Olympics, IOC members distinguished between the sports boycott of apartheid South Africa, which it supported, and the call to move or cancel the Moscow Games, which it opposed. President Killanin argued that the anti-apartheid campaign was initiated by fellow sportspersons about the human rights of persons within sport, something for which the IOC must accept responsibility, but that it had neither desire nor ability to intervene with the Soviet Union over Afghanistan, the target of the 1980 boycott campaign. These steps took the Olympic Movement into a policy field where the growing *de facto* concern for human rights jostled uneasily with the traditional culture of non-intervention.

Towards the language of human rights

During the Samaranch years, the IOC assumed further responsibility for the ethical and social conditions governing/affecting Olympic sport, increasing its use of the language of human rights, while admitting more than 50 new NOCs and several new International Federations (IFs) 'into the tent'. In response to the worldwide explosion of women's participation in sport, it significantly increased the number of sports and events they could enter, and elected women to the membership. Through Olympic Solidarity, it steered the largest share of the revenue it earned from television agreements into the training of athletes and the technical preparation of coaches, officials and sports administrators, with a disproportionate share going to the global south. It consolidated links to the United Nations system, signing cooperation agreements with most agencies and in 1993, initiating the Olympic Truce at the General Assembly. It strengthened the International Olympic Academy and encouraged the creation of National Olympic Academies, with the explicit purpose of broadening the commitment of athletes and young sports leaders to humanitarian values. Through Olympic Aid, it provided vaccines and emergency assistance for children and youth in countries ravaged by disease and war. It established the International Court of Arbitration for Sport to protect athletes from unfair or arbitrary decisions, with a special division for the Games to provide virtually instantaneous resolution of disputes and appeals. It proclaimed a 'responsible concern' for environmental issues, and committed itself to 'sustainable development in sport'.

Obviously, there were limits to these initiatives. The IOC turned a deaf ear to the appeal of equity advocates that all NOCs be required to enter female as well as male athletes in the Olympic Games – in Barcelona, 35 of 169 NOCs entered male-only teams – and made halting efforts to strengthen the role of women in leadership.[19] Critics increasingly pointed to the 'say do gap' between the idealistic language of the Olympic leadership and their actual practice. But the Samaranch-led IOC clearly committed itself to a humanitarian agenda and the spirit, if not the letter, of human rights.

It was this promise that fed the IOC's escalating legitimacy crisis during the 1990s. The crisis exploded in 1998 in response to the Salt Lake City bribery scandal and Samaranch's seeming indifference to doping at the discovery of a portable Festina doping lab and the arrest of the entire team during the Tour de France. But it had been building for many years, most tellingly among the thousands of volunteers on whom the Movement depended. It drew upon the growing corporate movement to social responsibility, accountability and transparency and the support of human rights. In this environment, with Senate hearings in the United States, pressure from sponsors, the expulsion and resignation of 10 IOC members, all under the glare of the international media, the IOC re-affirmed and strengthened the Olympic Movement's moral agenda. The subsequent reforms created the IOC Ethics Commission and the World Anti-Doping Agency, promised a stronger commitment to education and culture, provided for the direct election of athletes to the IOC, streamlined the bid process, and committed the IOC to transparency and accountability.[20] Today's *Olympic Charter* resonates strongly with the language of human rights. The 'fundamental principles of Olympism' seek to create 'respect for universal fundamental ethical principles', promote 'a peaceful society concerned with the preservation of human dignity', and enshrine 'the practice of sport as a human right, without discrimination of any kind'. The current *Charter* also calls upon the IOC to 'protect the independence of the Olympic Movement', to 'act against any form of discrimination', and to 'support the promotion of women in sport at all levels and in all structures with a view to implementing the principle of equality of men and women', and 'oppose any political or commercial abuse of sport and athletes'.[21]

Given this history and aspiration, it should not be surprising that the IOC came under criticism for its timidity during the spring and summer of 2008. One can well understand the desire to cooperate with the host government in the interests of a successful Games, but cooperation need not mean capitulation. According to Monique Berlioux, former IOC director, when IOC president Henri Baillet-Latour saw the anti-Semitic signs in Germany prior to the 1936 Winter Olympic Games, he:

> [R]equested an interview with Hitler. After the customary courtesies, he said, 'Mr. Chancellor, the signs shown to the visitors to the Games are not in conformity with Olympic principles.' Hitler replied, 'Mr. President, when you are invited to a friend's home, you don't tell him how to run it, do you?' Baillet-Latour thought a moment and replied, 'Excuse me, Mr. Chancellor, when the five-circled flag is raised over the stadium it is no longer Germany. It is Olympia and we are masters here.' The signs were removed.[22]

In 2008, after years of human rights talk, the IOC repeatedly backed away from any opening that would have enabled it to put its own stamp on the way the issues unfolded. 'We are not a political body, we are not an NGO', Rogge said in response to questions about China and Tibet, in attempt to justify the IOC's refusal to interfere in the internal affairs of the host nations. That comment only served to raise eyebrows because the *Charter* clearly states that the IOC is 'an international non-governmental not-for-profit organization'.[23] While silent on the chill against athletes and media, Rogge was quick to criticize one of the most accomplished performers in Beijing, Jamaican sprinter Usain Bolt, for apparent grandstanding at the conclusion of his world record gold medal in the 100 metres.[24] Such scolding suggested that the IOC was fully in step with the Chinese Government in its heavy-handed security of the Beijing Olympics.

At the same time, the IOC made little effort to create a space for, let alone encourage, the intercultural dialogue among people of different political, social and cultural values and practices that constitutes the Olympic Movement's historic ambition. To be fair, this was a difficult challenge given the security requirements. But in other ways, the staging of the Games in a state-controlled society with deep collectivist traditions presented an easier opportunity to argue from the recognition of difference to the necessity for dialogue, because there was much less chance that the ideologies of liberal individualism would render the task unimportant. The particular contribution of the Olympic Movement, as John MacAloon has argued: 'is not to eliminate (cultural) differences but make the world safer for them'.[25]

The distinct history and accomplishment of China and its people presented many such openings. Yet neither in the build-up to the Games, in the Olympic Village, nor across the Olympic city, did very much of this happen. Many NOCs stationed their athletes in other countries right up until their events, even if it meant that they missed the opening ceremonies. From all reports, attempts at people-to-people contact beyond souvenir shopping were actively discouraged. The only internationalism celebrated was the pursuit of the podium in sport. Despite the dramatic athletic performances, something was lost at the Beijing Olympics. The Olympic Movement threw away the rich opportunities that the human rights debate and the Games could have provided for genuine exchange between participants from different backgrounds and the development of new narratives of understanding. Many Chinese learned much more about the west than the west learned about China as a result of these games. While the IOC succeeded in anchoring the most populous nation in the world 'inside the tent', that significant accomplishment came at the cost of its historic promise of intercultural understanding and its developing agenda to advance human rights.

New century, new possibilities

It is time for a new paradigm of Olympism and human rights. In the first place, the tent is now full, with 205 national communities represented, and all genders, classes, religions and persons with disabilities involved in significant ways. Given the prestige of the Olympic Movement, the visible symbolism of inclusion in the community of nations that the opening ceremonies of the Olympic Games confers, and the IOC's close associations with that other symbol of international legitimacy, the United Nations, it is unlikely that any National Olympic Committee or International Federation will leave. Just as the crisis of 1999 led the IOC to impose new higher standards of personal conduct upon members that reflected the best practices of international governance, the IOC should now consider new higher standards for NOCs, IFs, and Organizing Committees (OCOGs) that reflect the recent advances in human rights.

Secondly, the principle of non-intervention in the affairs of sovereign states that shaped the IOC's formative years is now being supplanted by bold new ideas about the responsibility to protect, the importance of human empowerment as a precondition of human security, and the contribution of sport and culture to empowerment. The principle of non-intervention was intended to protect states and alliances of states from outside military attack. Even if it was not always accepted that particular states had the best interests of their citizens at heart, it was felt that states were sovereign actors and must be respected. The Universal Declaration on Human Rights and the various international conventions elaborating on those rights have been written from this perspective, and call upon states to guarantee them. But in recent years, particularly after the genocides in the former Yugoslavia and Rwanda and the explosion of humanitarian disasters in many parts of the world, it could no longer be seriously maintained that relying upon states to protect citizens was sufficient. With the collapse of the Soviet Union and the end of the Cold War, much of the pressure for powerful alliances to defend the sovereignty of errant member states evaporated. Moreover, it came to be recognized that what happens in any country is shaped by forces and conditions well beyond a state's control. As the United Nations Development Program (UNDP) observed in 1994: 'Famine, disease, pollution, drug trafficking, terrorism, ethnic disputes, and social disintegration are no longer isolated events that are confined within national borders. Their consequences travel the globe.'[26] As a result, while the concept of sovereignty still carries considerable weight, the international community is moving towards a different paradigm whereby respect for sovereignty is contingent upon respect for human rights.

Two emerging ideas flow from this realization – the responsibility to protect and the responsibility to empower. According to the responsibility to protect, on those occasions where a state cannot or will not protect its citizens from ethnic cleansing and mass killing, there is an international responsibility to intervene to protect.[27] The responsibility to empower flows from the realization that it is not enough simply to prevent violence to ensure effective security; humans must also have the capacity to control their own lives with dignity and adequate means. As former UN secretary general Kofi Annan explained in the introduction to the 2003 report of the Commission on Human Security, *Human Security Now,* human security

> embraces far more than the absence of violent conflict. It encompasses human rights, good governance, access to education and health and ensuring that each individual has opportunities and choices to fulfil his or her potential.[28]

The world is no longer prepared to leave security and human rights completely up to nation states.

A third emerging idea brings these developments to a place the Olympic Movement readily understands. If human security requires citizens to be empowered to shape their own destinies, then they need to enjoy not just freedom from want but the freedom to learn and make their own culture, including their own values, norms and beliefs and their forms of creative expression.[29] 'People's horizons extend far beyond survival to matters of love, culture and faith', argued the Commission on Human Security.[30] I would just add sport.

Toward a renewal of Olympism and human rights

This changing context and the experience of Beijing suggest that the Olympic Movement needs a full and open debate about its commitment to a humanitarian agenda, including the realization of human rights, and how it can pursue it in the months and years ahead. From my vantage-point, it should become more interventionist, not less. The IOC should carry out the recommendations of the 2000 Commission about Olympic Solidarity, humanitarian activities, education and culture and bring these in line with the emerging international strategies on human security.[31] It should require National Olympic Committees to report on the education, health and safety of athletes and the extent of 'sport for all' in their countries, post these reports on the its website, and make the results the subject of an international evaluation.

Rather than bow to the pressure of Olympic hosts as it did in Beijing, it should guarantee the full rights of athletes and other Olympic participants and use its moral authority to strengthen human rights and human security in the host countries. To do this effectively, it must make the protection of the rights of peaceful expression of athletes, journalists and citizens a condition of future host contracts. Just as it invited Greenpeace to monitor the environmental practices of the 2000 Games in Sydney, it should commission Amnesty International (or another independent human rights body) to monitor the protection of these rights during the Games and publish their findings. It should require bid committees to propose ways to stimulate peaceful intercultural exchange between Olympic participants and let them know that these proposals will be heavily weighted in the evaluation process. I would also recommend that it require bid cities to submit a social equity plan to enhance human security and social development during the course of Olympic and Paralympic Games and the host city to provide annual reports on implementation, and require Olympic sponsors to demonstrate fair labour practices and environmental best practice.

None of these are utopian suggestions. Some Olympic leaders were embarrassed by the chill on athletes' and journalists' rights in Beijing, and are not prepared to see it repeated. In Lausanne, IOC staff have begun to collect data on the extent of participation among children and youth in selected countries from around the world, in a commendable start to monitoring and evaluation. In Vancouver, the Organizing Committee for the 2010 Winter Olympic and Paralympic Games has set an ambitious sustainability target for itself, and not only publishes its own annual progress report, but in conjunction with the IOC has commissioned independent monitoring.[32] The Chicago City Council unanimously approved a binding commitment to minority participation, affordable housing, community enhancement and other social goals in conjunction with its bid for the 2016 Olympics.[33]

To be sure, an increasing number argue that such steps have nothing to do with high performance sport and the pursuit of the podium. At a recent conference at the University of Toronto on the implementation of the 1999 Olympic reforms, several participants argued that the IOC should 'get out of the values education business and admit that it is really only about sport'. President Rogge seemed to lend support to this view when he told the IOC's 120th session in Beijing that 'we are first and foremost an organization devoted to sport'. But as the outpouring of public opinion during 2008 amply demonstrated, the world expects a higher standard.

Notes

1. 'China: The Olympics Countdown – Broken Promises'. Amnesty International (AI), August 30, 2008. http://www.amnesty.org/en/china-olympics; 'China: Olympics Harm Key Human Rights'. Human Rights Watch (HRW), August 6, 2008. http://china.hrw.org/press;) 'China: As Paralympics Launch, Disabled Face Discrimination'. HRW, September 5, 2008. http://china.hrw.org/press. For one journalist's account, see Vicki Hall, 'Hitting the Wall in China: Media Covering the Beijing Olympics were Promised Complete Freedom, But the Reality was Something Different – and a lot Scarier', *Edmonton Journal*, September 28, 2008.
2. AI, 'China', 16–17.
3. HRW, 'China: As Paralympics Launch, Disabled Face Discrimination'. September 5, 2008. http://china.hrw.org/press/news_release/china_as_paralympics_launch_disabled_face_discrimination.
4. R. Juilliart, 'Freedom of Expression is a Human Right', April 10, 2008. http://www.olympic.org/uk/news/olympic_news/full_story_uk.asp?id=2535; G. Kingston, '"Shut Up or Stay Home", Pound tells Athletes: Olympians who Speak Out in Beijing "Will be Excluded"', *Vancouver Sun*, April 12, 2008; N. Mulvenney, 'Athletes Want Guidance on Freedom to Speak in Beijing'. http://uk.reuters.com/article/topNews/idUKPEK13287020080408.
5. Associated Press, 'China revokes ex-speedskater Joey Cheek's Visa', August 6, 2008. http://www.msnbc.msn.com/id/26047166.
6. AI, 'China'.
7. R. Mickleburgh, 'Politics Unravels Aboriginal Athlete's Plan to Wear Traditional Garb', *Globe and Mail*, August 19, 2008.
8. Associated Press, 'Italy praises athletes' human rights gestures', *International Herald Tribune*, August 24, 2008. http://www.phayul.com/news/article.aspx?id=22617&article=Italy+praises+athletes'+human+rights+gestures&t=1&c=1.
9. France 24, 'Athlete marks first protest action over Tibet', June 1, 2009. http://observers.france24.com; S. Oster, 'A Hairless gesture of ... something', *China Realtime Report*, August 20, 2008. https://www.phayul.com/news/article.aspx.
10. Kingston, '"Shut Up or Stay Home"'.
11. HRW, 'China: Olympic Sponsors Ignore Human Rights Abuses', September 9, 2008. http://china.hrw.org/press/news_release/china_olympic_sponsors_ignore_human_rights_abuses.
12. 'A Black Eye for the IOC', *National Post*, August 1, 2008; 'Beijing Olympics Tainted by Censorship', *Globe and Mail*, July 31, 2008; 'Silent Protests', *Maclean's*, September 8, 2008.
13. Lee, 'Earthquake Changed Canada's Mind on Olympic Boycott – Pound'.
14. Kidd, 'Montreal 1976', 194.
15. AI, '2008 Annual Report for USA', May 30, 2009. http://www.amnestyusa.org/annualreport.php?id=ar&yr=2008&c=USA.
16. United Nations General Assembly, 'Sport for Peace and Development: Building a Peaceful and Better World Through Sport and the Olympic Ideal'. October 31, 2007. http://multimedia.olympic.org/pdf/en_report_1247.pdf.
17. Arbena, 'Mexico City 1968', 175–6.
18. Cf. Hoberman, *The Olympic Crisis*; S. Brunt, 'Power and Might', *Globe and Mail*, August 2, 2008.

[19] By 2004, the number of teams had grown to 201 while the number without women had dropped to nine, but with only 12 of 112 members, the organization is still a long way from parity at the key leadership level; see Chappelet and Kubler-Mabbott, *The International Olympic Committee*, 22, 81.

[20] Mallon, 'The IOC Bribery Scandal', 11–27.

[21] IOC, *Olympic Charter* (2007), February 11, 2010, 14–15. http://www.olympic.org/Documents/Olympic%20Charter/Charter_en_2010.pdf

[22] Berlioux, 'The History of the International Olympic Committee'.

[23] IOC, *Olympic Charter* (2007), February 11, 2010, 29. http://www.olympic.org/Documents/Olympic%20Charter/Charter_en_2010.pdf

[24] Canadian Broadcasting Corporation, 'Rogge says Bolt should "Show more respect"', August 21, 2008. http://www.cbc.ca/olympics/athletics/story/2008/08/21/olympics-athletics-roggebolt.html

[25] MacAloon, *Intercultural Education*, 21.

[26] United Nations Development Program, *Current History*, 229.

[27] Welsh, 'From Right to Responsibility'; see also International Commission on Intervention and State Sovereignty, *Responsibility to Protect*.

[28] Commission on Human Security, *Human Security Now*, 4; Bajpai, 'The Idea of Human Security'.

[29] Clarkson, 'Broadening and Deepening'.

[30] Commission on Human Security, *Human Security Now*, 4.

[31] International Olympic Committee, 'Report by the IOC 2000 Commission to the 110th IOC Session'. Lausanne, December 11–12, 1999. http://multimedia.olympic.org/pdf/en_report_588.pdf, 14–19.

[32] Van Wynsberghe, 'The Olympic Games'; Vancouver Winter Olympic and Paralympic Organizing Committee 'Sustainability and Aboriginal Participation'. 2010. http://www.vancouver2010.com/en/sustainability-and-aboriginal-parti/-/31640/toq5zj/index.html.

[33] City of Chicago, 'Memorandum of Understanding'. March 2009. http://www.chicago2016.org/Portals/0/WhyChicago_OurPlan/MOU%20FINAL.pdf.

References

Arbena, J. 'Mexico City 1968'. In *Encyclopedia of the Modern Olympic Movement*, edited by J. Findlay and K. Pelle, 175–84. Westport, CT: Greenwood, 2004.

Bajpai, K. 'The Idea of Human Security'. *International Studies* 40, no. 3 (2003): 195–228.

Berlioux, M. 'The History of the International Olympic Committee'. In *The Olympic Games*, edited by Lord Killanin and John Rodda, 12–22. New York: Collier, 1976.

Chappelet, J.-L., and B. Kubler-Mabbott. *The International Olympic Committee and the Olympic System*. London: Routledge, 2008.

Clarkson, S. 'Broadening and Deepening: A Cultural Approach to Achieving Human Dignity'. In *Human Cultural Security*, edited by Pia Kleber. Forthcoming.

Commission on Human Security. *Human Security Now*. New York: United Nations, 2003. http://www.humansecurity-chs.org/finalreport.

Hoberman, J. *The Olympic Crisis: Sports, Politics and the Olympic Order*. New Rochelle, NY: Aristide Caratzas, 1986.

International Commission on Intervention and State Sovereignty. *Responsibility to Protect*. Ottawa: International Development Research Centre, 2001.

Kidd, B. 'Montreal 1976'. In *Encyclopedia of the Modern Olympic Movement*, edited by John Findling and Kimberly Pelle, 191–8. Westport, CT: Greenwood, 2004.

Lee, J. 'Earth quake Changed Canada's Mind on Olympic Boycott–Pound'. *Vancouver Sun*, August 5, 2008.

MacAloon, J. *Intercultural Education and Olympic Sport*. Montreal: Canadian Olympic Association, 1986.

Mallon, B. 'The IOC Bribery Scandal'. *Journal of Olympic History* 8, no. 2 (2000): 11–27.

Van Wynsberghe, R. 'The Olympic Games Impact (OGI) Study and the 2010 Winter Olympic Games: A Study in Monitoring the Games' Sustainability'. Paper presented to the conference: 'Olympic Reform: A Ten-Year Review', University of Toronto, May 19, 2009.

Welsh, J. 'From Right to Responsibility: Humanitarian Intervention and International Society'. *Global Governance* 8, no. 4 (2002): 503–521.

The tricolour in Beijing: Indian sport, Olympism and nationalism

Boria Majumdar[a] and Nalin Mehta[b]

[a]Senior Research Fellow, University of Central Lancashire, Preston, UK; [b]Global Fund, Geneva, Switzerland

This paper deals with the impact of the Beijing Olympics on Indian sport. After winning her first ever individual gold medal in Beijing Indian sport appeared poised for take-off, if there was a fundamental systemic overhaul. Beijing, in other words, presented Indian sport with an unprecedented opportunity. This paper examines how Olympic sports became central to the Indian sporting imagination post-Beijing and what the country needs to create a sporting culture. It suggests that, unless a sporting culture is created, then Beijing will have proven to be a false dawn.

Introduction

When Sir Dorabji Tata organized the first modern meet of Indian athletes with an eye on the 1920 Antwerp Olympic Games, he found that despite running barefoot their performance compared 'well with the times done in Europe or elsewhere'. Suitably impressed, Tata personally financed three of the best runners for Antwerp, a move that in his own words: 'Fired the ambition of the nationalist element in the city'.[1] Eighty-nine years after that wind-swept day in Pune, when Tata first dreamt of an individual Olympic gold for India, shooting prodigy Abhinav Bindra finally found the Holy Grail at the 2008 Beijing Games. As the Indian tricolor was hoisted in Beijing, the poise and pride on the bespectacled shooter's visage spoke to a billion Indians, becoming a leitmotif of gung-ho chest thumping in media commentaries and nationalist iconography. In a country undergoing a media revolution like no other – India now has more than 50 24-hour satellite TV news networks alone – the Beijing victory created an unprecedented national frenzy.[2] In a country with a population of one billion, and a competitive media industry looking for new heroes and new stories, the lone gold medal was justification enough to spark off celebrations worthy of a nation that was topping the medals tally.

For Indian sport, Beijing proved to be a watershed. It was much more than a sporting spectacle not just because India's performance at Beijing was its best ever at the Games, but also because it heralded the promise of a new beginning for Indian sports. Bindra was not an aberration. His performance was followed by near-podium finishes in badminton, tennis and archery. Just when it was turning out to be a tale of so near yet so far, Vijender Kumar (bronze in boxing, 75 kg) and Sushil Kumar (bronze in wrestling, 66 kg freestyle) ensured that the Indian tricolour went up twice more at Beijing. Their achievements, analysed for hours on television, turned them into national celebrities overnight. If the media catharsis that followed was any indication, for the first time, Olympic sports, apart from hockey, were at the centre stage of what could be termed as the national consciousness. It was an indication that decades of ill treatment and neglect, which had reduced Olympic sport to a footnote in India, might just be about to change. At a time when the country was reeling under the impact of serial blasts in Gujarat and Karnataka,[3] the medal successes helped emphasize the point that across contexts and time frames an Olympic gold can catapult sport to the forefront of a nation's imagination.

Three major themes emerged in the discourse that followed: a renewed media focus on Olympism as a nationalist playing field, the promise of a new Indian Olympic culture and the fear that without systemic change in Indian sporting structures, this would be yet another false dawn.

The Bindra moment

For the first time in Indian Olympic history, the media appropriated these accomplishments in a manner associated commonly with cricket – a non-Olympic sport in which the nation dominates. All of a sudden, Bindra was flooded by sponsorship offers that had long since been reserved for over-pampered cricket stars alone. A poll in *Times Now*, India's most popular English-language TV news channel, revealed that the national religion of cricket had slid in the popularity charts. According to the survey, 53% of sports fans in Chennai and 44% in Kolkata were glued to the Olympics. In contrast, 41% of sports fans in Chennai and 29% in Kolkata watched the Indian cricket team in action against the Sri Lankans. In Mumbai, an amazing 64% of the fans interviewed were unaware of the ongoing cricket series between India and Sri Lanka.[4]

The medal haul – by Indian standards – it seemed, had suddenly woken up the country to the significance of the Olympics as an event that Indians could win at as well. The medal winners seemed to satisfy a national yearning and in the process made a statement about the significance of sport in an era of escalating political turmoil. Olympic success, the victories demonstrated, held the promise of uniting Indians across the country. With some of India's greatest sporting achievements at the Olympics coming at a time when the nation was seeking answers to sudden terror attacks, their impact was all the more visible. In the days before the Olympic Games, most Indians were grappling with the political crisis at hand and were hardly concerned about what the small contingent of 56 could achieve in Beijing. So much so that Suresh Kalmadi, president of the Indian Olympic Association (IOA), had issued a statement asking sports fans not to expect miracles from the athletes. Set against this backdrop of gloom and limited expectations, India's successes shone even brighter.

The success of the three Beijing winners was as much a testament to their own skills as it was a metaphor for the larger story of India. They had arguably shattered the grand narrative of failure that has characterized Indian sport just as the emergence of the IT industry in the 1990s signified the end of the 'Hindu rate of growth' that had defined the economy since the 1950s. In a manner similar to the way in which Narayan Murthy or Azim Premji – founders of the IT giants Infosys and Wipro – had created the self-belief necessary for Indian business to act as a global player after decades of isolationism and the license-permit raj,[5] so did the Beijing victories usher in a new era of self-confidence in sport. As John MacAloon argues, the Olympics are a 'crucible of symbolic force' into which the world pours its energies and a stage upon which, every four years, it plays 'out its hopes and its terrors'.[6] For every Indian, that terror always came in the form of a question: A billion people and no gold medal. Why? Beijing provided that answer, and hence the nationalist frenzy that ensued.

The annals of Indian sports writing have been full of complaints about sporting failures. Analysts have blamed the system, they have blamed the politicians who run it, they have even questioned Indian genetics. Every four years, it has become a collective national ritual to blame everyone else when found wanting in the global mirror of the Olympics, only to move on and repeat the same catharsis four years later. The Beijing athletes showed that it is possible to succeed in spite of the system. The Bhartiya Janata Party's late General Secretary and former cabinet minister Pramod Mahajan once said, only half-jokingly, that the Indian IT and beauty industries rose to great heights only because the government did not realize their significance until they had already made a mark. Abhinav Bindra's success too followed a similar template, at least with respect to the national sporting superstructure. Born into affluence and the luxury of an indoor shooting range in his backyard, he emerged as a child prodigy, only to taste initial defeat at Sydney (2000) and Athens (2004). He could as easily have given up, blamed the system and have been content with his World Championship and Commonwealth Games medals, but he persevered. It is a victory born out of the pain of loss and an iron will to succeed. Here at last was India's answer to those that point to the success of Surinam's Anthony Nesty or that of the Ethiopian runners, for that matter. It is indeed possible to succeed without access to government-sponsored sporting facilities. This is not to argue against creating efficient systems – that would be a terrible folly – but in sports there are moments when all it boils down to is self-belief.

Legacy of Beijing 2008

Does the Beijing victory mean the arrival of a national Olympic culture for India? Or will Indians clap their hands in glee and return to their daily dose of cricket once the euphoria recedes? The three medals won at Beijing could certainly be the catalyst to help correct years of frustration at India's poor sporting performances. With various state governments promising to set up academies to promote boxing, wrestling and shooting, India does look poised to have an Olympic sporting culture of its own, but in the euphoria of victory it is important to remember that at least 15 corporate houses turned down pleas to sponsor the Indian shooters before the Olympics. The Beijing winners deserve the highest accolades and corporate coffers have opened up for them like Aladdin's cave, but the true legacy of this victory will lie in whether money can now be made available to build the training superstructure for other athletes.

This is no flash-in-the-pan success. Bindra, for instance, was only part of a phalanx of world-class Indian shooters that have emerged in the past decade. Beijing was his moment but each member of the Indian shooting team was capable of winning a medal. Similarly, Vijender Kumar was part of a boxing team in which his compatriot Akhil, and not he, was tipped for a medal in the run up to the Games. His defeat of the reigning world champion, Russian Sergei Vodapoyanov, in the 54 kg pre-quarter-final round turned him into a national hero before he crashed out in the quarter finals, just like his 19-year-old roommate Jitender Kumar, who fought valiantly despite 10 stitches on his chin. This is the terrifying beauty of sport, its unpredictability. This is why we watch it because it showcases all that is glorious and tragic about human nature; all that is uncertain and indescribable. The key for the future is to invest in having enough people at the top echelon of any sport, for one to click when the moment comes.

What now of the future? There are many in India who look longingly across the border at China's awe-inspiring sporting machine. The Chinese too built their success by focusing on key sports initially – gymnastics, table tennis, badminton and athletics. India, however, cannot hope to replicate the Chinese model blindly. The organization of Indian sport is far too complicated and far too political to allow for a uni-linear approach like the Chinese or the East Europeans before them.[7] Like Indian democracy, Indian sport too has evolved its own unique model, distinct from everyone else. When Kapil Dev's unfancied team won the cricket World Cup in 1983, no one could have predicted that the surprise victory, coinciding with the television revolution, would ignite deeper processes that would ultimately turn India into the spiritual and financial heart of global cricket. Now the Beijing success has created another opportunity that if harnessed well could well usher in a new era in Indian sport. As Bindra grabbed gold and the boxers charged through the early rounds, for the first time, a national television audience, led on by a cheerleading media, focused on Olympic sports. The fact that the entire boxing team had emerged from the small north-Indian town of Bhiwani with few facilities, or that Sushil Kumar had trained in Delhi's Chatrasal stadium with rotting wrestling mats and 20 other wrestlers as roommates provided too irresistible a story of human triumph against all odds. The hype was such that even the Haryana Chief Minister turned up at Vijender's house to watch his semi-final bout. It was a televised photo opportunity for the politician, but also an event that led government officials to build a new paved road overnight to show their boss that developmental schemes were working. Similarly, the Delhi Chief Minister immediately announced a huge cash award for Sushil Kumar and in early 2009 he was still busy travelling across the country for virtually daily felicitation functions.

When K.D. Jadav won India's last wrestling medal at the Helsinki Olympics in 1952 the celebrations at home were extremely muted, restricted to the sports pages of newspapers, unlike the mega hype now around Sushil Kumar and the new phalanx of Indian boxers. To compound Jadav's agony, the political class gave the victorious hockey team of 1952 a tumultuous welcome in ceremonies across the country while he had to make do with a localized cavalcade of a hundred bullock carts from his native village. In 1952 hockey was a potent symbol of Indian nationalism and Jadav, despite winning independent India's first individual Olympic medal, was left to ultimately die in poverty. He was forced to sell off his wife's jewels to build a modest cottage and won a posthumous Arjuna award – India's highest award for sportspersons – only in 2001. In sharp contrast, governmental coffers have already opened up for the Kumars from Beijing and much more corporate largesse is on the way. Even more so, in a nation starved of sporting glory, the intense media focus on the Beijing battlers has turned them into new nationalist heroes. Clearly the registers of iconicity have changed in the intervening years, with individual Olympic success becoming an important barometer of nationalist triumph.

What explains the change? Let us be clear: this is not necessarily about some newly found love or understanding of sports. There is a marked disjuncture between the hype about a resurgent India that the Beijing boys supposedly represent and the reality. On the morning of Sushil Kumar's bronze medal win most media outlets carried online stories saying he had 'crashed out' of the Olympics. There was an even an undertone that he had somehow wasted his first round bye. Few, at least on television or in the immediate internet discourse, remembered the repêchage rule[8] until the Jat from Najafgarh pleasantly shocked the nation with his marathon string of victories to clinch bronze.

As reporters struggled for epithets about a shining India, nothing characterized the madness better than the television scrum at Bhiwani. On the day of the two boxing quarterfinals, the squadron of satellite broadcast vans from various channels stationed at Jitendra Kumar's village of Devsar cut and run as soon as he lost. Their destination: Vijender's village of Kalua, 10 km away, in anticipation of his fight. With TV channels looking to maximize costly resources, this was partly understandable, but as one reporter on the spot asked: 'Has Jitender's village suddenly ceased to be a symbol of the new resurgent India we are talking about simply because he lost?' This, after all, was a

20-year-old gallantly fighting the weight of history with 10 stitches on his chin, but all that mattered it seems was the ruthless logic of victory. The hype was about nationalism, pure and simple and that tells us something for the future as India hopes to build on the successes of Beijing.

Television has certainly helped create a national public focused on boxing, but with all of India glued to the gripping celebrations in Bhiwani, at least one TV editor is said to have gloated in private that the channel had turned the boxers into heroes. Nothing could be further from the truth. The media went to Bhiwani and to the boxers because it needed the story. TV reporters, expecting awe-stuck country bumpkins, were received with a busy matter-of-factness in a town that is used to winning medals. It is just that it took an Olympic medal for the rest of India to wake up to it. Bhiwani today is home to at least 1,500–2,000 regular boxers and 20,000–25,000 active sportspersons. It alone has produced 14 Arjuna awardees and is part of an economy that thrives on local sportsmen who regularly make it to the sports quotas of the paramilitary forces, the army and the police. The seeds of the boxing renaissance here, planted by the legendary Captain Hava Singh, founder of the Bhiwani Boxing Club, are yielding fruit after years of nurturing. While India celebrates the spirit of Bhiwani it is important to remember that sporting success is not a pack of instant noodles.

In 2004, the ruling Bhartiya Janata Party fooled itself into believing that five years of 8% economic growth on paper had all but assured its victory. Sure of sweeping back to power, it over-confidently called a general election six months before time, ran a campaign focused on the catchy tagline 'India Shining' and was duly voted out of power by the majority of Indians who had been left out of the success of the economic reforms. There is now a danger of a generic 'India Shining' kind of discourse subsuming the real achievements and the real resurgence of the Beijing athletes. The boxers have emerged from a town which sometimes goes for days without electricity, where the rains have made it impossible to drive a car faster than 5 km/hour on most roads and where most people had to rely on inverters to watch the home boys win. In such a setting, sport has emerged as a way out for many. The real success of Bhiwani lies in the rock solid confidence of the new generation of athletes and a nascent public-private partnership which has allowed them to transcend a system used to mediocrity. They have not been content to merely repeat the past and this is the new Indian spirit that needs to be celebrated.

Like K.D. Jadav 56 years ago, virtually every winning athlete from Bhiwani in the past – at the Commonwealth Games, the Asiad and the SAF Games – has been welcomed home by celebratory motorcades of locals, except that they were rarely noticed by the mainstream press. Perhaps, the next time things will change, with a more concerted national focus on sport – an approach where the Akhils and the Jitendras who did not win are not forgotten.

In an atmosphere of relative optimism, a note of caution is necessary. India's sporting scene is in crying need of an overhaul and three individual medals can only create a possibility for such a change to come about. Unless the government, sports administrators, the IOA and, finally, the corporations come forward to embrace Olympic sport, Beijing 2008 will remain an exception to the rule. Private efforts, such as the Mittal Champions Trust and Olympic Gold Quest Foundation, must contribute more towards Indian sport. Tough questions need to be asked. What happened, for instance, to the Indian Army's celebrated Mission Olympics and can it be integrated with the larger national effort?

Mission Olympics – strength turned weakness

The Army's Mission Olympics plan was put into practice in 2001 when the then Army Chief General S. Padmanabhan, concerned about the lack of Olympic success, set up the Army Sport Institute (ASI) in Pune under Col. M.K. Naik, a former Asian Games gold medallist in rowing. Naik visited sport institutes across the country to study their shortcomings and set about creating an international standard sporting academy. Key sports disciplines were identified and his officers then recruited budding youngsters from across the country who had excelled at the sub-junior and junior levels. Once selected, the boys were recruited to the rank of havaldar (a police rank between inspector and constable) with a monthly income of Rs 6,000–8,000. Their living costs – travel, clothes, food and other essentials – became the responsibility of ASI, which was based upon a Rs 60 crore allocation from the Defense Ministry. According to Naik, the training had one aim: 'We want them to remember at all times that they are here to get India an Olympic medal.'[9]

By itself, such an academy is not novel. The Chinese have long had such training institutions aiming for Olympic glory, so have the Australians. What is unique about India is that here it is the Indian Army that has taken the lead, in consonance with its wider objective of safeguarding national notions of pride and honour. Met with widespread media approval, one reporter called it 'an emergency rescue act by the Army'.[10] By 2008, 115 sports cadets were training at the ASI. According to the Army: 'The potential candidates are selected primarily based on performance in a structured selection process, without any reservation/quotas of any kind.'[11]

In some senses, the new Olympic mission of the Army built upon long-standing structures of attracting sporting talent at various regimental training centres. For instance, the Punjab Regiment, composed of artillery and engineers, had always followed a practice of hiring talented children from their recruiting bases for special Boys Companies with a view to building their own talent pool. These were later recruited as soldiers. In 2008, 952 sports cadets were being trained in 15 such Boys Companies across the country's regimental centres. The ASI simply borrowed this template. The difference was that, this time, the Olympics was an explicit goal, not just regimental glory.

In a marked departure from the past, the ASI also brought in foreign coaches. By 2003, foreign specialists had been hired for boxing, sports medicine, archery and general theory.[12] This openness is a welcome departure from the hide-bound past and the Army's sport training is well spread across specialized centres across the nation.

However, its biggest weakness lies within the system itself. While the whole effort is admirable, the Army remains largely closed to outsiders. These facilities continue to be restricted to military men and women alone. This begs the question: Would it not make a big difference if civilian medal hopefuls like Anjali Bhagwat, Mansher Singh, Manavjit Singh and Abhinav Bindra were given the opportunity to use the facilities and the equipment at the Army's excellent shooting ranges? To give another example, in 2007, National Cadet Corps cadets stood second only to the Army in the junior shooting national championship, winning 34 medals in various categories. Many of its young shooters beat army marksmen, but there is no institutionalized mechanism to co-opt them for further training in the armed forces, the paramilitary forces or the state police forces. Most of these NCC shooters currently come from low income backgrounds and without institutional support their talent may well be lost to India.[13]

The Army, it must be acknowledged, remains suspicious of outsiders. For instance, when I first contacted the Army in 2005 for data on Mission Olympics, I thought it would be the easiest thing in the world. This, after all, was a showcase project of the Army and had been widely publicized already. I thought the Army's publicists would jump at the idea. Yet, I was first curtly informed by the then spokesperson in Delhi that he was only authorized to give such information to journalists, not to writers. 'Call the Director General Military Training', he said and hung up. When I found the military training department's numbers, the colonel there proved most courteous on phone, but he too said he would need special clearance to release such data. When repeated written requests were stonewalled with the standard 'no clearance yet' response, I decided to use the time-tested method of New Delhi: contacts. Through the good offices of family friends, I personally spoke to at least three senior generals in Army headquarters to get the data we wanted on Mission Olympics. Everyone was sympathetic, but nothing moved. In the end, a full year after my initial inquiries, a senior defence journalist, well respected in Army circles, helped me get the data. It was as if I had been fishing for the Army's best kept secrets, troop deployments and the like. The point of narrating this experience is that while the Army continues to be a bulwark of the nation, following its highest traditions in matters of sport, perhaps, it could do with a fresh outlook and the refreshing air of transparency. Until it breaks out of its splendid isolation and embraces the winds of change holistically, the task of winning Olympic medals will not get easier.

Conclusion

While India lauds Bhiwani for what it has done to place boxing on the national map, it is time to replicate such achievements across the country. With boxing being a television-friendly sport and with 24-hour television channels multiplying almost daily, the media would surely embrace boxing if properly marketed and managed. With such a systemic overhaul, India can expect more medals in boxing in the 2012 Games and Vijender's bronze will then have the significance of being more than an Olympic medal in the overall sporting context.

If India fails to take advantage of the fertile condition created by Beijing, its lasting legacy will have been confined to sports history books by the time of the next Olympics. A senior journalist had asked Abhinav on his return to India: 'Is this Abhinav's gold or India's gold?' Abhinav, the epitome of political correctness, was quick to suggest that it was India's without question. If there is a systemic overhaul, thanks to Abhinav and his colleagues, it will certainly be India's gold for all time. However, if a fundamental transformation of sporting infrastructure in India is not brought about, Abhinav's gold will remain his, a moment of individual brilliance lost amidst countless failures since independence.

Notes

[1] Nalin Mehta, 'Smile, Sir Dorabji', *The Indian Express*, August 12, 2008, 8.
[2] For the astonishing expansion of Indian satellite television see Mehta, *India on Television*. For the massive expansion of the Indian newspaper industry and its 'mass-ification' see Jeffrey, *India's Newspaper Revolution*.
[3] The two Indian states of Gujarat and Karnataka were rocked by serial bomb blasts in July 2008. Overall there were more than 20 instances of bomb blasts across India in 2008 alone.
[4] Boria Majumdar, 'Seize this Moment', *The Times of India*, August 25, 2008.
[5] India followed a policy of import substitution between 1947 and 1991, a phase known as the license permit Raj. Post-1991 has been a phase of liberalization of the Indian economy.
[6] Quoted in Mehta, 'Smile, Sir Dorabji'.

[7] For the Chinese model of sporting success see, for instance, Hong, Mackay and Christensen, eds, *China Gold*.
[8] It allows a lucky loser to come back after losing the first bout and still be in contention for a medal.
[9] Faisal Sharif, 'Indian Army Launches Operation Olympic Medal', September 4, 2003. http://www.rediff.com/sports/2003/sep/04spec.htm.
[10] Ibid.
[11] Col. Ajay Das, SC, Dir ALC, ADGPI. Email correspondence on February 21, 2008. I am grateful to Srinjoy Chowdhary for facilitating this data from the Army.
[12] Sharif, 'Indian Army Launches Operation Olympic Medal'.
[13] Figures from directorate general, NCC, Ministry of Defence.

References

Hong, Fan, Duncan Mackay, and Karen Christensen, eds. *China Gold: China's Quest for Olympic and Global Glory*. Great Barrington, MA: Bershire, 2008.

Jeffrey, Robin. *India's Newspaper Revolution: Capitalism, Politics and the Indian Language Press*, 2nd ed. New Delhi: Oxford University Press, 2003.

Mehta, Nalin. *India on Television: How Satellite News Channels Change the Way We Think and Act*. New Delhi: Harper Collins, 2008.

Index

Page numbers in *Italics* represent tables.
Page numbers in **Bold** represent figures.

175

INDEX

Close, P.: Askew, D. and Xu, X. 136
Cnaan, R.: *et al* 40
Columbia Journalism Review 141–2
communication platform 69–74; cultural
    ideas 72–4; international cooperation 70–2
'communitas' 33, 75–7, 85–6
Confucius 29, 31–2, 149; Harmony 149; *The
    Analects* 32
Cornford, T.: and Song, G. 107
Costas, Bob 79
Cotter, C. 42
'Created in China' 73, 142
Cricket World Cup (1983) 170
Cull, N.J. 132
Cuskelly, G.: *et al* 41

Daily Yomiuri 148
Dalai Lama (14th) 114–22; Middle Way
    Approach 115
Dayan, D.: and Katz, E. 76–7, 133; and
    Price, M. 17
de Coubertin, Pierre 5, 10–12, 160
Declaration of Human Rights 111
deLisle, J. 134
Deng Xiaoping 125
Deutsche Welle radio station 111
Dev, Kapil 170
Dewan, S. 138
The Digital Divide 96
Douglas, M. 33
Dream for Darfur 135
Droit, J. 7

Eason, K. 134
Economy, E.: and Segal, A. 136
Eifling, S. 141
English People's Daily Online 137–8
Espinoza, Maria Rosario 61

Fairbank, J. 34
Falun Gong 120
Federer, Roger 82
Fine Arts in Olympic Games and Everyday
    Life Exhibition (1906) 11
Finlay, C.: and Xin, X. 3, 132–56, 159
The Forgotten Olympic Art Competitions
    (Stanton) 12
Foucault, M. 112–13
Free Tibet campaign (2008) 21, 135
Freeman, K. 158
Friedman, T. 28
Fukuda, P.M. Yasuo 143, 150

Garcia, B. 10–11
Ge, Prof. Jianxiong 99
Gee, J. 43
Geertz, C. 30, 32–3

Geng, Xin 149
German Railway Publicity Bureau 7
Global News 143, 145–6, 150
Global Times 57–8, 149
The Globe and Mail 158
Gluckman, M. 27
Gosper, K. 158
Granbassi, M. 158
Greenpeace 164
Guangdong Television 89–95; ratings analysis
    92–5, *94*; strategies 91–2
Guangzhou Daily 124

He, Wenna 106
Henry, I.: and Al-Tauqi, M. 135
Hero (Zhang) 32
Hill & Knowlton Inc. 71
Hill, D. 18
Hitler, Adolph 7–8; Olympic Games (1936)
    17, 28, 135, 160, 162
Hjortzberg, O. 6–7
Hobsbawm, E.: and Anderson, B. 134
Hohlwein, L. 7–8
Horne, J.: and Whannel, G. 3, 16–26
Howe, L. 33
Hu, President Jintao 71–3, 143, 145, 148
Huang, Y. 3, 89–95
Hughson, J. 3, 5–15
human rights 111–31, 157–66; after Beijing
    157–65; opening ceremony 123–6; politics
    126–7; torch relay 114–20; Universal
    Declaration of Human Rights 160, 163
Human Rights Magazine 122
Human Rights Watch 135, 157–8
Human Security Commission Report (2003)
    164
Humphrey, C.: and Laidlaw, J. 34
Hunan Satellite TV Station 91; Olympic
    Games, Just do it 91
Hundred Year Humiliation 34–7
Hwang, Y. 3, 111–31

Idem, J. 158
India: National Cadet Corps 172
Indian Olympic Association 168
Indian sport: legacy of Beijing 169–73;
    Olympics and nationalism 167–74
Inglis, D. 10–11
Institute of Japanese JCC New Japan 149
International Broadcasting Centre (IBC) 84
The International Journal of Cultural Policy
    10
International Olympic Committee (IOC) 7,
    158; Ethics Commission 161
Ishihara, Shintaro 45

Jadav, K.D. 170–1

176

INDEX

Origins of English Individualism (Macfarlane)
33

Padmanabhan, Gen. S. 172
Peaceful Rise foreign policy 70, 138
Pearl River Channel 92
People's Daily 119, 121–4, 143, 145
People's Liberation Army (PLA) 121–2
*People's Mobile Newspaper on Olympic
Games* 107
'People's Olympics' 112
Phelps, M. 106, 140
Phoenix Satellite Television 145
Pinette, M. 158
posters: art 7–8; cultural legacy 5–15;
Cultural Olympiad 10–12; inspired by sport
12; politics 8–10; purpose 5–7
Potter, J.: and Wetherell, M. 43
Pound, R. 158
The Power of the Poster (Ades) 7
Premji, A. 168
Preuss, H. 41
Price, M.: and Dayan, D. 17
Project (119) 142
Pryde, James (The Beggarstaffs) 8
Puncog, Qiangba 117

Qinghai-Tibet Railway 115
Qui, Zhenhai 145

Rauschenburg, R. 9
Renmin Daily 107
Reporters Sans Frontières 135, 137
Richardson, S. 158
Riefenstahl, L. 7–8; *Olympia* 7–8
Roche, M. 17, 79
Rogge, J. 136, 158–9, 162, 165
Rorty, R. 127
Rothenbuhler, E. 86
Rothstein, E. 137
Ruskin, John 6
Russo, C. 158

Samaranch, J.A. 159, 161
The Sankei Shimbun 148
Sarkozy, President N. 159
School for Oriental and African Studies
(SOAS) 1
Segal, A.: and Economy, E. 136
Shin, Anbin 139–40
Short, J. 17
Shue, H. 118–19
Sichuan earthquake 120–3, 139–40, 147–8,
151
Singer, M. 30
Singh, Hava 171
Singh, Manavjit 172

Singh, Mansher 172
Smith, B. 135
Song, G.: and Cornford, T. 107
Sontag, S. 7
South Africa National Olympic Committee
(1963) 160
Southern Metropolitan Daily 56
Stanton, R. 12; *The Forgotten Olympic Art
Competitions* 12
State Administration of Radio, Film and
Television 90–1
Stebbins, R. 41
Steiner, A. 45
Stevenson, Sarah 61
Study Times 98
subpolitics 23–4
Sysimetsa, I. 7

Taiwan Democratic Progressive Party 120
Tang, I. 140–1
Tata, Sir D. 167
Tibetan Independence 113–20; Serf's
Emancipation Day 119; Torch Relay 118
Tibetan National Uprising Day 114
Tibetan Youth Congress (TYC) 116
Times Now 168
Times Online 134
Timmers, M. 6–9, 13
Tomlinson, A. 8
The Torch Relay (2008) 3, 16–26, 60–3, 91,
114–20, 136–9, 147; boycott 18–19;
celebrity involvement 19–22, 139–41;
journey of harmony 18, 114; print media
coverage 19–22
Turner, V. 27, 33–4, 78

United Nations Development Program
(UNDP) 45, 163
Universal Declaration of Human Rights 160,
163
The USA Today 141

Van Der Westhuizen, J.: and Black, D. 135
van Gennep, A. 33
Van Kuyck, M. 7
Vazquez Rana, M. 158
Verbruggen, H. 159
Victoria and Albert (V&A) Museum of
Childhood 5, 7
Vodapoyanov, S. 169
volunteers 40–52, 71; cheer squads 48; media
representation 42–8
vortextuality 23

Wang, Nan 83
Wang, Yifu 83
Wasserstrom, J. 47

 Routledge
Taylor & Francis Group

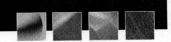

Soccer & Society

EXECUTIVE ACADEMIC EDITOR:

Boria Majumdar, *University of Central Lancashire, UK*

Soccer & Society is the first international journal devoted to the world's most popular game. It covers all aspects of soccer globally from anthropological, cultural, economic, historical, political and sociological perspectives. *Soccer & Society* encourages and favours clearly written research, analysis and comment.

To view free articles please visit **www.tandf.co.uk/journals/fsas** and click on News & Offers.

To sign up for tables of contents, new publications and citation alerting services visit **www.informaworld.com/alerting**

 updates
Taylor & Francis Group

Register your email address at **www.tandf.co.uk/journals/eupdates.asp** to receive information on books, journals and other news within your areas of interest.

Powered by
informaworld

For further information, please contact Customer Services at either of the following:
T&F Informa UK Ltd, Sheepen Place, Colchester, Essex, CO3 3LP, UK
Tel: +44 (0) 20 7017 5544 Fax: 44 (0) 20 7017 5198
Email: subscriptions@tandf.co.uk
Taylor & Francis Inc, 325 Chestnut Street, Philadelphia, PA 19106, USA
Tel: +1 800 354 1420 (toll-free calls from within the US)
or +1 215 625 8900 (calls from overseas) Fax: +1 215 625 2940
Email: customerservice@taylorandfrancis.com

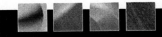

View an online sample issue at:
www.tandf.co.uk/journals/fsas